Shamans of the Lost World

Issues in Eastern Woodlands Archaeology
Editors: Thomas E. Emerson and Timothy Pauketat

SERIES DESCRIPTION: Issues in Eastern Woodlands Archaeology emphasizes new research results and innovative theoretical approaches to the archaeology of the pre-Columbian native and early colonial inhabitants of North America east of the Mississippi River Valley. The editors are especially seeking contributors who are interested in addressing/questioning such concepts as historical process, agency, traditions, political economy, materiality, ethnicity, and landscapes through the medium of Eastern Woodlands archaeology. Such contributions may take as their focus a specific theoretical or regional case study but should cast it in broader comparative or historical terms.

Scholars interested in contributing to this series are encouraged to contact Thomas Emerson, ITARP-Anthropology, 23 East Stadium Drive, University of Illinois, Champaign, IL 61820; teee@uiuc.edu.

BOOKS IN THIS SERIES:

Chiefdoms and Other Archaeological Delusions, by Timothy R. Pauketat

In Contact: Bodies and Spaces in the Sixteenth- and Seventeenth-Century Eastern Woodlands, by Diana DiPaolo Loren

War Paths, Peace Paths: An Archaeology of Cooperation and Conflict in Native Eastern North America, by David H. Dye

Shamans of the Lost World: A Cognitive Approach to Prehistoric Religion of the Ohio Hopewell, by William F. Romain

The Eastern Archaic, Historicized, by Kenneth E. Sassaman

Shamans of the Lost World

A Cognitive Approach to the Prehistoric
Religion of the Ohio Hopewell

William F. Romain

ALTAMIRA
PRESS

A division of

ROWMAN & LITTLEFIELD PUBLISHERS, INC.
Lanham • Boulder • New York • Toronto • Plymouth, UK

Published by AltaMira Press
A division of Rowman & Littlefield Publishers, Inc.
A wholly owned subsidary of The Rowman & Littlefield Publishing Group, Inc.
4501 Forbes Boulevard, Suite 200, Lanham, Maryland 20706
http://www.altamirapress.com

Estover Road, Plymouth PL6 7PY, United Kingdom

British Library Cataloguing in Publication Information Available

The hardback edition of this book was previously catalogued by the Library of Congress as follows:

Library of Congress Cataloging-in-Publication Data

Romain, William F., 1948–
  Shamans of the lost world : a cognitive approach to the prehistoric religion of the Ohio Hopewell / William F. Romain.
    p. cm. — (Issues in Eastern Woodland archaeology)
  Includes bibliographical references and index.
  1. Hopewell culture—Ohio. 2. Shamanism—Ohio. 3. Indians of North America—Ohio—Religion. 4. Indians of North America—Ohio—Antiquities. 5. Hopewell Site (Ohio) 6. Ohio—Antiquities. I. Title.
  E99.H69R66 2009
  299.7'971—dc22   2009015776

ISBN: 978-0-7591-1905-5 (cloth : alk. paper)
ISBN: 978-0-7591-1906-2 (pbk. : alk. paper)
ISBN: 978-0-7591-1907-9 (electronic)

Contents

Acknowledgments

This book would not have been possible without the help and support of many people. I am very grateful to AltaMira Press acquisitions editor Jack Meinhardt for giving this work consideration. Thanks also to editors Marissa Parks and Karen Ackermann at AltaMira. And I owe a huge debt of thanks to series editors Thomas Emerson and Timothy Pauketat for their continued support and encouragement.

A number of friends and colleagues read parts of earlier versions of the manuscript and offered valuable comments. My sincere thanks to Jarrod Burks, Jean McCoard, Dick Shiels, and Jay Miller. Thanks also to the anonymous reviewers who offered valuable criticisms. Shortcomings and errors are my own fault.

Thanks are extended to persons at several institutions. At the Peabody Museum of Archaeology and Ethnology, Harvard University, Susan Haskell provided time and space for my study of the Turner Collection. Thanks also to Helen Najarian and Genevieve Fisher at the Peabody Museum, Harvard University, for facilitating various permissions. At the Field Museum of Natural History in Chicago, Allison English graciously helped as my photographic assistant. Thanks also to Jennifer Pederson Weinberger at the Hopewell Culture National Historical Park for allowing me to examine materials at that location.

Special thanks are extended to several persons at the Ohio Historical Society. Bill Laidlaw, Rachel Tooker, Jim Strider, Angela O'Neal, and Teresa Carstensen facilitated my requests for permissions and photographs. Sincere thanks also to Martha Potter Otto, Bradley Lepper, Karen Hassel, and Raleigh Denig for help in accessing the OHS collections.

I thank Jim Harrison and Kristen Wiley at the Kentucky Reptile Zoo for posing live copperhead and timber rattlesnakes so I could photograph them. Thanks also to Jim and Eileen Wicker at Raptor Rehabilitation of Kentucky, Inc. for helping me photograph raptors at their center. Thanks to Michael Pogany at the Columbus Zoo and Aquarium for allowing me access to their cougars.

Many more kind people provided permissions, documents, information, and other support, including Yaron Antebi, Bruce R. Baby, Jack Blosser, Daniela Bono, Ayla Bouvette, Marti Chaatsmith, Robert Converse, Frank L. Cowan, Dwight Cropper, Christiane Cunnar, Laura Erickson, Robert Hall, George Hamell, George Horton, Jim and Allison Kalb, Duryea Kemp, Rick Perkins, Matthew Purtill, Greg Rouse, John C. Rummel, Lee Rothenberg, Nick Saunders, Hans Schick, Charles Scott, Geoffrey Sea, Jeff Smith, Curtis Tomak, Charla Tootle, Robert G. Vernon, Chris Young, and John T. Zubal. My sincere thanks to all. My apologies if I forgot someone.

I would also like to acknowledge an intellectual debt I owe to several scholars, including David W. Penny (*axis mundi* and three-tiered universe); Thomas Emerson, John G. Douglas, and John E. Kelly (quadripartite division of space); Martin Byers and Robert Hall (world renewal); Warren DeBoer and N'omi Greber (cosmic duality); and George E. Lankford (rotated cosmograms). Much of my work has been inspired by or is built directly upon their earlier insights.

Special thanks are extended to my wife, Evie Romain. For more years than I care to count, Evie has patiently tolerated my scholarly pursuits and has accompanied me on many unique adventures, including mushroom hunts, surveying expeditions, aerial reconnaissance missions, Indian pow-wows, and an untold number of conferences.

Last, but not least, special thanks to my mother, Frances Spania Rothenberg. Since I began my Hopewell investigations more than thirty-five years ago, not a single week has gone by where she did not offer thoughtful insights and encouragement. Thanks, Mom—this one's for you!

CHAPTER ONE

Introduction

It is not so much that shamanism is the root of all religion as that all religion is in sober essence shamanism. (La Barre 1970:223)

Blood and brains mixed with sweat on the face of the shaman as he pounded the head into a pulp. Freshly severed from its body, the head belonged to a soul who, either voluntarily or perhaps not so voluntarily, was fated to end corporeal existence with his or her head bashed into the stone altar.

This scene is not fiction. It is not something I made up. Rather, it describes an event that archaeological evidence shows occurred roughly two thousand years ago. The scene describes what was found in a Hopewell burial mound. Among the questions raised by this event are: What possible motivation could there have been for one human being to methodically bash in the brains of another? What were the final thoughts of the deceased? What were the thoughts of the mace-wielding perpetrator as he carried out his bloody act? And what about the onlookers—what were they thinking?

Questions such as these are the fair subject of inquiry in a field known as cognitive archaeology, defined as "the study of past ways of thought as inferred from material remains" (Renfrew 1994:3). To this we might add that cognitive archaeology includes the study of what people in the past thought and why. Among the expressions of human thought studied by cognitive archaeologists are prehistoric religious beliefs and rituals, cosmology, ideology, and iconography. At the risk of oversimplifying the matter, useful working definitions are provided by David Hurst Thomas: "[R]eligion is a specific set of beliefs based on one's ultimate relation to the supernatural"; "cosmology is the study of the universe as a whole . . . how the various parts fit together and what laws they obey"; ideology is "a systematic body of concepts and beliefs—often political in nature—about human life or nature"; and iconography is the "study of how people use art forms to represent their . . . beliefs" (1999:302–304).

In the chapters that follow, we will explore these subjects as they apply to the Hopewell. What we will find with reference to the grizzly scene above is that religious beliefs likely motivated the actions of the shaman; that is, religious beliefs likely resulted in the particular behavior that, in turn, left the material evidence we now consider. For those same religious reasons, the shaman's actions were probably endorsed by witnesses to the act. The final thoughts of the deceased will forever remain a mystery. It is likely, however, that he or she understood the concepts involved. But what exactly were the beliefs that resulted in what we find in the material record?

Arguably, shamanic concepts are at the essence of humankind's oldest religious expressions. And there is certainly a tremendous body of evidence indicating that shamanic beliefs and rituals played a central role in prehistoric Native American life. Accordingly, it is to the subject of shamanism that we turn to for answers.

The cognitive sciences, with their emphasis on empirical methodology, offer the potential to help us understand prehistoric shamanism. The problem, however, is that in looking to the literature concerning prehistoric shamanism, one is hard-pressed to find approaches that rely on emerging data from the cognitive sciences. There are occasional notable exceptions (e.g., Mithen 1996, 2006; also see Renfrew and Zubrow 1994). For the most part, however, where cognitive approaches are found, the usual argument is that either entoptic phenomenon or hallucinogenic drugs played a central role in early religious beliefs. But surely humankind's enduring relationship with the spirit world is based in something more profound than an occasional lunch of magic mushrooms.

In recent years, a promising way forward has appeared in the cognitive science of religion (e.g., Lawson and McCauley 1990; Guthrie 1993; Boyer 1994; Barrett 1997; Atran 2002; McCauley and Lawson 2002; Pyysiäinen 2003; Whitehouse 2004; also see Andresen 2001; Pyysiäinen and Anttonen 2002; Whitehouse and Martin 2004; Whitehouse and McCauley 2005; Tremlin 2006). This approach recognizes that religious beliefs and practices are directly related to, or are emergent by-products of, psychological functions that, in turn, result from our cognitive evolutionary development.

Tremendous progress has been made in the cognitive sciences and specifically the cognitive science of religion. What has been slower in coming, however, is consideration of how shamanism relates to theories and data in these fields. Little mention of shamanism is found in the literature devoted to cognitive science or the cognitive science of religion. Yet, as discussed later in this chapter, the cross-cultural expression of shamanism is recognized by a considerable number of anthropologists and ethnologists. Countless books and articles have been written on the subject, and archaeologists have shown that shamanic concepts predate Buddhism, Christianity, Islam, and the world's other major religions by tens of thousands of years. Given this, one might think shamanism would be of vital interest to those who study how human beings came to believe in gods and spirits.

Having made these observations, what I propose to do in the pages that follow is consider in detail a particular example of prehistoric shamanism using an approach that is informed by the cognitive sciences and the cognitive science of religion, as well as by archaeology and ethnology. To that end, the focus of my investigation concerns the religious beliefs and practices of "classic" Hopewell—Native Americans who lived in central and southern Ohio roughly two thousand years ago. My objective is simple: to show from their material remains how Hopewell expressed what I believe to be core attributes of an archetypal shamanic worldview.

Using Hopewell as a case study, I hope to show that a model of shamanism grounded in the cognitive sciences can be successfully used to inform us with regard to prehistoric religious beliefs. Thoughts matter. For thousands of years, religious thoughts have significantly affected the lives of millions of people and changed entire cultures. To better understand ourselves and the impact of our religious thoughts, we need to look for the common ground between the cognitive sciences and archaeology. In particular, we need to bring into sharper focus the landscape that exists between psychological and biological explanations of ritual and belief and the material record of our past.

Hopewell Defined

The term *Hopewell* derives from the name of Mordecai Hopewell, a Civil War veteran who owned a unique piece of property in Ross County, Ohio. In the 1800s a large concentration of prehistoric Indian mounds was discovered on his property. Upon excavation, these mounds were found to contain significant numbers of burials, caches of exotic materials, and many examples of exquisite artwork. As is common even today, the property owner's name was applied to the site, and, in this case, also to the people buried in the mounds.

The term *Hopewell*, however, is problematic. To begin with, it is not a Native American name, and many Native Americans object to a European name given to people they consider their ancestors. Archaeologists, on the other hand, are quick to point out that the name does not refer to a specific group of people; rather, it is an archaeological term used to describe "a broad interregional network—concentrated in what is now southern Ohio—of economic and political contacts, beliefs, and cultural traits among different Native American groups from 200 b.c. to 500 a.d." (National Park Service 2001:15). Dates for the Hopewell florescence are now considered shorter in duration than indicated by the National Park Service definition. Mark Seeman (2004:59) and Bradley Lepper (2004:73), for example, consider Hopewell in southern Ohio to range from about a.d. 1 to a.d. 400. A more significant problem, however, is that no one is quite sure what specific traits comprise the supposed "interregional network," given that clear differences exist among groups.

Confounding the difficulty, as Darlene Applegate (2005:6–7) points out, is that the term *Hopewell* has been and continues to be used by archaeologists as the name for a culture, period, style, tradition, interaction sphere, climax, complex, and phenomenon.

My own taxonomic preferences follow those of archaeologist N'omi Greber, who explains, "For both 'Adena' and 'Hopewell,' my units of thought are peoples and groups of peoples" (2005:20; emphasis in original). This approach recognizes that there are differences between groups. As the archaeological record demonstrates with respect to burial modes and earthwork configuration, for example, the practices of people of the Hopewell culture who lived in the Scioto River Valley differed from those living in the Little Miami River Valley. Accordingly, I think it makes sense that if we insist on applying a name to Hopewell peoples who lived in distinct ecological regions, we might, as Greber suggests, apply such names as "Central Scioto Hopewell" and "Middle Muskingum Hopewell" (39; also see Seig 2005:183–84). What these groups and others have in common—and what, to my mind, delineates Hopewell—is that they shared a worldview that was expressed in a similar and uniquely flamboyant way. As I will show, this worldview can be described as shamanic.

I should also note that although archaeological evidence for Hopewell groups is found throughout eastern North America, the present study is mostly limited to Ohio Hopewell—traditionally considered to be representative of classic Hopewell. Figure 1.1 shows several of the Ohio Hopewell sites mentioned in this text.

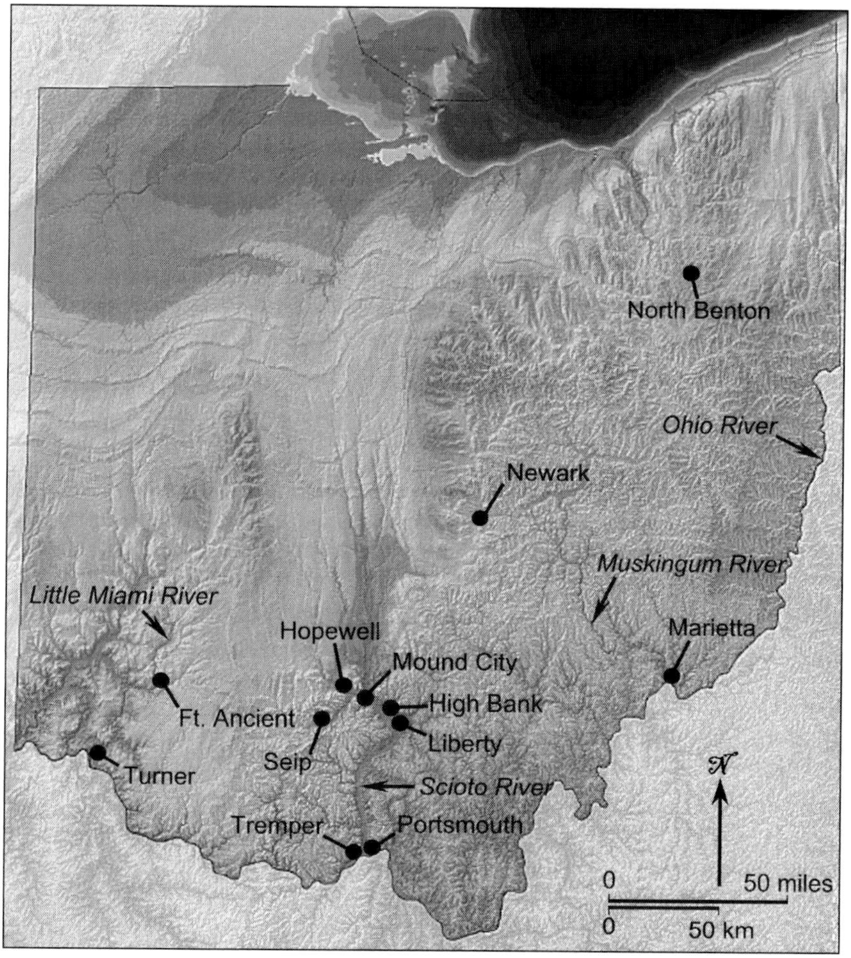

Figure 1.1. Shaded elevation map of Ohio showing selected Hopewell sites. Map by the Ohio Department of Natural Resources, locations added by William Romain.

People of the Ohio Hopewell culture were hunters and gatherers. They were also fishers and growers of weedy seed plant foods. They lived in small hamlets or villages scattered along the major river valleys of southern Ohio. Hopewell people crafted a stunning array of exquisitely designed items, often made from exotic materials including obsidian from the Yellowstone area, mica from the Carolinas, and shell from the Gulf Coast.

Perhaps the Ohio Hopewell are best known, however, for their huge, geometrically shaped earthworks. Situated where the present-day cities of Newark, Chillicothe, Cincinnati, Marietta, and Portsmouth are located, many of these earthen enclosures are larger than several football fields. Most often they are in the shape of circles and squares, but ellipses, octagons, and other shapes are also found.

The subject matter of this book is Hopewell shamanism. Occasionally, however, discussion will turn to the Adena. People of the so-called Adena culture lived in an area encompassing southern Ohio and extending into parts of Kentucky, Indiana, and West Virginia. Adena sites range from about 500 B.C. to A.D. 100 (Clay 1992:77). Until a few years ago it was generally accepted that Adena preceded Hopewell, with the view that Hopewell was an elaboration of Adena. More recent studies, however, suggest a more complicated picture, with Adena and Hopewell partially overlapping both geographically and temporally (Otto and Redmond 2008). Further, as mentioned above, both Adena and Hopewell were made up of different groups of people. In any event, what makes Adena significant to the present discussion is that many of the shamanic themes found in Hopewell are expressed in Adena using the same design elements. In fact, Beth McCord and Donald Cochran suggest that, at least for east-central Indiana, Adena and Hopewell "represent different parts of a single ceremonial system" (2008:359). In a similar vein and based on the evidence from Kentucky, Jimmy Railey proposes that "Adena should be viewed as an early regional expression of Hopewell rather than as its predecessor" (1996:100).

I like Anthony Aveni's way of thinking about the relationships: "[L]et's not think of Adena, Hopewell, and Mississippian peoples as different and distinct from each other. Instead, we should imagine them as blends of people who changed culture through time" (2005:57). Having said this, and with apologies to my Native American friends, I use the terms *Adena* and *Hopewell* in lieu of accepted alternatives and with the understanding that they are heuristic devices.

Shamanism Defined

A number of writers have commented that there is no commonly accepted or agreed-upon definition for *shamanism* (Hamayon 2001:3; Bowie 2000:191; Hutton 2001:vii). Others argue that shamanism is a Western conceptual category having no existence on its own, imposed on a disparate variety of beliefs and practices (Klein et al. 2001:229). Alice Kehoe (2000:101–102) has argued that the term *shaman* should be limited to Siberian ritual practitioners.

To be sure, shamanism means different things to different people. Part of the problem is that shamanism assumes many different guises. Shamanism in Siberia, for example, differs in its external manifestations from shamanism found in South America or South Africa. Even in Siberia, shamanism takes different forms (Hamayon 1994). In this, perhaps there is much to be said for use of the term *shamanisms* (Thomas and Humphrey 1994:6). Yet another difficulty is that indigenous cultures do not refer to their religious beliefs as shamanic in the same way that others might characterize their religion as, for example, Christian, Buddhist, or Hindu.

In general, however, I think the criticism that there is no commonly accepted definition for *shamanism* is overstated. As archaeologist Thomas Emerson (2003:1–2) points out, it is true that shamanism is not a religion, per se, in the sense that its practitioners have a shared history; neither is it a church, cult, dogma, or doctrine. However, as a working definition drawn from a number of sources (Eliade 1964; Harner 1988:7; Clottes and Lewis-Williams 1998:19), we can consider shamanism to be a complex of beliefs and practices based in the notion that spirits pervade the cosmos and that these spirits can be personally contacted for specific purposes, through altered states of consciousness.[1] *Spirit* in this case means an animating force or vital power.

Studies by Lewis-Williams and Pearce (2005), Winkelman (2004), Whitley (2000), Furst (1977), La Barre (1972), Harner (1990 [1980]), Wilbert (1972), Lommel (1967), Eliade (1964), and others have documented the universal, cross-cultural aspects of shamanism. As Michael Winkelman explains:

> Empirical studies based on worldwide samples, systematic cross-cultural research, and formal quantitative analysis . . . establish that there are universals of shamanism and that the concept of the shaman has a cross-cultural, or etic, status. Shamanism is not an arbitrary or culturally specific concept but a specific complex of characteristics found in the magico-religious practitioners of hunter-gatherer and simple pastoral and agricultural societies around the world. (2004:195)

In chapter 2, I will outline some of the universal characteristics of shamanism. It is this "complex of characteristics" that comprise what I refer to as the archetypal shamanic worldview.

As to the objection that shamanism is a Western or academic conceptual category having no existence on its own, I have no quarrel with that. Shamanism is a mental construct in the same way that communism and democracy are. In the case of shamanism, as explained by anthropologist Ronald Hutton: "Shamanism . . . is . . . a scholarly construct, used to group together beliefs and activities across the world which have some apparent relationship [or apparent similarity] with those observed in Siberia" (2001:vii). What we are really talking about is a particular worldview made up of assumptions.

These assumptions have a presence in the mind of the individual that results in real behaviors. To some extent the assumptions that make up a person's worldview are idiosyncratic as well as culture specific. There are, however, cross-cultural commonalities, or shared cognitive attributes that derive from our embodiment in the world. It is these commonalities that give rise to the archetypal shamanic worldview.

The idea of an archetypal shamanic worldview is not new. Clearly, Mircea Eliade (1964) and Weston La Barre (1970) had that in mind; as did anthropologist Peter Furst when he proposed that the "shamanic worldview" is the "common property of humankind" (1994a:2, 4). Interestingly, these statements anticipate the conclusions of investigators today drawn together in the emerging field known as the cognitive science of religion. For example, Harvey Whitehouse, an anthropologist and leading expert in the cognitive science of religion, refers to an "invariable core of all religious thinking and behavior—a universal religious repertoire"(2007:218). According to Whitehouse:

> Humans everywhere (and throughout the opaquely visible past) have entertained notions of *essentialized religious coalitions, supernatural agency* and of *life after death*; have attributed misfortune and luck to *transcendental causes*; have assumed that certain features of the natural world were *created by intentional design*; have performed *rituals* and endowed them with *symbolic meanings* and have regarded certain kinds of *testimony or obligation as divinely 'given'* and unchallengeable. (218; emphasis in original)

In the chapters that follow, we will find that the universal repertoire Whitehouse identifies is manifested or given specific form in the shamanic worldview.

In the same way that use of the term *shamanism* raises objections, so too, the word *shaman* is problematic. Many Native Americans object to use of the term *shaman* to describe their ritual practitioners. Some, such as Inez Talamantez, go as far as to maintain that "they are stealing our religion by calling our medicine men shamans. . . . Our language does not know shamans, and that name is only used by neo-shamans; not our chanters" (paraphrasing of remarks attributed to Talamantez, in Hutton 2001:158). In the opinion of like-minded persons, *shaman* implies a deceitful trickster, charlatan, or conjurer. That is not the meaning intended here.

At the same time, however, we need to acknowledge that many of the terms preferred by persons who object to the term *shaman* have their own problems. The term *medicine-man*, for example, ignores female as well as gender-variant ritual practitioners. Terms such as *spiritual leader, doctor,* and *healer* fail to communicate the ecstatic aspect of interaction with the spirit world and ignore practices that sometimes include malevolent acts.

The origin of the word *shaman* is usually attributed to the language of indigenous Tungus-speaking groups located in Siberia (Vitebsky 1995:10; Shirokogoroff 1935:269; but see Lyon 1998:278–79 for differing theories). In common usage, however, the term has evolved from its strict application to specific Siberian ritual practitioners to one that includes a wide range of persons having special knowledge of the spirit world. In common usage, the term is often used synonymously—if incorrectly—with medicine-man, holy person, healer, witch doctor, magician, curer, and sorcerer. Other magico-ritual experts can include spirit mediums, midwives, herbalists, astrologers, dream interpreters, snakebite curers, seers, diviners, soothsayers, and witches. The question is: Who among these persons should be considered shamans?

Comparative religion expert Mircea Eliade (1987:4–6) distinguishes the shaman by his or her ability to communicate directly with spirits and soul travel to other worlds, including the upperworld and lowerworld, through altered states of consciousness. By this definition, not every medicine-man, herbal doctor, bonesetter, or fortune-teller is a shaman. Nor is every spiritual leader, or tribal priest a shaman.[2]

With reference to Hopewell, Christopher Carr and D. Troy Case (2005b:181–82) introduce the term *shaman-like practitioner*. Carr and Case propose that shaman-like practitioners, as distinguished from shamans, are more specialized in their activities and do not engage in soul travel as a routine matter to accomplish their purposes. The term *shaman-like practitioner* takes into account the findings of Winkelman (1989, 1990, 1992), who explains that there are differences among magico-ritual experts in societies of differing complexity. Thus, while the "classic" shaman is found in small-scale hunter-gatherer groups, magico-ritual experts tend toward more diversified and specialized roles as societies evolve along a continuum that includes simple horticultural societies; more complex, large-scale, agriculturally based societies; and class societies. At the complex end of the spectrum, for example, in large-scale, agriculturally based and politically integrated societies, magico-ritual practitioners include specialized chief-priests as well as a retinue of politically less powerful, healers, mediums, diviners, and witches.

The distinction Winkelman makes is useful at many levels. Hopewell can perhaps be characterized as falling in to the lower to middle range of Winkelman's continuum—that is, hunter-gatherer-horticulturalists not politically integrated above the community level. Accordingly, the term *shaman-like practitioner* is applicable in a variety of Hopewell contexts. At the discussion level of individual burials, however, I find it impossible to distinguish a shaman from a shaman-like practitioner. And so, even though the term may be useful in certain contexts, in the present work the term *shaman* is used for what may include a range of shaman-like practitioners.

Piers Vitebsky points out that in Siberia and Mongolia, "there were many different kinds of 'shaman,' even within the same group or encampment. Some were healers, others were finders of game, still others warded off evil spirits, or contacted the dead" (1995:34–35). The same appears to be the case in North America. While shamans found in some groups are "general practitioners" who engage in a variety of shamanic tasks, other groups have specialist shamans who excel at curing, hunting or war medicine, divination, or other roles (Lyon 1998:278).

In the broadest sense, then, a shaman is a person who deliberately uses altered states of consciousness to access non-ordinary reality to gain power or information, or to manipulate life forces or spirit entities. Information sought may relate to the cause of an illness, future events, the location of lost souls, and other matters. The manipulation of life forces or spirits is usually for the purpose of causing changes in this world such as healing, weather control, and bringing in game.

Shamans can be male or female (Tedlock 2005; Nelson 2008), or gender-variant (Conner 1993). Shamans are recognized for their abilities by the social group in which they live, and they are called upon to interact with the Otherworld on behalf of both the community and individuals. Community-oriented shamanic activities might be directed toward hunting success, favorable weather, crop fertility, and other matters. More individually oriented tasks might include escorting a deceased person's soul to the Otherworld, healing a sick person, retrieving a lost soul, or causing someone's illness or death. The extent of leadership exercised by shamans with reference to communal activities, warfare, and food procurement differs among cultures. In virtually all cases, however, the power wielded by shamans can be used for benevolent or malevolent purposes. Powerful shamans are sometimes feared for their potential to turn their abilities to witchcraft. Many cases are known of shamans using their powers to protect their community by causing harm to their enemies, and cases are known where shamans have tried to kill each other using their powers (Lyon 1998).

The preceding gives a general view of the shaman. And so, although I am sympathetic to the concerns of those who object to use of the term *shaman* (especially in connection with Native American religious practices), I find no other instantly recognizable term that might alternatively serve as an umbrella for the cross-cultural range of magico-ritual practitioners who hold worldviews having the same underlying core attributes and who use altered states to interact with the spirit world. For the time being, I am obligated to use the term *shaman*.

Archaeological Indicators of Shamanism

From an archaeological perspective, the question is whether it is possible to recognize shamanism in the archaeological record. As archaeologist Colin Renfrew has pointed out, "The archaeologist . . . cannot observe beliefs: one can only work with material remains, the consequences of actions" (1985:12). Religious symbols and ritual activities, however, offer the possibility of leaving material evidence, and so it is to that kind evidence that we need to look. Since the evidence for symbols and rituals is central to the reconstruction of ancient thought, it is useful to briefly consider what is meant by these terms—even if, unfortunately, space limitations constrain our discussion.

Symbols

A symbol is a representational form or image that stands for something else. Many of the symbols we will consider were probably religious symbols. Following Eliade (1959:88), by religious symbol I mean a symbol that functions within the context of religious experience or conception. In turn, many—but not all—religious symbols derive from natural phenomena. In other words, they are based in what archaeologist David Whitley (2005:81) calls natural models. Hopewell symbols draw heavily from natural models, especially avian predators. Whatever their form, though, religious symbols represent an aspect of the world or cosmos that is not immediately evident in the realm of everyday experience. As explained by Douglas Allen, religious symbols "point beyond themselves to 'something' transcendental, supernatural, transhistorical, transhuman" (2002:150).

Another characteristic of religious symbols is that they tend to reveal the inter-related nature of things. As anthropologist Victor Turner explains, "a dominant symbol is a *unification of disparate significata*. . . . [T]heir very generality enables them to bracket together the most diverse ideas and phenomena" (1967:28; emphasis in original). By way of example—and as I hope to convince the reader in chapter 4—in their symbolism, Hopewell copper plates integrate diverse phenomena to include the solstice directions, world quarters, and raptors. What might otherwise be thought of as unrelated phenomena are, in the copper plate symbol, bound together in a structurally interrelated system.

Related is that religious symbols are capable of expressing and reconciling paradoxical or contradictory aspects of reality (Eliade 1959:101). The

Chinese Taijitu is an example. In this symbol, representing the principle of yin and yang, opposite aspects of the cosmos are shown to be part of the same reality. As I will demonstrate in chapter 4, a similar expression is found in the Turner monster engraving.

The meaning of a religious symbol is not always straightforward. In fact, Turner (1967:30–32) proposes that there are two kinds of symbols: dominant symbols and instrumental symbols. Dominant symbols occupy a central place in rituals and carry their meanings across multiple rituals. Instrumental symbols are, in a sense, modifiers; that is, when situated with a dominant symbol, they identify the specific meaning intended for the dominant symbol. A Hopewell example is provided by black obsidian and white quartz biface blades. It is likely that these blades were used in a variety of rituals. As such, large biface blades would be considered dominant symbols. The specific meaning for a particular blade, however, becomes manifest depending on its color, which in this instance is an instrumental symbol. Presumably, black blades symbolized one set of concepts, whereas white blades symbolized something else.

Religious symbols are often polysemic, or "multivocal," meaning they can have multiple meanings and "may stand for many things" (Turner 1967:50). A Hopewell example is again provided by the falcon symbol. In later chapters, we will consider evidence showing that the Hopewell used the falcon as a symbol for the upperworld, solstice directions, mythical Thunderbirds, and perhaps shaman status.

A related issue is noted by archaeologist C. Wesley Cowan. As Cowan (1996:133) points out, the meaning of a symbol might be known only to its creator. Alternatively, it might be known to a wider group—such as a clan or lineage—but not to anyone outside the group. Or it may be that the meaning of a symbol is known to all Hopewell people, but not to non-Hopewell peoples.

For the archaeologist, the question is whether or not the polysemic meanings for a symbol are arbitrary. If they are entirely arbitrary, we would have little hope of understanding any prehistoric symbol. Fortunately, though, Renfrew (1985:13) points to three attributes of symbols that argue against this potential dilemma: (1) the relationship between a symbol and its meaning may become conventionalized—that is, the symbol may be repeatedly used to convey the same meaning; (2) symbols are often used together in the same context, thus allowing the assumption of meaning in less apparent contexts; and (3) the form of a symbol is not entirely arbitrary, but instead often relates graphically to its intended meaning or concept. In archaeological contexts, these attributes, related essentially to matters of context and redundancy, provide important clues to the meaning of a particular symbol.

For the individual, religious symbols ultimately serve to elucidate the place of humans in the world of existence. Eliade explains: "The religious symbol translates a human situation into cosmological terms and vice versa; more precisely, it reveals the continuity between the structures of human existence and cosmic structures" (1959:103).

For the archaeologist, symbols hold the potential of revealing the world-view of the culture under study, if we find, with Geertz, that culture is a "historically transmitted pattern of meanings embodied in symbols, a system of inherited conceptions expressed in symbolic forms by means of which men communicate, perpetuate, and develop their knowledge about and their attitudes toward life" (1973:89).

Rituals

Ritual behavior is engaged in by both humans and animals. Bees, pigeons, whales, and wolves, for example, all exhibit ritual behaviors likely to have had adaptive significance. With reference to human behavior, however, Turner defines ritual as "a stereotyped sequence of activities involving gestures, words, and objects, performed in a sequestered place, and designed to influence preternatural entities or forces on behalf of the actors' goals and interests" (1977 [1972]:183). As I will demonstrate in later chapters, this definition appears to effectively capture the intent of Hopewell religious rituals.

Rappaport (1979:179–82) distinguishes two classes of messages that are transmitted through rituals: indexical and canonical. Indexical messages provide information concerning physical, mental, or social states to others. Canonical messages are "concerned with the enduring aspects of nature, society, or cosmos, and [are] encoded in apparently invariant aspects of liturgical orders" (182). We can apply these distinctions to the archaeological correlates of ritual behavior. What this means for Hopewell is that, while indexical expressions of ritual behavior will differ from each other in terms of location, timing, number of participants, objects utilized, and so on, canonical messages as expressed in the liturgical order of things will remain fixed. Thus Hopewell canonical messages concerning the dualistic nature of the cosmos, for example, will find expression through the juxtaposition of complementary opposite, or mirror images rendered variously in copper, bone, and earth. Indeed, it is canonical information relative to ritual behavior that allows us to gain some understanding of Hopewell religious beliefs.

Cognitive anthropologist Maurice Bloch (1992) proposes a useful theory that offers insight into the psychology of religious ritual. In Bloch's view, human societies recognize that life proceeds through a process of birth, growth, reproduction, aging, and death. This "vital side" of life is characterized by its transience. At the same time, however, human societies construct transcendent and permanent worlds that exist beyond biological processes. These transcendent and permanent worlds provide a sense of stability in an ever-changing environment, structure out of chaos, and meaning out of transience.

Humans connect to this "world beyond process" through rituals (Bloch 1992:4). They do this by symbolically sacrificing the ritual initiate or participant. This moves the initiate into a liminal state that allows the person to participate in the immortality of the transcendent entity—even if only momentarily. According to Bloch, the ritual sacrifice through which the initiate becomes joined with the transcendental is typically accomplished through violence, which can include body mutilation of the participant and/or the killing of living creatures.

Bloch proposes that this construct accounts for the near-universal occurrence of a three-phase structural pattern found in religious rituals, namely: initiatory symbolic death, joining with the transcendental, and reincorporation with the here and now. The operational concept is that "by leaving this life, it is possible to see oneself and others as part of something permanent, therefore life-transcending" (1992:4). Among the rituals that Bloch proposes to incorporate this structural commonality are initiations, marriages, funerals, and spirit possessions.

Bloch's thesis provides a convincing explanation of the rationale and mechanism by which, for example, the hunter assimilates the transcendent vitality of his prey. As such, Bloch's thesis can be used to help interpret Hopewell collections of predator, or "power" animal body parts, as discussed in chapter 5.

An evolutionary basis for religious ritual is proposed by anthropologist Brian Hayden (2003:29–34). It is Hayden's contention that religious rituals were adaptive and even selected for through natural selection. Hayden's thesis is that emotional bonds between individuals (such as male and female partners, parents and children, and siblings) lead to social alliances. Social alliances are critically useful to human survival as a way of ensuring or fostering mutual aid. Such bonds are especially important during times of ecological stress. One way in which emotional bonds and the potential for mutual aid can be expanded beyond the immediate family group is through shared experiences to include ecstatic religious rituals. Among the experiences Hayden identifies as contributing to shared emotional bonding within such rituals are feasting, gift giving, and altered states brought about by rhythmic singing and dancing and various stress-related techniques. The result, according to Hayden is that "[t]his bonding is, in essence, what I suggest the original function of religion was among hunter-gatherers. . . . Groups that had the potential for such religious emotions and used them by holding rituals in which participants entered into ecstatic states, communicating with common deities or totemic ancestors, would be more likely to survive because of mutual help in times of need" (32). We will return to this theme in chapter 7. Conceptually related is the idea that rituals demonstrate the participant's commitment to the group's ideology (Gintis, Smith, and Bowles 2001; Sosis 2003).

Reaching deeper into our cognitive makeup is the hazard-precaution model put forth by cognitive anthropologists Pascal Boyer and Pierre Liénard (2006; also see Liénard and Boyer 2006). In this view, most rituals have a range of common themes. These themes include a concern with purification and pollution, protection against invisible dangers, and the creation of special space. Concern with these themes originates in a mind-brain system referred to as the hazard-precaution system (HPS). This system is not the same as fear systems that respond to actual dangers (e.g., Le Doux 2003). Rather, the HPS serves to monitor potential danger clues and indirect signals of threats to include predation by large animals, intrusion or assault by strangers and other individuals, contagion and contamination, loss of social status and exclusion from the group, harm to offspring, and probably other threats. When activated by clues of potential danger, the HPS motivates the individual toward appropriate precautions, which include washing, cleaning, contact avoidance, safety-checking the environment, delineating special space, avoiding particular places, and monitoring others' behavior. Examples of ritual precautions include immersion in water for spiritual cleansing and purification, chasing away disease spirits that are a source of contamination by blowing smoke, and the circumambulation of space to designate a special protected area. Many more examples could be cited. The point is that, according to Boyer, "religious rituals are highly stylized versions of precautionary procedures" (2008:1039). Further, "[r]ituals are compelling because specific aspects of human cognitive architecture make these behavioral sequences attention-grabbing, intuitively appropriate, and compelling" (Liénard and Boyer 2006:814). In this view, our proclivity toward religious ritual is a by-product of our cognitive evolution.

Further Thoughts

Based on the multiplicity of viewpoints and issues noted above, as well as others, it is clear that the interpretation of prehistoric religious beliefs and practices offers its share of challenges and difficulties. In spite of the difficulties, however, I would follow the lead of archaeologist Ian Hodder (1992:123) who points out that the problems are not insurmountable; rather, they are similar to those faced by archaeologists every day. As I will explain in more detail in chapter 2, whether we are looking at subsistence systems, social structures, political systems, or religious beliefs and practices, informed inferences and interpretive hypotheses are the result when seeking explanations for what we find in the archaeological record. Indeed, it is informed inference and interpretive hypotheses that, for better or worse, make archaeology more than a mere exercise in the quantification of potsherds and projectile points.

The book is structured in the following manner. Chapter 2 provides an overview of the theories, methods, and assumptions that have guided my investigation. In chapter 3 the physical appearance of Hopewell shamans is considered. Chapters 4 and 5 explore the structure and nature of the Hopewell universe. In chapter 6 I discuss the roles Hopewell shamans may have played. Chapter 7 looks at how Hopewell shamans accomplished their objectives. Chapter 8 provides a few concluding remarks.

CHAPTER TWO

Theoretical Background and Methods

Accounts of prehistoric shamanism vary in method and theory. Some emphasize the importance of altered states of consciousness (e.g., Lewis-Williams and Dowson 1988; Clottes and Lewis-Williams 1998); others are more concerned with art and iconography (Pasztory 1982; Freidel, Schele, and Parker 1993; Reilly 1996). Some rely heavily on ethnographic analogies (e.g., Whitley 2000); others are not so inclined (Bahn 2001:69–72). Against this varying backdrop, it is important to identify one's theoretical position and methodological approach, for, as E. Thomas Lawson and Robert McCauley point out, "theories guide interpretation" and "no datum is self-interpreting" (1990:10). The purpose of this chapter, therefore, is to identify the theoretical and methodological approaches that have guided the present inquiry.

In the chapters that follow, we will be concerned with Hopewell expression of what has been referred to as a "shamanic worldview" (Furst 1994a:2). Actually, a more precise term might be *archetypal shamanic worldview*. By this I mean a biogenetically generated set of concepts, or recurring ways of thinking, that underlie or are implicit in the religious beliefs and practices of humankind. As discussed in more detail later in this chapter, what I mean by *biogenetically generated* is that the core concepts of the shamanic worldview result from how the human mind-brain operates—which, in turn, is largely determined by the genetically hardwired structure of our nervous system.[1] As Todd Tremlin explains, "The conceptual range of the human mind is constrained by its own processing methods and by the patterns and tools it uses to interpret and organize the world. There are only so many ways we can think about things" (2006:91).

With this understanding, in what follows, the terms *shamanic worldview* and *archetypal shamanic worldview* are used synonymously.

The notion of a fundamental worldview common to humankind has been discussed by Donald Brown (1991), Michael Kearney (1984), Robert Redfield (1953), and others. To begin with, however, it might be helpful to define what is meant by the term *worldview*. Kearney provides a useful definition:

> [E]ach society is a particular arrangement of ideas and behavior. The overall cognitive framework of these ideas and behavior is that society's worldview. Another way of stating this is that a world view is the collection of basic assumptions that an individual or a society has about reality. (42)

Like the term *shamanism*, worldview is something of an academic construct. In truth, no one carries a worldview around in his or her head. Rather, what we possess as individuals are certain images and assumptions that together comprise what the investigator calls a worldview. Problematic too is that the term *worldview* lumps together under the rubric of sameness what is really a range of similar, but not quite identical images and assumptions held by individuals within a society. For these reasons, the terms *worldview* and *shamanic worldview* are used herein as heuristic devices.

The Shamanic Worldview

Having introduced the concept of worldview, we can now consider what is meant by *shamanic worldview*. As explained by Furst (1994a:2), the shamanic worldview expresses a certain "philosophy" or approach to the world. The shamanic worldview has its origins in the Paleolithic period, when humans lived as hunters and gatherers. Since 99.5 percent of human existence occurred during this time period (Hayden 2003:22), it is not surprising that the kind of creature we are reflects our background as hunter-gatherers. With reference to this Paleolithic world, we can surmise that our earliest ancestors were compelled to find order in their world. As James Ashbrook and Carol Rausch Albright explain,

> humans keep trying to make sense of what we experience. As a result, we keep organizing the random and disorganized—both things and ideas. This propensity contributes to what matters to our survival—and to what is significant for who we are. (1997:8)

Our propensity to find or create order allows us to do something of considerable value: It allows us to predict future events based in our apprehension of the regularities and connections between things. In other words, if, out of the myriad of sensory data we perceive, we are able to distinguish a pattern to things, we are then in the position of being able to predict: if A, then B; or if C, then D. This enhanced ability in humans allows us to predict future events and has provided us with the means to outsmart every other creature on the planet, the result being that most of the time, humans are hunters rather than prey.

Our need to find or create order may be driven by the mind-brain's causal operator (Newberg, d'Aquili, and Rause 2001:50). We will explore the concept of the causal operator in more detail later in this chapter. For now, we begin with the thesis that "the mind brings things to awareness, it discloses and presents the world" (Thompson 2007:13). Further, it is the mind that creates meaning for what we apprehend. That is to say, "a cognitive being's world is not a prespecified external realm, represented internally by the brain, but a relational domain enacted or brought forth by that being's autonomous agency and mode of coupling with the environment" (15). There are constraints, however, on what the mind-brain is capable of bringing to awareness. The result is that as a function of how our mind-brains are structured, the physical form and limitations of our bodies, and the nature of the world around us, the relational domains or cognitive worlds enacted by humans have commonalities among individuals and cultures. These commonalities contribute to what I refer to as the *archetypal shamanic worldview*. The essential aspects of this worldview are essentially the same cross-culturally and deep into prehistory—even if the specific content differs among peoples as the result of cultural setting, environmental influence, and unique historical tradition. Pearson explains it this way: "Although the topographical details of the shaman's universe may differ from culture to culture and from place to place, the fundamental structure is the same" (2002:69).

Given this, it is possible to construct a model of the shamanic worldview, where model means a theoretical construct consisting of interrelated variables or attributes, used in this case to help us understand what we find in the archaeological record. In developing the shamanic worldview model that follows, I have relied primarily on the work of Eliade (1964), Furst (1977), Lewis-Williams and Pearce (2005), Tuan (1977), von Gernet (1992a), Whitley (2000), and Winkelman (2004).[2]

The archetypal shamanic worldview model posits certain core traits or attributes. Chapters 4 and 5 provide detailed discussions, relevant citations, and cross-cultural examples showing how this model finds support in both the cognitive neurosciences and ethnographic data. By way of introduction at this point, however, I propose that key features or attributes of the shamanic worldview include the following:

1. The shamanic universe is holistic and dualistic. All things are interconnected and part of a greater reality (Harner 1988:10). At the same time, the shamanic universe is comprised of binary sets or opposite pairs, often balanced or mediated by a third element or feature.
2. The shamanic universe is multi-layered in its vertical aspect (Eliade 1964:259; Furst 1976a:151). These layers include some combination of earth and sky; earth, sky, and beneath earth; or earth, sky, and water. These locations have cosmic or spirit analogues often expressed as upperworld, this world, and lowerworld.
3. The layers or realms of the shamanic universe are connected by a central axis or *axis mundi* that extends vertically (Eliade 1964; Furst 1976a:151). As the *axis mundi* serves to connect the cosmic realms, it is often used by the shaman to soul travel to these other worlds. The *axis mundi* can by symbolized by a tree, a column of smoke, a ladder, a ray of sunlight, a rainbow, or in many other ways.
4. The shamanic universe also extends in the horizontal plane. Often, this plane is divided into four basic directions or quadrants (Furst 1976a:151). Often, each direction or quadrant has a particular color, animal, spirit, element, time of day, and/or other phenomenon associated with it.
5. The center of the shamanic universe is located on the *axis mundi* at the intersection of the cardinal directions, or world quarters (Tuan 1977:149).
6. Time in the shamanic universe is oriented to periodic events that include solar and lunar cycles, seasons, and life cycles.

In addition to the structural features noted above, the shamanic universe has qualitative features that include the following:

7. The shamanic universe has hidden dimensions or realms not normally visible or accessible. As explained by Christina Pratt, "[R]ealms of the spirit world are not geographically removed from the everyday world. All the worlds occupy the same space, but the spirit world spaces are only accessible to some us of some of the time" (2007:465). Portals to the spirit world can include graves, specially constructed structures, and special landscape features.

8. The shamanic universe is animistic:[3] "All phenomena in the environment are animated by a life force or soul" (Furst 1976a:152). In some sense, all things are alive, including humans, animals, plants, rocks, rivers, mountains, tools, weapons, pottery vessels, figurines, and so on.

Related to this is the widespread belief that the essential life force or soul of humans and animals resides in their bones: "Humans and animals are reborn from their bones" (Furst 1976a:152). Also related and common is the belief that living beings have more than one soul (Hultzkrantz 1953). In a simplified version of this belief, a person can have a body-soul that remains with the corpse after death and a free soul that, upon death of the body, leaves this world on a journey to a land of the dead.

Closely tied to the idea of life force, spirit, or soul is the concept of power. As Kearney explains:

> Power is essentially an inherent aspect of creation; it is a vital force, an energy that pervades the world and is responsible for virtually everything that happens. It is like electricity in that it too is ubiquitous, occurring in some degree in all things, but unevenly. That is, it tends to be concentrated in certain special objects, places, or persons. (1984:148)

James Pearson provides a good explanation of why power is useful for the shaman:

> Form, space, and time are all rendered mutable and malleable under the influence of power. A shaman has the ability to draw a land form toward him or travel through space, transformed into some other creature, such as a bird, bear, or mountain lion. He might use power to bring sacred time into the present so that he can interact with supernatural beings from that otherworldly time. (2002:71–72)

In the shamanic worldview, power can be obtained from plants, animals, and humans, as well as spirit beings.

9. The shamanic universe is one of metamorphosis and transformation. There is "a primordial capability of people, animals, and spirits to assume each other's forms" (Furst 1976a:152). Further, there is a "qualitative equivalence between humans and animals" (Furst 1994a:20). Outward physical appearance is only an incidental attribute of an entity's life force and is subject to change. As S. M. Shirokogoroff explains with reference to the Tungus worldview, "human beings and

other creatures are places for vital life force energies that could alternatively be situated elsewhere" (1935:190). The result is that in the shamanic world, nonhuman entities such as upper- and lowerworld creatures can assume a variety of shapes, including human form. So too, shamans are often believed to have the ability to change their form, often assuming the shape of an animal.

10. The shamanic worldview is concerned with the relationship between predators and prey. Or, to phrase it a bit differently, the shamanic worldview is concerned with the relationship between humans and the plants and animals we eat. Shamanism was "born of the hunt" (Pearson 2002:148). To survive, humans need to eat. To obtain high-protein food, humans hunt and kill other animals. From this reality, humans create a web of spiritual beliefs and relationships with their prey (e.g. Bloch 1992; Burkert 1983). In the shamanic worldview, one of the most common of these beliefs involves the concept of reciprocity and the idea that plants and animals have spirit masters or mistresses. Many shamanic cultures believe that plants and animals willingly give up their lives so that humans can eat their flesh. In this view, since most animals can hide, fly, or outrun, outswim, and outjump humans, it is believed that if an animal gives up its life to the hunter, it is because it was willing to do so.

The other side of the equation is that the taking of a plant or animal life needs to be reciprocated by giving thanks and/or an offering. Thanks and offerings are made either to the slain animal itself or to animal or plant masters who control the release of animals and plants into this world. These spirit masters often appear as large members of the species. In the shamanic worldview, spirit or animal masters need to be propitiated in order to assure continued hunting or gathering success (Furst 1994b:2–3; Hamayon 1994:79). In some shamanic worldviews, if animals are treated with cruelty or disrespect, the animal masters may withhold game.

11. In the shamanic worldview, it is possible for humans to experientially engage and interact with the spirit world and spirit entities. Engagement occurs through altered states of consciousness. For purposes of this discussion, dreaming can be considered an altered state. Other kinds of altered states can be induced by a variety of methods, including the use of psychoactive substances, fasting, sleep deprivation, isolation, hypoxia, and pain, as well as prayer, hypnagogic visualization, and meditation. Pratt (2007:158, 457) distinguishes two "poles" of shamanic altered

states of consciousness: soul flight and embodiment trances. During soul flight trance, the shaman's soul or spirit travels to the Otherworld. In embodiment trance, an outside spirit entity or force is allowed to temporarily reside in the person of the shaman. Through embodiment trance the spirit is able to make its thoughts known—or, in the case of an embodied force, the force can be used by the shaman. Shape-shifting by shamans into animal form by invoking an animal spirit into the body is a form of embodiment trance. In both soul flight and embodiment trances, the shaman maintains control over the trance state. Spirit possession differs from embodiment trance; in possession, the trance state is not under the control of the person possessed.

I hasten to add a number of qualifiers to the above. First, the model I have presented is admittedly oversimplified. There are many aspects to and iterations of the key attributes noted. Further, not every attribute will always be readily apparent in every indigenous worldview or culture. In some cultures, certain attributes will have a visible presence; in others, the same attributes may be sublimated, fragmentary, morphed, or imprecise in their form. Attributes will also be expressed in different ways, some of which we may not recognize. Not all of the attributes will always be visible in the archaeological record. And although they are based in universal mind-brain structures and functions that are the product of human evolution, there is an element of observer subjectivity as to what attributes comprise the shamanic worldview. The above list could be expanded or collapsed in various ways (see, e.g., Furst 1976b:6; Schlesier 1987:45–49). The above list represents my understanding of what is central to the shamanic worldview.

So too, the material remains I have chosen to consider in the chapters that follow reflect a certain selectivity—based in personal decisions as to what I consider important to the points I wish to make and the data I am familiar with. The consequence is that the view of Hopewell religion presented here is neither exhaustive nor entirely objective.

Lastly, it is important to note that, although interrelated, the attributes that comprise the shamanic worldview each have their origins in different cognitive evolutionary backgrounds; that is, each attribute is the by-product of particular cognitive functions that evolved along different trajectories and for different reasons. The result is that the shamanic worldview probably did not suddenly emerge as a total package, with all of its attributes assuming equal weight, on an especially brilliant day in our past. More likely is that aspects of the shamanic worldview gradually came into focus over time, with its attributes finding differing cultural expressions at different times.

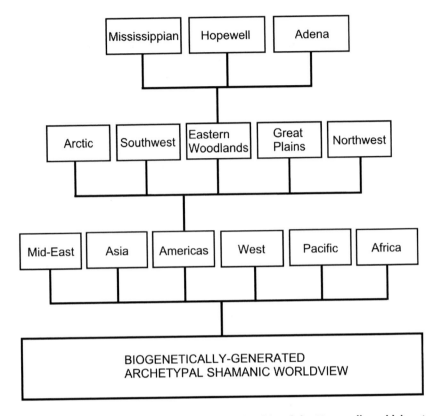

Figure 2.1. Schematic chart showing the relationship of the Hopewell worldview to the archetypal shamanic worldview. Drawing by William Romain.

Crucial to what follows, however, is an understanding of the posited relationships between the Hopewell worldview, other worldviews, and the archetypal shamanic worldview. Figure 2.1 shows an idealized representation of these relationships. With reference to this figure, we need not quibble over the geospatial categories depicted. The world could be divided up differently. What is important is that at the bottom of the figure we find the archetypal shamanic worldview made up of the attributes discussed; at the other end we find a number of specific Native American worldviews, including Adena, Hopewell, and Mississippian. (If we wished, we could further subdivide these worldviews into their own regional iterations and add dozens more.) As figure 2.1 implies, although Adena, Hopewell, and Mississippian worldviews differ from each other in their details, each worldview has its common origin in a biogenetically generated set of attributes, referred to as the *archetypal shamanic worldview*. Further, any specific worldview will have various attributes in common with its relatives at the next lower structural level. Thus, for example, Adena, Hopewell, and Mississippian worldviews have features in common with all Eastern Woodlands worldviews; so too, all Eastern Woodlands worldviews have features in common at the Pan-American level, and so on.

An analogous situation is found in what it means to be an individual. Even though each of us is different from everyone else, there are nevertheless attributes we have in common with members of our family, members of our ethnic group, members of the human species, and so on. The fact that there are cultural and other differences among people does not preclude the fact that we share fundamental similarities. Cognitive scientists Edouard Machery and H. Clark Barrett explain:

> [I]f there were no human nature, huge swaths of the social and biological sciences, notably medicine, that aim at producing general knowledge about our species would be bound to fail. It would be pointless to study human livers, because there would be nothing that one could say about human livers in general. This is clearly wrong in both theory and practice. Generalizable claims about human physiology are clearly possible, as are claims about human cognition. (2006:13)

It is the commonalities in human cognition that allow us to consider the possibility of a biogenetically generated, archetypal shamanic worldview. This perspective accounts for the deep commonalities found among people and cultures without recourse to mystical connections or theories of migration or diffusion. It also accords with the earlier-mentioned notion that there are multiple "shamanisms."

In advocating this perspective, I do not mean to imply that because core aspects of the shamanic worldview are common to humankind and extend deep into prehistory, change has not occurred, or is irrelevant or inconsequential. In connection with Eastern Woodlands religious beliefs, for example, it is quite clear that significant changes occurred during the thousands of years from Paleo-Indian times, through Hopewell, to later Mississippian and Historic periods. Generally, the roles of magico-ritual practitioners became more diverse and specialized as the socioeconomic complexity of these cultures increased. Moreover, the way in which shamanic concepts were expressed in early hunter-gatherer groups differed from how they were expressed by later horticultural and agricultural groups. If one were to look at two side-by-side representative displays—one of Mississippian symbols and the other of Hopewell symbols—the differences would be immediately apparent.

At the same time, however, when we penetrate the surface of Mississippian symbolism, we find the same shamanic worldview attributes that are found in Hopewell. For example, with reference to Mississippian symbolism, archaeologist Thomas Emerson (2003, 1997) finds expression of a dualistic, quadripartite division of the cosmos; use of altered states of consciousness; spirit helpers; soul flight; and human-animal transformations—all of which are found in Hopewell. The difference is the manner of expression.

So how are we to account for such similarities and differences? Because we have biogenetically generated mind-brains that are fundamentally the same, and because we are embodied in a physical form common to humans, and because we exist in a world that has the same physical laws everywhere, the cognitive results are much the same. It is these similar end results, or broad conclusions, that make up the archetypal shamanic worldview. Differences presumably are the result of climate, geography, subsistence basis, culture history and social interaction, modes of information transmission, and idiosyncratic factors. As explained by Whitehouse, however, the result is that "regardless of local histories of cultural innovation and transmission, our fixed, generic cognitive capacities churn out more or less the same kinds of religious outputs in all places and at all times" (2007:229).

The consequence in terms of cosmology, for example, is that the Chinese sage will likely conclude that the world has four quarters, as will the Inca priest, as will the Navajo medicine-man, as will the Siberian shaman. The concept of a quadripartite cosmos in the horizontal plane will be expressed a bit differently by each, but there is a good likelihood that each would recognize the underlying concept expressed, for example, in the cardinal alignment of a temple built in a different region's capital city. In some extreme cases—such as the case of the jungle-bound Amazonian shaman. The shaman may never have seen the distant horizon, but even in that unlikely circumstance, he or she would likely reference the four basic directions to the human body. When standing on a riverbank, for example, our jungle-bound shaman might refer to upstream, downstream, this side of the river, and across the river—thus creating an orthogonal directional system referenced to his embodied perspective.

As people's situations changed over time and as humans expanded into new and unique environments, the attributes that make up the shamanic worldview found expression in countless different ways. But always, the same core attributes were at the heart of it all.[4] In some cultures certain attributes are emphasized, while others find minimal expression. As observers, the more core concepts we are able to identify, the stronger our assessment that the culture or religious system under study is "shamanic." But as mentioned earlier, there are many shamanisms, and all religions incorporate shamanic concepts.

In this regard, it might be useful to address the matter of Western worldviews as related to the archetypal shamanic worldview. It has been suggested that in about the third millennium B.C., a "breakout" or transformation occurred in the Mesopotamian world that led to Western civilization (Lamberg-Karlovsky 2000). One might think that the shamanic worldview disappeared with the advent of Western civilization; however, that notion would not be correct. If I might use the example of Western Christian religious belief, most Christians believe in a vertically tiered cosmos, with avian angels above and reptilian demons below, and humankind balanced between. Clearly four cardinal directions are recognized, and every church that has a steeple is, in effect, an *axis mundi* connecting this world to the upperworld. Most people still live in a universe of hidden dimensions shared with angels and demons, ghosts and spirits. And we attribute animacy and social motives to cars, boats, and planes—giving them personal names and cursing them when they misbehave. Magical transformation or transubstantiation is a frequent Sunday occurrence as millions consume the wine and bread that are the blood and body of Christ. Counterintuitive agents that include vampires, werewolves, and Transformers are a frequent theme of television and movies. Many are in contact with the Otherworld through dreams, séances, and prayer. And we hope to exercise control over games of chance using personal rituals and exhortations that include yelling at and coaxing horses, dice, and machines. Millions seek to know future events through horoscopes and astrology. Indeed, if the everyday lives of civilized Western people are any indication, then the core of the Paleolithic archetypal shamanic worldview is still very much with us. What seems to have changed is that in Western Abrahamic religious traditions, a monotheistic God now rules. This God can be described as a personal attachment figure that has evolved as a byproduct of social-cognitive mechanisms used to negotiate various kinds of relationships, including "attachment, kinship, social exchange, coalitions, and dominance hierarchies" (Kirkpatrick 2008:65; also see Kirkpatrick 2005; Wenegrat 1990).

Methodological Tools

Not too long ago, many archaeologists were of the opinion that it is not possible to know what was in the minds of prehistoric peoples (e.g., Prufer 1996:415; also see Hill 1994) or that "archaeologists are poorly trained to be paleo-psychologists" (Binford 1972:127). For archaeologists of this persuasion, the assumption was that, since matters of prehistoric ideology and religious belief involve questions related to meanings—rather than physical qualities that can be measured, tested, and verified—the resulting interpretations amount to mere speculation.

Archaeological theory involves complex issues, with an extensive literature. Unfortunately we do not have the space to explore that literature, except to comment that today, increasing numbers of archaeologists recognize that although the concept of proof is useful in logic and mathematics, in archaeology the results of our investigative efforts are usually interpretive hypotheses (Whitley 2005; Shanks and Hodder 1995). This is not to say that interpretive hypotheses cannot be scientific—if by *scientific* we mean amenable to evaluation by empirical data.

In this view, there are many different kinds of evidence that can be used to infer to an interpretive hypothesis—such as theories and data derived from the cognitive neurosciences, morphological and contextual analyses, and ethnographic analogies. Together, these and other lines of evidence can be thought of as interwoven strands in a cable, as contrasted to chainlike positivist arguments (Wylie 1989; Lewis-Williams 2002:102–103; Whitley 2005:71–78). In this analogy, chainlike arguments rely on the strength and connection of individual links that comprise the argument. If a single link in the chain is weak or fails in terms of logic or evidence, the argument falls apart. In cabled arguments, however, multiple strands of diverse evidence are woven together so that where there is a break or weakness in one line of evidence, other strands compensate and sustain the argument.

Following upon this, the ability of an interpretive hypothesis to account for what we find in the archaeological record can be evaluated in terms of its strengths and weaknesses, following—in a general sense, a Bayesian perspective (Buck, Cavanagh, and Litton 1996; Bernardo and Smith 1994). In this assessment, the matter is not one of establishing absolute truth; rather, it is a matter of establishing likelihood. The idea is aptly summarized by Clive Ruggles:

> The key principle in the Bayesian approach is to express one's state of knowledge about the domain of current interest in the form of a probability distribution of the parameters of some model, "probability" being taken in the sense of "degree of belief." (1994:500)

Where multiple interpretive hypotheses exist, the preferred hypothesis will generally be the one that accounts for the greatest amount and diversity of data, successfully fits within larger models and overall theory, is internally consistent and logical, is such that empirical facts can be deduced from it, and offers the ability to generate new insights and research questions.

To summarize, in the chapters that follow, I do not pretend to "prove" what the Hopewell thought or believed about the world around them. Rather, I seek to understand Hopewell through the model or "lens" of shamanism. Toward that end, we will find that certain interpretive hypotheses are strongly supported by the available data; others, less so. Listed below are several of the multiple lines of evidence I will draw upon in this effort.

Cognitive Neuroscience

Cognitive neuroscience refers to the study of the biological mechanisms that underlie cognition. In practical usage, the term overlaps with subdisciplines including cognitive psychology, neurobiology, and psychobiology. The value of cognitive neuroscience for archaeology is that it provides a bridge, or link between archaeological remains and the thought processes of the ancient people who created those material remains.

Earlier mentioned—but worth repeating—is that, based in the findings of cognitive neuroscience, the position taken here is that there are fundamental similarities in shamanism around the world and deep into prehistory. These similarities result from the structure and function of the mind-brain, how the world is structured, and how we perceive and adapt to the world through our bodies. The result, as explained by Lewis-Williams and Pearce is that, "[a]lthough each society's cosmology is unique, nevertheless there are broad structures that derive from the brain" (2005:11). Winkelman articulates the same idea:

> The fundamental similarity across time, space, and cultures in the phenomena of shamanism indicates that these traditions developed from a common psychobiological basis. The cross-cultural distribution of fundamental aspects of shamanism reflects an underlying psychobiological basis and its adaptive consequences. These universal and cross-cultural characteristics of shamans reflect biosocial and neurophenomenological structures that constitute the primordial basis for religion. (2000:71)

The nature of the neurobiological structures that Lewis-Williams, Pearce, and Winkelman refer to is currently the subject of intense study. Unfortunately, a Grand Unified Theory for all the subdisciplines that make up cognitive neuroscience has yet to be realized. Indeed, because the mind-brain is so complex, with so many different cognitive systems, networks, and explanatory levels involved, it is unlikely that one theory or one approach will ever answer all our questions. As a consequence, in what follows, I have drawn from a number of theories, hypotheses, and explanations.

Specifically, I have drawn from the work of d'Aquili, Laughlin, and Mc-Manus (1979; cognitive operators); Fauconnier and Turner (2002; conceptual blending); Lakoff and Johnson (1999; embodied mind); Guthrie (1993; animism and anthropomorphism); Boyer (2001; counterintuitive concepts); Leslie (1995; intentional agents); Barrett (1997; agency detection); Premack and Woodruff (1978) and Bering (2002; Theory of Mind); and others. This does not mean I subscribe to everything these investigators propose. Indeed, even these subject matter experts sometimes disagree with each other. Rather, each theory provides yet another piece of the puzzle in our understanding. Two of these theories are of sufficient importance to the present study to warrant introduction at this point. They are the theory of cognitive operators and the theory of conceptual blending.

Cognitive Operators
Recent approaches to human cognition suggest that the mind relies on a variety of mechanisms to help us respond to different kinds of problems or situations. Researchers describe these mechanisms in different ways. Barrett (2004), for example, refers to *mental tools*. Boyer (2001) describes *inference systems*. Baron-Cohen (1995) uses the term *neurocognitive mechanisms*. A number of researchers refer to *mental modules* (Fodor 1983; Gazzaniga 1988; Pinker 1997; Barkow, Cosmides, and Tooby 1992; Mithen 1996; Sperber 1994). Among the earliest investigators to think along these lines were d'Aquili, Laughlin, and McManus (1979), who described what they call *cognitive operators*. Cognitive operators are similar to modules.

Opinions differ with regard to mind-brain modularity. Fodor (1983), for example, considers the mind's modularity to be limited (i.e., only a few modules). Tooby and Cosmides (1992) argue for a "massive modularity" (i.e., hundreds or even thousands of different modules). Mithen (1996) describes a "cognitive fluidity" among mental modules. What all these approaches have in common, however, is the notion that when confronted with a particular kind of problem, the mind uses a specialized mental tool, or a combination of tools to solve the problem. When faced with a different kind of problem, the mind uses other tools. Among the tools or mechanisms Barrett (2004:5) identifies, for example, are an agency detection device, face detector, living-thing describer, and intuitive morality facilitator. In this sense, the modular mind has been compared to a Swiss Army knife (Cosmides, Tooby, and Barkow 1992).

Undoubtedly, things are more complicated than suggested by any of the above conceptions. It is also important to recognize that for many investigators, terms such as *mental modules* are intended more as metaphorical descriptions of functional aspects of the mind-brain than as literal entities. Having said that, however, it is noteworthy that d'Aquili, Laughlin, and McManus (1979) find cognitive operators to be associated with specific areas of the brain—recognizing of course, that each specialized area is part of an interconnected system that gives rise to mind-brain functions. D'Aquili, Laughlin, and McManus base their opinion on the results of single photon emission computed tomography (SPECT) and positron emission tomography (PET) scans.

In any event, Newberg, d'Aquili, and Rause (2001) propose that the mind's cognitive operators include (1) a holistic operator, which allows us to view things as a whole; (2) a reductionist operator, which enables us to apprehend the parts that make up a whole; (3) a causal operator, which gives us the ability to perceive cause-and-effect relationships; (4) an abstractive operator, which allows us to form general concepts from individual facts; (5) a binary operator, which helps organize what we see by simplifying or reducing relationships to a series of opposites; (6) a quantitative operator, which allows us to apprehend such things as time and distance; (7) an emotional value operator, which assigns an emotional feeling to what we apprehend allowing us to react appropriately; and (8) an existential operator, which provides us with a sense of what is real. According to d'Aquili and Newberg (1999:51) it is the combined functioning of these cognitive operators that gives rise to our sense of mind.

The cognitive operator theory will no doubt undergo modification as new insights are gained. Further studies are needed to assess the extent to which cognitive operators and/or other mental modules are associated with specific areas of the brain. It is also the case that cognitive operators or mental modules account for only part of what it means to be human. Nevertheless, the cognitive operator theory is useful in that it provides us with a springboard for the discussions that follow.

Conceptual Blending

The second cognitive theory that will play a prominent role in the chapters that follow is conceptual blending. Elaborated upon by Fauconnier and Turner (2002) and based in part on work by Lakoff and Kovecses (1987) and Lakoff and Johnson (2003 [1980]), in its simplest form conceptual blending holds that by subconscious process, elements and relations from two input mental spaces are projected into a third mental space termed *blended space*, or simply *the blend*. In turn, "the blend develops emergent structure that is not present in the inputs" (Fauconnier and Turner 2002:42). Of crucial importance to creative thinking is that we can "run" the blends by treating them as simulations, thus creating alternative scenarios and potentially significant insights. As I will demonstrate later, conceptual blending can be used to help explain many different kinds of shamanic transformations.

With conceptual blending, we enter the realm of imagination, and, as we will discover, shamanism is very much dependent on imagination. In this regard I am reminded of research involving a female chimpanzee named Panpanzee (Jaffe 2006:155–56). Reportedly, Panpanzee would pretend to groom a doll, picking imaginary "bugs off her body and feed[ing] them to the doll." Moreover, Panpanzee would offer some of the imaginary bugs to her human caretaker, Liz. Of considerable interest is that when Liz offered imaginary bugs back to Panpanzee, the chimp would accept and eat the phantom bugs. In this interaction it might be said that the chimp and human created a shared social world comprised of invisible bugs as distinguished from "us"— with the further implication that it is acceptable for "us" to eat the bugs. (See Byrne [1995] for additional examples of pretend play in chimps and gorillas.) I propose that the mental leap from imaginary bugs to imaginary spirits and imaginary worlds is not very great. Indeed, I would suggest that imagination lies at the essence of shamanism and the associated rituals that go with it. Boyer expresses a similar opinion:

> From childhood, humans form enduring, stable and important social relationships with fictional characters, imaginary friends, deceased relatives, unseen heroes and fantasized mates. . . . It is a small step from having this capacity to bond with non-physical agents to conceptualizing spirits, dead ancestors and gods, who are neither visible nor tangible, yet are socially involved. (2008:1038)

In short, the core assumptions that underlie what follows are (1) the mind-brain is comprised of mental tools, operators, or modules, designed to solve problems found in our evolutionary past; (2) these modules and their functions evolved over millions of years as the result of natural selection; and (3) because the mind-brain is structured the same among human beings as a species, "the way people think and the ideas they produce are largely the same for everyone everywhere" (Tremlin 2006:8). The further implication is that these psychobiological commonalities have resulted in an archetypal shamanic worldview that has an observable set of core attributes.

Indeed, it is this commonality in mind-brain structure and function that allows us some idea of how the Hopewell viewed the cosmos, for one of the implications in accepting the idea that shamanic concepts have their origins in the structure and operation of the human brain is that core elements of the shamanic worldview will be found not only in our Paleolithic past (Lewis-Williams 2002), but also in the beliefs of the earliest peoples who migrated to the Americas (Furst 1977:20). From this it follows that if core elements or central shamanic themes are still found among Historic Native American groups, then it is likely that temporally intermediate peoples such as the Hopewell also held these core beliefs (also see von Gernet 1992a:137).

Morphological Analyses

Another kind of evidence that can help us understand prehistoric religion is morphological analysis. Morphology refers to the form and structure of an object. In the case of the Hopewell, morphological analyses of their earthworks and smaller artifacts offer the potential of providing a tremendous amount of information. The presumption is that these objects reflect implicit cosmological beliefs and that certain of these beliefs can be identified through analyses of such variables as shape, size, proportion, and composition.

Consideration of shape and size with respect to Hopewell earthworks, for example, can provide significant insights relative to Hopewellian concepts of geometry and units of measure. Composition refers to the manner in which individual parts are combined to form a whole. Composition with respect to Hopewell material remains will focus on two concepts or themes: (1) bilateral symmetry and (2) complementary opposites. As I will demonstrate, consideration of these concepts offers the possibility of drawing strong inferences about how the Hopewell structured space.

Contextual Analyses

For a variety of reasons, it is often difficult to know the meaning of a symbol drawn from a prehistoric culture separated from us by thousands of years. Helpful in this regard, however, is consideration of the context in which the symbol is found. Indeed, whether an ancient symbol is as large as Stonehenge or as small as a king's scepter, to successfully interpret an object's meaning, its context needs to be taken into account. As explained by Hodder, context means "all those associations which are relevant to its meaning. This totality is of course not fixed in any way since the meaning of an object depends on what it is being compared with, by whom, with what purpose and so on" (1992:14). Contextual analysis thus presumes that the meaning of an object is found in its relationships to other things. Indeed, it can be said that the meaning of an object is bounded by its relational context.

For example, many meanings have been attributed to Stonehenge. However, the "meaning" of the structure depends on the ideology of the viewer as well as the historical context within which it is being considered. In the case of the king's scepter, what is nothing more than a piece of decorated metal takes on grave significance when considered as a symbol of the king's authority. In the chapters that follow, we will find that contextual analyses figure prominently in assessing the symbolic meaning of Hopewell objects.

Analogical Reasoning and Ethnographic Data

One of the implications of the idea that core shamanic attributes are common to Historic Native American groups, the Hopewell, and earlier peoples is that it allows us to use ethnographic analogy to help interpret what we find in the archaeological record. In other words, within certain constraints, we can use ethnographic data to help us understand what we find in the Hopewell record.

Archaeological use of ethnographic analogy is not without potential problems, however. There is the danger of falling into the trap of claiming similar uses for objects or meanings for symbols that superficially resemble each other, only to find upon critical review that the analogical inferences do not hold, usually due to exceptions or counterexamples being pointed out. To better understand how I propose to apply ethnographic analogy to the Hopewell case, it is useful to unbundle the concept. Three issues are involved: (1) analogical thinking; (2) ethnographic data; and (3) the archaeological application of ethnographic data.

When confronted with unknown or novel situations, the human mind tries to make sense of the new by reference to what it already knows. In more precise terms, we use analogical reasoning "to understand the target domain by seeing it in terms of the source domain" (Holyoak and Thagard 1995:2). *Source domain* means the knowledge with which we are already familiar; *target domain* means the less familiar piece of knowledge we wish to understand. For example, to describe the structure of an atom, we might say: "The atom is like a miniature solar system." In this case, we are using an image that is familiar to us (the solar system), to describe the less familiar structure of the atom. The source domain is the solar system; the target domain is the atom. Human cognition relies heavily on analogical reasoning.

The second issue mentioned above is the matter of ethnographic data. Ethnographic data provide real-life descriptions of cultural phenomena. Ethnographic analogies utilize ethnographic data to help us understand things we find in the past. In such cases, ethnographic data provide the source domain, while the target domain is the prehistoric thing we seek to understand.

As to the archaeological application of ethnographic data, the observations of archaeologist Alexander von Gernet are useful. Von Gernet

(1992a:137) makes the point that in our efforts to understand prehistoric beliefs (von Gernet uses the example of a prehistoric Iroquoian site), we need to recognize that the belief system in question will not be "entirely unique" but rather will reflect a combination of features. Von Gernet explains that, in the case of the prehistoric Iroquois, these features will include (1) pan-human principles that derive from a universal neurological functioning of the brain; (2) Pan-Amerindian features; (3) pan-northeastern features; and (4) idiosyncratic features. In the Hopewell case, we need to change "pan-northeastern features" to "pan–Eastern Woodlands features."   Each of these levels provides a potential source domain for ethnographic analogies. For example, based on the work of van Gennep (1960), we know that humans universally engage in rites of passage. Since there are no known exceptions to this, we can infer with a high degree of probability that the prehistoric Hopewell also celebrated rites of passage.

At the next level, based on his review of ethnographic data, Nicholas Saunders (2004:123) finds that, "conception of the earth as a living entity" is Pan-American in extent. Specifically, "conceptualization of the earth as a sacred, female, living entity is widespread across the Americas. It is part of a worldview that sees the physical world and its natural phenomena as animated by, and infused with, spirit force" (125). Given the Pan-American nature of this belief, it is likely that it has a deep time line and that the Hopewell held similar beliefs.

On the pan–Eastern Woodlands level, we find in the ethnographic literature that giant serpents and panthers were associated with the lowerworld, while thunderbirds, eagles, and falcons were associated with the upperworld. These associations are found not in a single story, but rather in the myths and legends of Native American peoples across the Eastern Woodlands—again suggesting a deep time line. From this and symbolic analyses based in natural models, it is reasonable to infer that the Hopewell also associated serpents and panthers with the lowerworld and raptor birds with the upperworld.

In each of these and similar cases, the credibility of the analogical inference is supported by (1) "the existence of constraints on infinite variability in human symbolization and belief" (von Gernet 1992a:137) and (2) the conservative nature of shamanic ideology in terms of change over the millennia. As to the first point, there are constraints that limit what humans believe and how we express those beliefs. Constraints include limitations imposed by the range of our sensory capabilities, limitations imposed by the neurobiology of our brains, limitations associated with the form of our bodies, and limitations imposed by the mechanics of the physical world in which we live. For example, although we believe our senses provide a complete and objective representation of the world around us, the fact is that our sensory capabilities are limited and biased in particular ways. We are not able to see ultraviolet, X-ray, or infrared light. So too, our sense of hearing is limited. Bats, rats, and mice can hear much higher frequencies. Likewise, our sense of smell is limited. Dogs, cats, and other animals are able to distinguish many more odors than we are, and at greater distances.

Physical limitations imposed by the neurobiology of our brains include a finite memory capability and limit to the speed at which we are able to process information. Other constraints dictate how we process the limited sensory data we receive. Limitations imposed by the form of our bodies include forward-facing eyes that constrain our field of view, lungs that require air for breathing, locomotion using legs rather than wings, and so on. Limitations imposed by the mechanics of the world we live in are a function of the fact that we live in three-dimensional space subject to particular laws, such as the law of gravity. These constraints establish the range and character of our interactions with the environment and directly influence what we perceive, how we perceive it, and what we believe about the world. The result, as Steven Pinker explains, is that "contrary to the widespread belief that cultures can vary arbitrarily and without limit, surveys of the ethnographic literature show that the people of the world share an astonishingly detailed universal psychology" (1997:32).

As to the second point concerning the conservative nature of change in shamanic concepts over time, von Gernet notes that "evidence for long-term continuities in the ideational domain . . . is particularly salient in the New World, where uniformities in native belief systems transcend significant spatio-temporal boundaries" (1993:77). Indeed, it is the position taken here—based on multiple examples, including the Maya, Inca, Navajo, Iroquois, and others—that the underlying shamanic ideology that von Gernet refers to continues to persist in the Americas, not only across boundaries of space and time, but also in spite of changes in subsistence from hunting and gathering to horticulture, in spite of changes in political systems from clan and village headmen to empires and countries, and in spite of changes in demographics caused by disease, disaster, and war. Even in the face of these and other significant changes, the core elements of the shamanic worldview are still visible in native cultures throughout the Americas.

A related point is that, as Hall (1997:504–505), von Gernet (1992b:178) and von Gernet and Timmins (1987:41) explain, a direct continuity in cultural forms or particular design features need not be demonstrated for ethnographic analogies to be useful in understanding prehistoric beliefs. Similar motifs, designs, and symbols can manifest themselves quite independently and repeatedly across time and space, given the existence of an underlying substratum of core beliefs. As Hall points out, we are "not suggesting direct continuity of particular cultural forms as much as the persistence of culturally transmitted beliefs and understandings which manifest themselves in many different but recognizably related ways" (504–505).

In short, isolated similarities in form do not necessarily imply identical meanings across time. Rather, it is the occurrence of multiple exemplars from within the source domain that lends credibility to the analogical bridge between past and present (Wylie 2002:150). From this, it follows that unless alternative meanings from within the source domain can be shown, the analogical bridging argument between past and present is without challenge, and other interpretations are less plausible.

Summary

The present study is based in the following ideas: (1) there is an archetypal shamanic worldview comprised of identifiable core attributes; (2) this worldview is an emergent property of our cognitive architecture and interaction with the world during hunter-gatherer times; (3) there are constraints that shape and limit the parameters of this worldview; and (4) the core attributes of the shamanic worldview are found in all religions, including Hopewell.

Having said this, I again want to emphasize that in advocating this view I am not presuming that religious beliefs and practices were static for the Hopewell. Clearly, religious beliefs and practices change over time—as do social, political, economic, and other aspects of any culture. What I am proposing is that even though change occurs, it is possible to identify core shamanic concepts in all religious worldviews, including Hopewell. In the present study, in order to better identify these core attributes, I have collapsed Hopewell time in such a way that the evidence for religious beliefs and practices is considered coeval. Some may consider this problematic. As a practical matter, however, most of the Hopewell sites from which the material remains discussed herein were recovered encompassed hundreds of years of use, and exact dates for construction episodes, individual burials, and deposits are not well established, if they are established at all. Further, it is possible that many of the more important objects expressive of Hopewell religious beliefs and practices were passed down through generations before being situated in their final depositional contexts.

My point is that in this particular study, I am not interested in parsing specific changes over the course of a few hundred years. For now, my more limited goal is to establish the broad outline of Hopewell religious beliefs and practices by reference to the shamanic worldview model and its cognitive sources. Toward that end, the following kinds of evidence are used: (1) theories and data from the cognitive neurosciences; (2) morphological analyses; (3) contextual analyses; and (4) ethnographic and ethnohistoric analogies.

The final point I would make is that in no way do I consider this to be a definitive study. No doubt there are other credible explanations that might be offered for the phenomena discussed here, and there are very likely theories or data I have failed to take into account. What follows should therefore be considered as a series of informed hypotheses and interpretations, supported to greater or lesser extent by the available data as I understand them. As archaeologist Ian Hodder once said, "There is no finality, and my interpretation is only a moment in a moving dialectic" (1992:160).

CHAPTER THREE

Hopewell Shamans

In this chapter we will consider the physical appearance of Hopewell shamans. Ethnographic and ethnohistoric literature tells us that the outward physical appearance of a shaman can vary depending on time, circumstance, and culture. Oftentimes, a shaman looks no different from anyone else in his or her society. Other times a shaman might appear quite different from other people, anatomically as well as in demeanor and clothing. In all instances, though, shamans are liminal persons—"betwixt and between" (Turner 1967:96–97), able to move between the world of humans and the world of spirits (Myerhoff 1976:103). As might be appropriate to their liminal status, many shamans are recognized for their shape-shifting ability, whereby they can transform their appearance, often appearing as part human, part something else, usually animal in nature. Thus Eliade (1964:156) explains that among Siberian peoples, for example, there were bear, reindeer, and bird shamans.

Like their Siberian counterparts, people of the Hopewell culture had bear, deer, and bird shamans. Additionally, there is intriguing evidence for Hopewell wolf and panther shamans, as well as an unusual dwarf shaman.

Bear Shamans

The bear is one of the largest, most powerful, and most intelligent animals in North America. It is also the most humanlike in appearance and habits. (See Hallowell [1926] for a list of similarities.) Perhaps it is not surprising, therefore, that humans might feel a kinship with the bear and that the bear might figure prominently in Native American beliefs. Indeed, Hallowell suggests that a "bear cult" was distributed across the circumpolar region of the Northern Hemisphere and that this cult extended deep into the Paleolithic. Veneration of the bear among Hopewell is evidenced by the large numbers of decorated bear teeth and bear effigy designs found in Hopewell contexts, as well as suggestive evidence for human-to-bear transformation.

Transformation from human to animal form is an ability attributed to many shamans, and in North America one of the most common guises was that of the bear (Lyon 1998:33–36). Åke Hultzkrantz tells of "so-called bear doctors, medicine men whose guardian spirit is the bear and who are transformed into bears as soon as they wear its hide" (1979:73). A story that illustrates just how convincing bear guises could be is related by John Heckewelder, based in an experience he had in Ohio:

> I was once walking through the street of a large Indian village on the Muskingum . . . when one of those monsters suddenly came out of the house next to me, at whose sight I was so frightened, that I flew immediately to the other side. . . . The juggler within the dress hearing what passed between us, began to act over some of his curious pranks . . . but the more he went on with his performance, the more I was at a loss to decide, whether he was a human or a bear; for he imitated that animal in the greatest perfection. (quoted in Wallace 1958:127)

The best representation of what is likely a Hopewell bear shaman—perhaps in the act of transformation—is provided by the Wray figurine (figure 3.1a). Discovered in 1881, the Wray figurine was found with a human skeleton interred in a mound in Newark, Ohio (Dragoo and Wray 1964). The figurine is 6 1/4 inches (15.9 cm) in height, 2 1/2 inches (6.4 cm) wide, and 2 1/2 inches (6.4 cm) thick.

Several lines of evidence support the notion that the Wray figurine represents a Hopewell shaman. To begin with, a human face is shown emerging from the neck of the bear. Of interest is that the human is wearing distinctive Hopewell earspools. From the hump on the creature's back (figures 3.1b and 3.1c), the bear appears to be a brown bear (*Ursus arctos*) or grizzly bear (*Ursus arctos horribilis*). Black bears lack such a prominent hump. What we have in the Wray figurine, therefore, is a composite human-animal image that essentially matches ethnohistoric accounts of what bear shamans looked like.

Next we find that the Wray figurine is shown holding an upside-down severed human head. It is difficult to know the symbolic message being communicated here; however, the handling of a severed human head is consistent with something a psychopomp shaman might do. Also worth noting is that

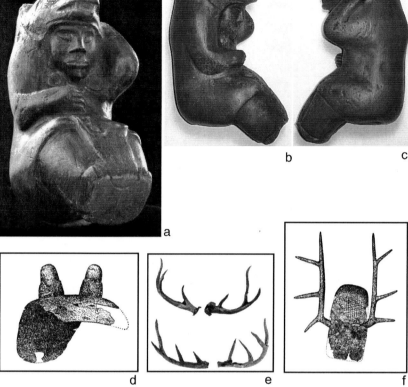

Figure 3.1. a. Wray figurine. Ohio Historical Society image #A3874/000001, used with permission. b. Replica of the Wray figurine showing its human side. Photo by William Romain. c. Replica of the Wray figurine showing its bear side. Photo by William Romain. d. Antler headdress from Hopewell site, mound 25, burials 260 and 261. From Moorehead 1922:fig. 12a. e. Deer antler headdresses from Mound City, mound 13, burial 4. From Mills 1922:fig. 69, used with permission of the Ohio Historical Society, scan provided by Arthur W. McGraw. f. Antler headdress from Hopewell site, mound 25, burial 248. From Moorehead 1922:fig. 11. Figures not to scale.

among some Native American peoples, the head or scalp was considered to be the seat of a person's soul (e.g., Lovisek 2007:53).

The notion that the wray bear shaman is in the act of transforming is suggested by the following. First we note that the piece is a three-dimensional sculpture that fits neatly into the hand of the viewer. The size and shape of the sculpture facilitates viewer manipulation of the piece through space. Next we note that the left arm of the creature is positioned so that from one perspective, the human operator inside the bearskin appears to be holding or propping up the bear head. Given the way the bear's head is firmly situated on the human head, however, the idea that the human is either moving the bear head up and down as a visor or propping up the bear head is not especially convincing. When we rotate the sculpture around its vertical axis, however, a different interpretation becomes possible. Figures 3.1b and 3.1c show what I mean. Viewed from the creature's right side, the face of the human operator is clearly visible (figure 3.1b). However, when the sculpture is rotated counterclockwise around its vertical axis, so as to show its other side, the human face disappears and only the bear is seen (figure 3.1c).[1] In this case, the left arm serves not to prop up the bear head but rather to conceal the human face—the result being that we see a bear with its hand to his head.

In essence, as the viewer rotates the sculpture through space, the human becomes the bear. Conversely, when the piece is rotated back the other way, the bear changes to human. We can further interpret the were-bear shaman as a liminal figure who in human form is holding a bear's head with his or her left hand, while in reversed bear form the bear is holding a human head with his or her right hand. In the Wray figurine, therefore, we find a simple visual illusion rendered in stone and reinforced in multiple ways, but one that is demonstrative of two shamanic concepts—first, transformation between living forms, and second, the notion that Hopewell shamans are capable of assuming animal or human form. In chapter 4, I will show how a similar three-dimensional transformation around a vertical axis finds another occurrence in the Turner monsters.

It is interesting that no other clear instances of bear shamans are found in the Hopewell record. However, another line of evidence suggestive of bear shamans is found in earlier occurrences in the Eastern Woodlands of cut and drilled bear skulls. According to Abel, Stothers, and Koralewski (2001) and Berres, Stothers, and Mather (2004), multiple examples of cut and drilled bear skulls—modified so they could be worn as masks—have been found. In Ohio these masks occur in Late Archaic and Glacial Kame contexts.

Deer Shamans

Furst (1976b:170) and La Barre (1970:176) point out that in Siberia, the shaman's regalia often included a cap or headdress crowned by either real cervid antlers or effigy antlers made out of iron. Notably, Michael Ripinsky-Naxon observes that "horns have continued to be associated with shamanism, in both hemispheres, since remote antiquity. They are believed to be the seat of shaman's power" (1993:44).

Deer antler headdresses are found in Ohio Hopewell, suggesting that the individuals who wore them were spiritually linked to deer or derived their power from the deer spirit. Given this shamanic association, it may be that the following individuals represent deer shamans.

Burial 4 in mound 13 at Mound City was found accompanied by three sets of effigy deer antlers made out of copper, two of which are shown in figure 3.1e. One set was described as 9 inches (22.9 cm) in length with no tines. The second set was about 6 inches (15.2 cm) in length with three tines on each antler. The third set, also about 6 inches (15.2 cm) in length, had four tines on each antler (Mills 1922:452). From perforations through the base of one set and cinch tabs at the base of the two other sets, it was clear to Mills (544) that the effigy antlers were fashioned so they could be attached to headdresses.

At the Hopewell site, a spectacular copper-covered wood antler headdress was found with burial 248 in mound 25 (Moorehead 1922:107; figure 3.1f). Based on its size and backward sweep, the headdress appears modeled after a set of elk antlers. Deer, elk, and caribou are all members of the Cervidae family. Of these animals, the elk (*Cervus canadensis*) is the largest. Accordingly, elk antlers would certainly be appropriate to a shaman-chief who might wish to communicate power and status.

Also found in mound 25, but with burials 260 and 261, was another copper-covered antler headdress (figure 3.1d). The antlers on this object, however, had been fashioned to resemble the first stage of antler growth (Moorehead 1922:110).

Assuming that deer antler headdresses imply shaman status or shamanic associations, then, like bear shamans, deer shamans appear to have a deep time depth in the Eastern Woodlands. Copper deer antler effigies were found, for example, in the Fisher mound, an Adena mound located in Fayette County, Kentucky (Webb and Haag 1947:76–77). Even earlier is a deer antler and skull headdress found with an Archaic period burial near Unionville Center, Ohio (Converse 2003:102).

Raptor Shamans

Cross-culturally, birds play a prominent role in shamanism. Their symbolic meanings are many. Raptors, for example, are often associated with shamanic activities—perhaps inspired not only by their impressive hunting skills, but also by their ability to fly so high as to be lost from view as they enter the upperworld (Pratt 2007:62). Thus raptors are often associated with soul flight and it is in the were-raptor form that the shaman often makes his or her journey to the Otherworld.

Among the indications that the Hopewell had bird shamans are two unique copper headdresses. Figure 3.2a shows the first of these headdresses. In this case, the object was found with an unnumbered burial in mound 7 at the Hopewell site (Shetrone 1926:37). Carr and Case (2005a:25) propose that the headdress represents a bird feather. I agree. Carr and Case do not provide reasons for their interpretation. I would point out, however, that the curved projections of the copper headdress resemble the stylistic manner in which feathers are rendered in another copper piece, found at Mound City (cf. figure 3.2b).

A second copper headdress that might indicate bird shaman status was found with burial 11 in mound 25 at the Hopewell site (figure 3.2c). In this case, the curved headpiece has two copper elements that Henry Shetrone

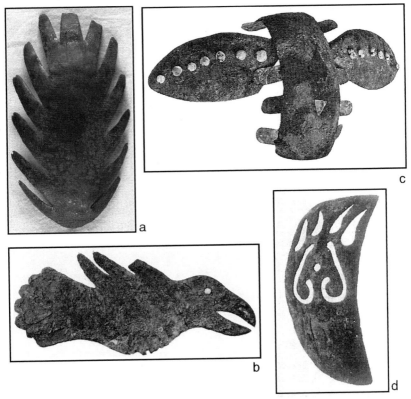

Figure 3.2. a. Copper headdress from Hopewell site, mound 7. Ohio Historical Society image #A0283/000457, used with permission. b. Copper raven effigy from the Hopewell site. From Moorehead 1922:Pl. 69(3). c. Possible bird effigy headdress from the Hopewell site, mound 25. From Shetrone 1926:fig. 106, used with permission of the Ohio Historical Society. d. Copper headdress with canine paw design from Hopewell site, mound 25, burial 4. From Shetrone 1926:fig, used with permission of the Ohio Historical Society. 105. Figures not to scale.

characterized as "large oval copper wings" (1926:68). Shetrone states that the headdress "probably was intended to represent a bird or a butterfly" (1930:fig. 61 caption). Of significance, the "wing" elements are described by Shetrone as moveble, as might be expected if they were intended as wings (or ears). Supportive of the wings interpretation, however, are the further observations of Shetrone who notes that attached to the headdress was a "bonnet-like appendage of woven fabric . . . and to this fabric had been sewed large pearl beads, bear claws, *bird feathers and the head of a small raptorial, presumably a hawk*" (1926:71–72; emphasis added).

Possible bird shamans are also found in burial 47 in mound 25 at the Hopewell site. In this case the burial was comprised of two extended skeletons. At the head of one skeleton a number of objects were found, including the "head of a small raptorial bird, presumably a hawk; and an image of an eagle's foot and claws cut from mica" (Shetrone 1926:95). Further, Shetrone describes the second burial in the following way: "On the chest of the skeleton to the north lay a second eagle foot, differing from the other specimen" (95).

The repeated avian symbolism, including an actual hawk skull and two cut mica effigy talons, suggests that raptors were of special significance in connection with these two individuals. Among many peoples, birds are believed to be spirit helpers as well as psychopomps, or soul escorts to the Otherworld. Based in this, the burial 47 individuals may have been bird shamans. Alternatively, the bird symbols might have been employed to carry these individuals' souls to the Otherworld. However, since most other Hopewell burials are typically not accompanied by birds or bird symbols, but presumably also had souls that traveled to the Otherworld, it seems more likely that the burial 47 individuals were bird shamans.

Further support for this interpretation is that a cut mica effigy of a human hand was found situated between the two burial 47 individuals. As discussed in chapter 5, the mica hand has equivalent size and shape relationships to one of the mica bird talons found with the burials. The intentional equivalency between bird and human symbols seems suggestive of human-to-bird transformation, as would be appropriate for bird shamans.[2] Also in a later chapter we will find further evidence for human-to-bird transformations in various designs found in the Adena tablets.

Wolf Shamans

In addition to bear, deer, and raptors, other animal shamans are found in Hopewell contexts. A possible wolf shaman is suggested by a copper headdress found with burial 4 in mound 25 at the Hopewell site (Shetrone 1926:63).

As shown by figure 3.2d, the headdress incorporates the cutout design of a canine paw print.[3] It is also the case that cut and modified wolf mandibles, as well as numerous perforated wolf teeth, were found with several burials at the Hopewell site. And while there are several possible explanations for wolf mandibles and teeth to have been collected and worn—including as decorative elements—it is also the case that many Native America stories tell of humans changing into wolves (see, e.g., Pijoan 1992:51–78).[4]

In any case, what seems certain is that wolf shamans predate Hopewell. In fact, wolf shamans seem to have been prominent among earlier Glacial Kame and Adena peoples (Converse 2003:117). At least three Adena examples of cut wolf maxilla apparently used to impersonate wolves are known (Webb and Baby 1957:61–71). The first example was found in an Adena mound known as site 6, at the Wright mounds site, in Montgomery County, Kentucky. The second was found in an Adena mound known as the Ayers mound in Owen County, Kentucky. The third was found in a mound associated with the Wolford Group in Pickaway County, Ohio. What all three wolf maxillae have in common is that they were cut and ground so that only certain of the upper teeth and palate remain.

In the case of the Ayers wolf maxilla, that object was found in the mouth cavity of the human burial it accompanied (Webb and Baby 1957:69). The human was a young adult male. Covering parts of the skeleton were pieces of leather, leading Webb and Baby to speculate that the individual had been buried with a wolf skin. Examination of the human skull indicated that it was missing the upper medial and lateral incisor teeth. Based on evidence of healing of the surrounding bone tissue, physical anthropologists determined that the incisor teeth had been lost or removed during life. The remaining teeth appeared healthy. Of considerable interest is that the wolf palate had been cut and ground in such a way that it fit perfectly between the human's missing incisor teeth. When the wolf maxilla was worn, the resulting appearance would have been a human with protruding wolf teeth. No doubt the visual effect of a were-wolf shaman would have been intensified had the person been wearing a wolf fur coat, as suggested by Webb and Baby. Significantly, the other two wolf jaws were cut and worked in the same way.

Panther Shamans

Figure 3.3a shows the replica of a smoking pipe found in mound 8 at Mound City. Unfortunately, the present whereabouts of the original pipe fragment is not known. Ephraim Squier and Edwin Davis describe the fragment as 3 3/8 inches (8.6 cm) in length and 1 7/8 inches (4.8 cm) in height. What the pipe seems to show is a human head with feline features, including powerful jaws and neck and short, pointed ears. Incised lines on the face—indicative of face painting, scarification, or tattooing—are suggestive of cat whiskers.

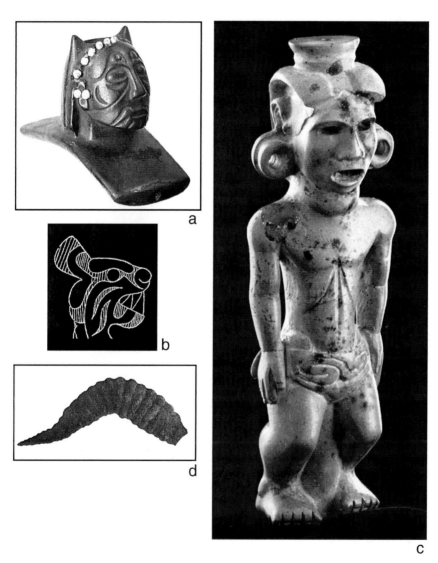

Figure 3.3. a. Human-feline pipe fragment (cast) from Mound City. Ohio Historical Society image #AV17, used with permission. b. Feline engraving on bone from the Hopewell site. From Moorehead 1922:fig. 64. c. Adena dwarf effigy pipe. Ohio Historical Society image #SC10, used with permission. d. Copper horn effigy from Mound City. From Mills 1922:fig. 70, used with permission of the Ohio Historical Society. Figures not to scale.

Originally, small pearls may have been set across the forehead and in the ears (Squier and Davis 1848:244). What the Mound City pipe seems to represent is a human—partially transformed or assuming the guise of a feline. Carr and Case refer to the figure as a "cat impersonator" (2005a:fig. 1.3 caption).

Of interest is that the pipe fragment resembles another feline face, engraved on bone, found at the Hopewell site (Moorehead 1922:159; see figure 3.3b). In both cases, curvilinear designs extend from the eye down the side of the face. Also relevant is that that several other Hopewell effigy smoking pipes also depict felines, albeit without human features. However, as discussed in chapter 7, these and other animal effigy pipes no doubt functioned as consciousness-altering devices, and in that role smoking pipes are implicated in the use of animal spirits as well as human to animal transformation.

Shamanic transformations between humans and felids are well documented throughout North and South America (Hamell 1998; Saunders 1998; Benson 1972). Variously referred to as cougar, mountain lion, or puma, the panther (*Felis concolor*) ranged across the Hopewell territory.

A number of cut panther jaws have been found in both Hopewell and Adena contexts. In Mason County, Kentucky, the upper jaw of a panther was found in an Adena mound. Similarly, a piece of lower jaw was found in an Adena mound in Pickaway County, Ohio (Webb and Baby 1957:66). The Mason County panther jaw had been cut, ground, and drilled; the Pickaway County panther jaw had been cut. In both instances, the manner in which the jaws were modified suggested to investigators that the jaws were used as mask elements (69), similar in concept to the wolf maxillae discussed earlier.

The Dwarf Shaman

One of the most intriguing pipes ever found in Ohio is shown in figure 3.3c. The pipe shows a dwarf. Known as the Adena pipe, the piece was found in Ross County, Ohio, in the namesake Adena mound (Mills 1902:475). Webb and Snow (1945:219) suggest that the pipe was made during Late Adena times, when Adena and Hopewell overlapped chronologically and geographically. In any event, the pipe is made of clay and is about 8 inches (20.3 cm) in height. It was found near the left hand of a burial that had been placed in a log tomb, near the base of the mound. The pipe had been sprinkled with red ocher.[5] A narrow chamber extends through its length.

Given that the pipe was found in a mound located in the heartland of Hopewell and that it dates to a time when Adena and Hopewell overlapped, there is little doubt that whatever core shamanic beliefs are represented in the Adena pipe were known to both Adena and Hopewell.

Two attributes suggest that the individual represented was a shaman. First, as mentioned, the figure shows a dwarf. A diagnosis of achondroplastic dwarfism was made based on the figure's "heavy set muscular body and a trunk of normal proportions, the stubby arms and legs, and the enlarged head . . . all very characteristic" (Webb and Baby 1957:55). Other details suggest the represented individual suffered from goiter and rachitis, or rickets (55). In addition to the abnormalities Webb and Baby note, features in the chest area suggest the possibility of skeletal deformities including *Pectus carinatus*, or "pigeon chest," and *Pectus excavatum*, or "funnel chest." "Pigeon chest" takes its name from a protrusion of the sternum and ribs resulting in a peculiar appearance that looks like the footprint of a pigeon, virtually identical to the peculiar design shown on the effigy dwarf's torso, except that in real life the deformity protrudes outward rather inward. In the case of "funnel chest," the main symptom is a depression in the center of the chest over the sternum, as appears in the sternum of the Adena pipe dwarf. Of interest is that "funnel chest" can result from rickets, consistent with Webb and Baby's diagnosis.

In any event, among Indians of the Historic period, dwarfs were widely believed to have superhuman powers. Many Native American myths and tales attribute magical powers to dwarfs (e.g., Eliade 1964:102; Lankford 1987). Among the Cherokee, for example, a race of "Little People," no taller than a man's knee, were said to live deep in the woods. The Little People had the power of invisibility and could cast magical spells (Mooney 1900:330–35). Among the Creek, children who were raised to be "wizards" were said to often meet with the Little People (Swanton 1946:714).

As to why dwarfs might be believed to have magical powers, it is clear that they are anomalies; that is, they fail to match our preconceived notions of what humans should look like. Although they might be adults in a functional sense, dwarfs are the size of children. Although the same as normal-size human beings in most ways, they are also sufficiently different as to occupy a different experiential space. In other words, dwarfs are liminal entities. As Turner explains, liminal entities are "neither here nor there; they are betwixt and between" (1969:95). As liminal entities, dwarfs provide a link between the ordinary everyday world and the extraordinary Otherworld.

Anthropologist Mary Douglas (1966) has pointed out that creatures and things that do not fit into normal categories of classification are often feared and thought to have superhuman powers. Not knowing for certain their real potential, we tend to overestimate the capabilities of unfamiliar creatures and the dangers of things that are unknown to us. No doubt this innate sense of caution served us well in our evolutionary past. If the Adena-Hopewell viewed anomalous things in the same tentative way, then it is likely that the peculiar-looking individual represented in the Adena pipe was thought to have special abilities.

A more specific attribute of the pipe that suggests the dwarf was a shaman relates to the function of the piece. Based on the hollowed-out chamber extending through the length of the object, it is generally accepted that the piece functioned as a pipe. Many examples of tubular pipes have been found in Adena contexts, so the idea that the dwarf piece could have been used in this way is reasonable.

As discussed in chapter 7, tobacco was known to both Adena and Hopewell peoples. Accordingly, if the Adena pipe was used to smoke, then tobacco—or some combination of tobacco and other substances—is implicated. People do not smoke inert substances. Whatever the substance being smoked, a physiological effect was the result. Associated with physiological changes are changes in mental states, which means an alteration in the state of consciousness. Altered states of consciousness, in turn, facilitate contact with the Otherworld—clearly a shamanic function.

Tube pipes, however, can also be used for sucking and blowing techniques associated with curing. If the Adena pipe was used in that manner, then a shamanic function is again implied, thus supporting the likelihood that the dwarf himself was a shaman. Indeed, in this piece, I believe we are looking at the image of a specific dwarf shaman who lived in real life.

Support for the notion that the pipe represents an actual individual comes from the discovery of a dwarf skeleton in an Adena mound near Waverly, Ohio. Webb and Baby (1957:55) identify the mound as Adena in origin; archaeologist Gerard Fowke described the skeleton as "a skeleton of peculiar form. It was not over five feet long, but the bones were very thick and the processes for attachment of the muscles were extraordinary in their development. The skull was nearly half an inch thick and of unusual size, mostly back of the ears, though the forehead was full and high. The teeth were large, hard, and but little worn" (1902:372).

Notably, Waverly, Ohio, is situated about 18 miles (29 km) south of the Adena mound where the dwarf effigy pipe was found. Also relevant is that in modern populations the incidence of achondroplastic dwarfism is rare—on the order of 1:26,000 to 1:40,000. Other types of dwarfism are even rarer. Typically, achondroplastic dwarfs are born to normal-size parents. Although it is difficult to estimate, in Ohio there may never have been more than a total of forty thousand Adena and Hopewell individuals combined. This would suggest that the occurrence of a real dwarf in that ancient population was a rare event. That probability, along with the geographic proximity of the

Adena pipe and dwarf skeleton combine to suggest that the Waverly dwarf and the Adena pipe dwarf shaman were perhaps one and the same. Perhaps the person buried with the Adena pipe was in some way related to the real-life dwarf, or perhaps the dwarf shaman was an ancestor or spirit guide for the person buried with the pipe.

Little Bighorn on the Scioto

"Little Bighorn on the Scioto" refers to an article by the same title written by archaeologist Warren DeBoer (2004). DeBoer's article concerns, in part, a peculiar item found with burial 12 in mound 7 at Mound City. Figure 3.3d shows the item: a copper effigy made to resemble a horn. Mills (1922:367) originally identified the piece as the effigy of a mountain goat horn. De-Boer makes a convincing argument that the effigy represents the horn of a bighorn sheep (*Ovis canadensis*). Bighorn sheep are not found in Ohio, but they are native to the American West in the same area where the Hopewell obtained their obsidian. Drawing upon Hamell's (1992) representation of the Iroquoian "World Rim" as a place where superhuman entities reside, and Miller's observation that "the farther one [goes] away from civilization, the more powerful the spirit acquired" (1999:58), DeBoer argues that the bighorn sheep effigy horn would have been a powerful statement of shamanic power given that it was modeled after a creature found far outside the boundaries of the Hopewell world, in the "Zone of Extraordinary Travels."

DeBoer reasonably suggests that the horn may have been part of a head-dress worn by burial 12, and that other items found with this individual, including bangles, copper turtle rattles, and a copper plate, comprised part of that individual's shamanic regalia.

Little can be added to DeBoer's proposal except to note that, as will be discussed in later chapters, the bangles and turtle rattles suggest that this individual was involved in percussion-driven rhythmic activities. Percussion driving and rhythmic dancing techniques are often employed by shamans to facilitate altered states of consciousness.

Summary

In this chapter, evidence was presented as to what Hopewell shamans may have looked like. Admittedly, the physical evidence is sparse. On the other hand, given the time depth and theoretical issues involved, perhaps we are fortunate in being able to identify any potential real-life shamans. Certainly, one of the most suggestive images is that of the Wray figurine, which appears to be a shaman in the act of transforming into a bear. The occurrence of bear masks in earlier cultural contexts within the region and references to bear shamans in the later ethnographic literature also support the notion that the Hopewell had bear shamans.

Evidence for deer shamans is more complicated. Several cervid antler headdresses were found with Hopewell burials. What is problematic about the Hopewell evidence is that the occurrence of a deer antler headdress with an individual does not unequivocally mean the person was a shaman. Cross-culturally, the ethnographic data show that in addition to shamans, warriors, chiefs, clan leaders, and others wore animal headdresses. Antlers and horns are often used as symbols of political and social authority. Accordingly, it is possible that Hopewell individuals buried with antler headdresses may have been political or social leaders.

On the other hand, what all these roles have in common is "power": power over people, power over things. What we also find is that power, in whatever form—sociopolitical, martial, or religious, often finds its legitimizing source in its connection to the spirit world through animal masters, gods, or totem animal ancestors. In other words, the individual is believed to draw power, authority, and legitimacy from the spirit world (Helms 1998:10–11). Arguably, animal headdresses symbolize those connections. As a consequence, I would propose that all power-symbol animal headdresses have an implicit shamanic aspect. Therefore, even if Hopewell cervid antlers were symbols of political and social power, a shamanic aspect is implicated.

Also worth considering is the set of effigy antlers found with burials 260 and 261 in mound 25 at the Hopewell site. As mentioned earlier, this antler effigy was made to resemble the first stage of antler growth. In this, an interest in the process of transformation seems implied; in turn, transformation is a common shamanic theme.

Evidence for raptor shamans is intriguing. As Whitley points out, flight is a "common shamanic metaphor . . . typically expressed through the use of avian imagery" (2005:119). In the case of the Hopewell, multiple lines of evidence support the notion that the Hopewell had raptor shamans. First, it was shown how one or two copper headdresses incorporate wing and feather motifs. Second, it was noted that actual hawk remains were found in association with at least two Hopewell burials. The occurrence of human-bird transformation imagery in the form of mica cutouts, as well as in the Adena tablets, was briefly mentioned.

Clearly, wolf shamans played an important role in Glacial Kame and Adena cultures. The evidence for Hopewell wolf shamans is not as strong. Indeed, the only evidence suggestive of Hopewell wolf shamans is a solitary canine paw design headdress found with burial 4 in mound 25 at the Hopewell site. While that headdress could indicate the individual's status as a wolf shaman, without corroborative data the headdress might alternatively indicate the individual's leadership or membership in a canine-related clan or lineage. At this point, all we can reliably conclude is that based on the canine paw headdress and numerous cut and drilled wolf jaws and teeth found with Hopewell burials (discussed in chapter 5), it is likely that spirit power was derived from the wolf.

Evidence was presented for several other kinds of shamans, including panther, dwarf, and ram. The Adena evidence of panther jaws used as mask elements supports the existence of panther shamans. Even more suggestive, however, is the Hopewell cat effigy pipe from Mound City. The design of the effigy pipe seems to combine human and feline features. The conceptual blending of human and animal attributes is a common shamanic theme. Contextually, the fact that a were-panther is represented on a Hopewell smoking pipe is of interest given that smoking pipes are mind-altering devices. In this object, therefore, we find transformational imagery embedded in what may have been the very device used to bring about a human-to-animal transformation.

In the case of the dwarf and ram shamans, these appear to be one-time occurrences. Given the rarity of dwarfism in life, we might not expect to find another Ohio Hopewell example of a dwarf shaman. In connection with De Boer's posited ram shaman, however, it is puzzling that no other Hopewell occurrences are known. Alternatively, of course, the copper horn could represent something other than a sheep shaman.

As a group, what is interesting about the Hopewell were-animal shamans is that they represent "counterintuitive" concepts (Boyer 1994, 2001). Counterintuitive concepts defy our expectations of normalcy. Comic book characters such as Superman, Spider-Man, and Falcon are counterintuitive agents in that their unique abilities violate our expectations of what humans are normally capable of. So too, ghosts, witches, and vampires are counterintuitive.

Hopewell shamans dressed in animal regalia are counterintuitive in the sense that various attributes of different animals were presumably assimilated by their human counterparts, the result being anomalous creatures that include humans with horns, were-bears that could talk, and humans with wolf teeth—all contrary to normal expectations.

Where counterintuitive agents become relevant is that, because they defy our expectations, such concepts are memorable (Boyer and Ramble 2001). Moreover, because properties belonging to separate ontological categories are merged through our mind's natural propensity for conceptual blending, the hybrid creatures we imagine are believable. Whether viewed through Hopewell eyes or our own, the peculiar creatures found in the Hopewell record basically make sense to us. And because these hybrid creatures are ambiguous and liminal in that they are part human and part nonhuman, they are able to act as intermediaries between this world and the Otherworld.

CHAPTER FOUR

Hopewell Cosmology: Part I

Viewed from a human perspective, the world moves in a dynamic, ever-changing whirl of activity. Things are in a constant state of change, forms are impermanent, beings are transitory, and transformations of one sort or another are the rule. Aware of this, humans strive to "stabilize and harness the energetic forces attributed to the universe and tangibly shape and concretize these dynamics in order to create at least the illusion of a certain amount of stability, order, and durability"(Helms 1998:164). One of the ways we do this is by imposing structural organization on the cosmos. As articulated by Tim Ingold, however, the origin of this "structure" lies within us: "The organization of environmental possibilities into a coherent system has its source within the individual, being a projection of its own internal organization onto the world outside its body" (1987:2). In the case of the Hopewell, this cosmological order provided the operational environment for the shaman, as well as a baseline for actions, including ritual behavior (in the sense of Bean 1977:128).

Holistic and Dualistic Aspects of the Cosmos

According to the cognitive operator model of the human mind proposed by d'Aquili and Newberg (1999:52), the holistic operator allows us to view things in a "big picture" way. Tentatively associated with the right parietal lobe, this operator helps us apprehend the seeming unity or oneness of the universe. It is this sentiment that led Pierre Teilhard de Chardin to comment:

55

Each element of the cosmos is positively woven from all the others. . . . It is impossible to cut into this network, to isolate a portion of it without it becoming
frayed and unraveled at its edges. All around us, as far as the eye can see, the
universe holds together, and only one way of considering it is really possible,
that is, to take it as a whole, in one piece. (1959 [1955]:44)

A similar idea is implicit in Native American cosmologies. As explained
by anthropologist Jay Miller:

Throughout Native America, there was a single, ultimate potency, known
by many terms and conditions, and so vast and awesome that all of it never
could be encompassed or understood. . . . Therefore, it was treated as a series
of manageable, discrete aspects of the whole. It has been compared to water in
that it was everywhere yet concentrated in specific locations, able to be named
and handled apart from the totality. The naming of different geographical sections of the water, or sky, or land, did not mean that they were fundamentally
separate. All shared a common underlying reality. (1988:95)

Among the Hopi, this "ultimate potency" is personified as "Giver of
the Breath of Life," breath meaning the spark of life Creator gives to living beings. The true nature of Creator, however, remains a mystery (Lyon
1998:101). Among the Creek, the ultimate potency was expressed in the
term *Hisákidamissi*, which meant "Master of Breath" (101).

Paradoxically, even though we sense the holistic, interconnected nature
of things, by function of the mind-brain's binary operator we are also inclined to order the world into dyads, or pairs of complementary opposites.
As explained by Andrew Newberg, Eugene d'Aquili, and Vince Rause, "The
binary operator. . . . enables the mind to make fundamental sense of things by
reducing the most complicated relationships of space and time to simple pairs
of opposites—up versus down, in versus out, left versus right, before versus
after, and so on" (2001:50).

The notion that the mind has a binary operator recalls the work of Claude
Lévi-Strauss. Lévi-Strauss (1963, 1966) posited universal structures for the
mind, based in pairs of binary oppositions including male-female, hot-cold,
cooked-raw, and so on. The essence of the approach Lévi-Strauss pioneered
is explained by British structural anthropologist Edmund Leach: "Binary oppositions are intrinsic to the process of human thought. Any description of
the world must discriminate categories in the form 'p is what not-p is not'"
(2001 [1982]:40).

Unfortunately, due to the limited state of knowledge at the time, particularly
with regard to the cognitive sciences, "old school" structural anthropologists

such as Lévi-Strauss and Leach were never quite able to account for how binary oppositions arose in the mind. Recently, however, a body of theory known as biogenetic structuralism has emerged (Laughlin and d'Aquili 1974; d'Aquili, Laughlin and McManus 1979; d'Aquili and Newberg 1999; Newberg, d'Aquili and Rause 2001). In this version of structuralism, it is the mind-brain's binary operator that accounts for binary oppositions. The theory holds that the binary operator arises from the genetically determined structure of the nervous system. In other words, our predilection to organize the world in terms of binary oppositions derives from the way our nervous system is structured.

Associated with the inferior parietal region of the brain (Newberg, d'Aquili, and Rause 2001:51), it is arguably the binary operator that gives rise to the archetypal shamanic worldview attribute of dualism. As human beings, perhaps the most fundamental question is: "To be, or not to be?"[1] From that polarity, we resolve the universe into additional dualities, such as movement and stillness, matter and energy, light and dark, approach and avoidance, pleasure and pain. In religious thought, the binary operator gives rise to linked opposites, including this world and Otherworld, Creator and created, body and soul, good and evil, heaven and hell. In one form or another, the notion of cosmic dualism is found in all religions.

In Native American cosmologies, cosmic dualism is expressed in the belief that everything has an opposite. As explained by Alana Cordy-Collins:

> One of the most pervasive aspects of Amerindian religion is the concept of dualism: the pairing and interaction of opposites. Dualism is recognized in the opposition of day and night, good and evil, cold and heat, right and left, but most importantly in the complementarity of male and female. (1983:42)

An example of this dualistic understanding is provided by the Osage Indians of southwestern Missouri. In Osage belief, the cosmos is divided into two realms—earth and sky. Earth is called Mother; sky is called Father. Life is the result of the interaction between earth and sky. Reflecting this duality in their tribal makeup, Osage clans were traditionally divided into two moieties. The *Ho-ga* moiety represented the earth, land, and water; the *Tsi zhu* moiety represented the sky.

Another example is provided by the Iroquois. According to the Iroquois, the dualistic nature of the world has its origins in Creation. As related by Fenton (1962:292–94), when the earth was created, the daughter of Sky-woman gave birth to twins. One twin was good-minded; the other twin was evil-minded. The good twin, known as Sky-holder or Creator, is associated with growth and fertility. The evil twin, Flint, is associated with winter and monstrosities. Where Creator caused things to grow, Flint offset that by creating frost—hence the alternating seasons.

Since dualism is based in a belief that reality is an arrangement of binary oppositions, dualism necessarily implies that in an ideal state, binary opposites will be balanced. By balanced I mean that opposites exist in a state of equilibrium, with opposing forces or elements within a dyad equal to each other. In this regard, there are two ways of visually expressing balance: (1) by symmetrical arrangement of design elements and (2) by certain asymmetrical arrangements of design elements. As both kinds of designs were used by Hopewell, it might be useful to briefly explain the difference.

The top view of a bird with outstretched wings provides an example of a symmetrical design. Looking down on the bird, the bird's right side and wing is a mirror image of its left side and wing; left and right sides are balanced along either side of a longitudinal axis that extends from head to tail.

In asymmetrical designs, balance is achieved by placing elements so the area of visual interest is evenly distributed. Asymmetrical designs can be of different types. Hopewell asymmetrical designs, for example, often incorporate complementary opposites. By complementary opposites I mean opposite patterns or geometric figures proportioned and situated so they appear visually balanced. An example might be a circle and square, each having the same approximate area, situated next to each other so they appear balanced and associated. By way of contrast, the positioning of a square next to a circle that is considerably smaller would not create a balanced asymmetrical composition. In this case the design would be asymmetrical and unbalanced.

In a dualistic universe, there is no contradiction in the expression of cosmic dualism by either symmetrical or balanced asymmetrical designs. By way of example, consider the traditional Chinese Taijitu. In this symbol we find opposite cosmic forces represented by two symmetrical teardrop-shaped design elements situated in a balanced relationship to each other.

At the same time, however, we can imagine a Chinese painting of an opposing tiger and dragon, also intended to represent opposite cosmic forces. The tiger and dragon are asymmetrical with respect to each other's form, but viewed together, they are expressive of the dualistic nature of the universe. Dualism therefore can be expressed through symmetry as well as balanced asymmetry.

In Hopewell, balanced designs that incorporate symmetrical and asymmetrical arrangements occur at multiple scales. Large-scale balanced space is evident in the layout of many Hopewell earthwork complexes. On a smaller scale, balanced space using multiple design elements is found in the design of many Hopewell pieces. Presented below are several Hopewell examples suggestive of a dualistic apprehension of space expressed through bilateral symmetry, balanced asymmetry, and complementary opposites.

Geometric Earthwork Morphology

There are two basic kinds of large scale Hopewell earthworks: irregularly shaped hilltop enclosures and geometrically shaped lowland enclosures. Both use man-made earthen walls or embankments to define their perimeters. Since the outline of a hilltop enclosure is in large measure determined by the topography of the hill itself, relatively few degrees of freedom were available to the Hopewell in terms of controlling the overall shape of these structures. Lowland geometric enclosures, on the other hand, were built in flat river valley areas. The result was that the shape of a lowland geometric earthwork was limited only by the designer's imagination.

Although the design possibilities for lowland earthworks were unlimited, two basic geometric shapes—circles and squares—predominate. Several major earthwork complexes are made up of a single circle and square or circle and octagon (see, e.g., figure 4.1a). These complexes include Circleville, Hopeton, High Bank, and the Seal Township Works, as well as the Newark Octagon and Observatory Circle. In these earthwork complexes there exists a visually balanced relationship between opposite circle and square or circle and octagon design elements.

Other earthwork complexes are made up of multiple circles and/or squares (see, e.g., figure 4.1b). These complexes include Liberty, Seip, Baum, Works East, and Frankfort (also known as Old Town Works). In these cases, asymmetrical balance between multiple design elements is accomplished in a variety of ways. In the case of Frankfort, Liberty, Seip, and Works East, for example, asymmetrical balance is achieved by placing a large circle between smaller circle and square elements.

Although other geometric shapes—including ellipses, unique polygons, and a handful of one-of-a-kind figures—are found in the repertoire of Hopewell earthwork designs, circles and squares predominate. Circles and squares can be thought of as complementary opposites. The repeated enclosure of landscape using these two fundamental shapes and the fact that the two shapes are repeatedly linked together suggests that the Hopewell thought of space in dualistic terms. (For earlier and similar arguments also see Byers 1987:219; Greber and Ruhl 2000:216–22; DeBoer 1997:234; Romain 1991a:33, 2004a:132).

Hopewell dualism goes beyond the matter of complementary opposite shapes, however. It appears that the Hopewell were also interested in equal or balanced quantitative relationships between circles and squares. An example

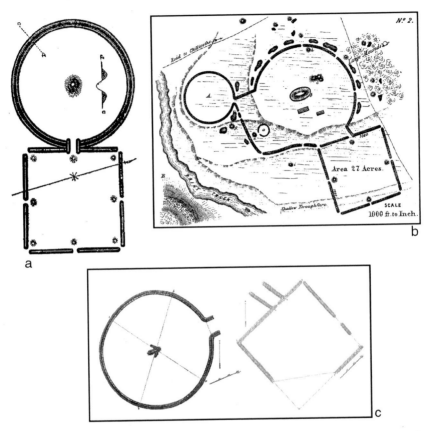

Figure 4.1. a. Circleville earthwork. From Squier and Davis 1848:fig. 10. b. Seip earth-work. From Squier and Davis 1848:Pl. 21, no. 2. c. Newark Great Circle and Wright Square. From Thomas 1894:Pls. 31 and 34. Figures not to scale.

is provided by the relationship between the Wright Square and Great Circle earthworks, located within the Newark earthwork complex (figure 4.1c).

The Wright Square and Great Circle are conceptually related in that they comprise a dyad consisting of circle and square (Romain 2000:fig. 2.1). The two earthworks are separated from each other by about 2,000 feet (853 m). From early maps (e.g., Wyrick, in Beers 1866) it appears that a parallel walled walkway originally extended between the earthworks, thus emphasizing their relationship. Moreover, survey data provided by Thomas (1894:462, 466) shows the perimeters of the two earthworks to be equal to each other to within 1.5 percent. The Great Circle is approximately 3,694 feet (1,125.9 m) in circumference, while the perimeter of the Wright Square is 3,744 feet (1,141.2 m). In this case, a quantitative equivalence is established between the two figures, thereby resulting in a balanced relationship. Additional examples demonstrating quantitative relationships between Hopewell earthworks are provided elsewhere (Romain 2004a).

Artifact Designs

A second category of evidence suggesting that the Hopewell recognized a dualistic nature to things is provided by the designs found in many of their smaller objects. The Rutledge salamander piece is a case in point.

The Rutledge Salamanders

The Rutledge salamander effigy was found in the Rutledge mound in Licking County, Ohio (Baby 1961a). The object is made of thin copper and is about 6 inches (15.2 cm) in length (figure 4.2a). Along with Skinner (1987:54), my interpretation is that the design shows the anterior halves of two salamanders facing in opposite directions.

Identification of the creatures as salamanders is indicated by the narrowing of their necks, as well as the presence of the crescent-shaped features just behind the limbs on the copper piece. These appendages correspond to the external plumelike gills found on certain salamander species, including mudpuppies (Behler and King 1979:281). Mudpuppies (*Necturus maculosus*) are found throughout southern Ohio (Conant and Collins 1998:420). Distinguishing them from many other salamanders, mudpuppies have four toes on their front feet (Behler and King 1979:281), as do the creatures found in the Rutledge copper piece.

In any case, the Rutledge salamanders provide a good example of bilateral symmetry. Each salamander is a mirror image of its opposite-facing companion; thus the two salamanders comprise a balanced dyad and a dualistic division of space. Also worth noting is the resemblance of the Rutledge salamander to the design found in the Gaitskill stone tablet (Skinner 1987:54).[2] The resemblance is shown in figures 4.2b–4.2d.

Mound City Vultures

Several copper effigies found in mound 13 at Mound City present interesting examples of repeated bilateral symmetry. Figure 4.3a shows two of these effigies, although Mills (1922:536) reported that three were originally found. Mills (fig. 64) identified the figures as eagles. Contrary to Mills, I concur with Merriam (1923), who proposed that the designs represent turkey vultures (*Cathartes aura*). Merriam did not offer any reasons for his opinion. My identification rests on the shape of the turkey vulture's beak, which is longer and thinner than the beaks of eagles or falcons (cf. figures 4.3b and 4.3c); the relatively

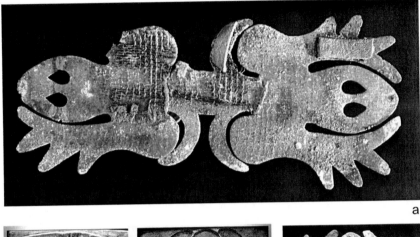

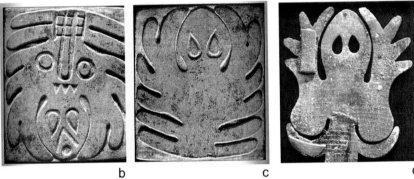

Figure 4.2. a. Copper salamander effigy from Rutledge mound. Ohio Historical Society image #A3490/000001, used with permission. b. Gaitskill Stone Tablet. Courtesy of the William S. Webb Museum of Anthropology, University of Kentucky. c. Rotated view of Gaitskill Stone Tablet (V-shaped and circle features removed by the present author). Courtesy of the William S. Webb Museum of Anthropology, University of Kentucky. d. Close-up view of Rutledge mound salamander. Ohio Historical Society image #A3490/000001. Figures not to scale.

small size of the eyes as compared to other Hopewell pieces that definitively show eagles and falcons; and the distinctive posture of the vulture resulting in its head appearing lower than the "elbow" joint of its wings (figure 4.3d). The downward projections on the copper pieces may represent legs.

Turkey vultures are common throughout southern Ohio (Romain 1991b). Several characteristics unique to the turkey vulture make it of possible interest to the Hopewell. For one thing, the turkey vulture feeds on carrion, or dead flesh. As Webb and Baby (1957:101) point out, the flesh-stripping behavior of the vulture has an analogue in the activities of Adena and

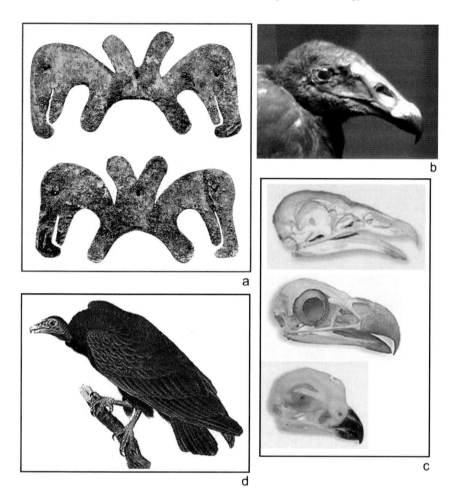

Figure 4.3. a. Copper bird effigies from Mound City, mound 7. From Mills 1922:fig. 64; used with permission of the Ohio Historical Society. Scan provided by Arthur W. McGraw. b. Close-up view of turkey vulture head. Photo by William Romain. c. Photos of bird skulls. Top to bottom: bald eagle, turkey vulture, peregrine falcon. Heads not to scale. Photos equalized in size to illustrate beak proportions. Skull photos courtesy of www.skullsunlimited.com. d. Detail of Audubon drawing of a turkey vulture. From John Audubon, *Birds of America*, 1840:Pl. II. Image courtesy of www.audubon.org/bird/BoA/BOA_index.html.

Hopewell shamans who dismembered and sometimes de-fleshed the deceased prior to interment. In this, the vulture may have had a role in helping to advance the deceased to the Otherworld if "sky burials" were part of Woodland burial practices. (See Buikstra, Charles, and Rakita [1998:89] for discussion of ravens similarly associated with the dead for Illinois Hopewell).

In any event, what is apparent is that in each of the vulture pieces, mirror-image symmetry is expressed in the relationship of opposite-facing heads. The symmetry of each piece is further reflected in the creation of a second copper piece (and presumably the lost third piece), which repeat the design of the first. The results are mirror-image bird heads memorialized as dyads and a dualistic use of space.

The Turner Turtle

Figures 4.4a and 4.4b show a unique discovery made in altar 3 at the Turner site (Willoughby and Hooton 1922:57). The discovery consists of two bone disks, each about 4 inches (10.2 cm) in diameter. Both disks were cut out of human parietal bone; both are engraved. Fastened together, the disks likely comprised two halves of a rattle (Mainfort 1986:70).

Several morphological attributes of the disks suggest a dualistic way of thinking about space. First, the disks are the same size and shape. If the two disks were removed from the same skull, then opposite sides of the head are represented. Also relevant is that in figures 4.4a and 4.4b, holes are shown penetrating through each disk in six different locations. The locations of the holes match their counterparts on the other disk. The implication is that the two disks were originally fastened together. That the two disks were made to fit together tells us that when assembled, the resulting object had distinct two sides.

More compelling evidence, however, comes from the engravings found on the disks. As Willoughby (1916:496) points out, the same design is found on both disks, but the designs are reversed; that is, the designs on the two disks are mirror images of each other. In their mirror-image symmetry, the two designs comprise a dyad made up of complementary opposites.

The question of what creature is represented in the engravings is of interest. I suspect a turtle is shown. The key to this puzzle is in the distinctive morphology of real turtles' front legs, and in particular the backward curvature of their legs. Figure 4.4d shows this characteristic shape, which matches the leg elements in the Turner disks. Other correspondences include claws and beaks. In the Turner disk designs, the posited feet have claws. Also in the Turner designs, as Willoughby mentioned, we find beak elements. Notably, real turtles have claws and sharp, horny beaks.

Recognition of the turtle elements in the disks is sufficient to establish the turtle motif. However, something else also appears to be expressed. It appears the designer intended that a whole turtle be manifested if the two disk designs are combined—as they would be, in a sense, if the two disks were fastened together.

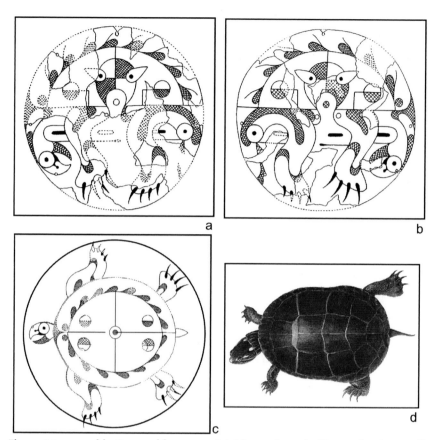

Figure 4.4. a and b. Engraved human parietal bones from the Turner site. From Willoughby and Hooton 1922:figs. 23 and 24, courtesy of the Peabody Museum, Harvard University. c. Turtle design by the author made from parts found in figures 4.4a and 4.4b. Drawing by William Romain. d. Dorsal view of painted turtle (*Chrysemys picta*). From Babcock 1919, as reproduced by the Center for North American Herpetology.

To see the turtle, the individual design elements in each piece first need to be separated. Once that is done, they can then be reassembled in their correct anatomical relationships. The process is roughly analogous to using Tinkertoy parts to create different designs. In any event, the end result of the operation is shown in figure 4.4c.[3] Importantly, the resulting turtle image was made entirely from the design elements contained in the two disks. I added nothing.

In additional to the morphological analysis just presented, the turtle interpretation finds support in other lines of evidence. Located near the turtle disks, a spatula-like object made out of "tortoise shell" also found in the ashes of Turner altar 3 (Willoughby and Hooton 1922:58). A tortoise is simply a land-dwelling turtle.

Also significant is that Mainfort (1986) documents the discovery of two unequivocal rattles, likewise made from human parietal bones, found at the Pinson Mounds site in Tennessee. The Pinson Mounds site is contemporaneous with Ohio Hopewell. In the case of the Pinson rattles, they were found at the knees of a human burial. The parietal bones making up each rattle were found still fastened together with thongs (70). Small quartzite pebbles were situated inside each rattle.

Related to how the Turner disks were used and what their engraved designs represent is the discovery at Mound City of eighteen copper rattles, found with burial 12 in mound 7. The rattles contained small pebbles or beads. Notably, the Mound City rattles were fashioned in the shape of small turtles.

What these discoveries tell us is that in Hopewell thought, rattles were associated with turtle symbolism. More to the point and based in their morphology as well as mirror-image designs, the Turner rattle incorporates dualistic themes at multiple levels.

Mound City Falcons
The next example of dualistic expression involves two bird effigies, made out of thin copper sheets. Shown in figures 4.5a and 4.5b, these effigies were found in mound 7 at Mound City (Mills 1922:537). Based on the bird's-eye markings, barred bellies, and "hooded" head markings, it has long been suggested that the effigies represent peregrine falcons (*Falco peregrinus*; Webb and Baby 1957:100; Penny 1985:185). Figure 4.5c shows a peregrin. I tentatively agree with this identification, although peregrines were probably not common in Ohio during Hopewell times and other falcons, such as the American Kestrel (*Falco sparverius*), have similar eye markings. The chest and "hooded" head markings on the American Kestral, however, are not quite the same as what is shown in the copper designs. In any event, female falcons of all species are larger than their male counterparts. In fact, female peregrines are up to one-third larger than males (Priebe 2000:19). Thus my contribution to the discussion is identification of the copper effigies as male and female. Figure 4.5a shows the male; figure 4.5b shows the female.

In figure 4.5a, the upper part of the bird's body is concave in shape, whereas the body in figure 4.5b is more convex. Hence, the body of the posited female bird in figure 4.5b is wider in girth. According to Mills, the bird in figure 4.5a is 12 1/2 inches (31.8 cm) long and 8 inches (20.3 cm) in overall width, while the companion bird in figure 4.5b is 13 1/2 inches (34.3 cm) in length and also

Figure 4.5.   a. Copper falcon from Mound City, mound 7. From Mills 1922:fig. 61; used with permission of the Ohio Historical Society. Scan provided by Arthur W. McGraw. b. Copper falcon from Mound City. From Mills 1922:fig. 60; used with permission of the Ohio Historical Society. Scan provided by Arthur W. McGraw. c. Peregrine falcon. Photo by William Romain. Figures not to scale.

8 inches (20.3 cm) in overall width (1922:537). The difference in size between the copper birds therefore corresponds to the proportional difference between male and female peregrines in life.

Several additional lines of evidence suggest that these birds comprised a male-female dyad. Stylistically, the two birds are rendered in the same way. Moreover, both birds have an identical number of tail feathers—seven. Next, the copper falcons were not only found in the same burial mound—in mound 7 at Mound City—they were also positioned so that one was situated in the northeast corner of the rectangular-shaped grave, while the companion figure was found in the southeast corner of the same grave (Mills 1922:313). The birds were therefore spatially related. Lastly, it is of interest to note that peregrine falcons are monogamous and mate for life (Priebe 2000:19). This is consistent with the notion that the two copper effigies represent a male and female pair.

In terms of size, stylistic rendering, spatial relationship, and natural relationship, the evidence suggests that a binary relationship was intended. In this case, the binary relationship is not one of mirror images; rather, the relationship is one of complementary male-female opposites, with duality expressed through sex.

The Turner Monsters

One of the most remarkable examples of Hopewell dualism is shown in figure 4.6a. What this figure shows is a fragment of human ulna bone, found in altar 1 at the Turner site (Willoughby and Hooton 1922:6–8). A series of lines have been engraved on the bone. Figure 4.6b shows the engraving as represented by Willoughby and Hooton (pl. 2). It was Willoughby's (1916:495) opinion that the design represented either a bison head, or other unidentified animal heads.

My interpretation is that two monsterlike spirit beings are represented— one male, the other female. The creatures appear when Willoughby's illustrations are turned upside down (see figure 4.6c). Figure 4.6d shows the details of this view.

Several observations suggest that the creature on the left is the complementary opposite of the one on the right. First are the horns—if that is what they are. On the left-side creature, the horns turn outward; on the right-side creature they turn inward. The shape of the left-side creature's head is defined by straight lines and is angular; the right-side creature's head is rounded. The mouth of the left-side creature shows barred teeth; the right-side creature's mouth is more rounded. Both creatures have what appear to be distended earlobes, as occurs due to wearing heavy earspools and as is represented in other Hopewell pieces.

Of central interest is the question of sex. Here things become more intuitive. I would propose, however, that interpretation of the features shown in the bottom half of both designs as sex organs is reasonable.

Also of interest is that a second creature closely resembling the posited Turner female monster occurs in a discovery made in mound 25 at the Hopewell site. In this case, however, the creature is found in the design of a copper piece (see figures 4.8c and 4.8d). An enlarged detail of the Hopewell site, mound 25 piece is shown in figure 4.6e. At least eight design similarities between the Turner engraved design and Hopewell site copper design are apparent: (1) the overall shape of the two heads are similar—both are more or less apple-shaped; (2) both designs have inward-curving bifurcated elements

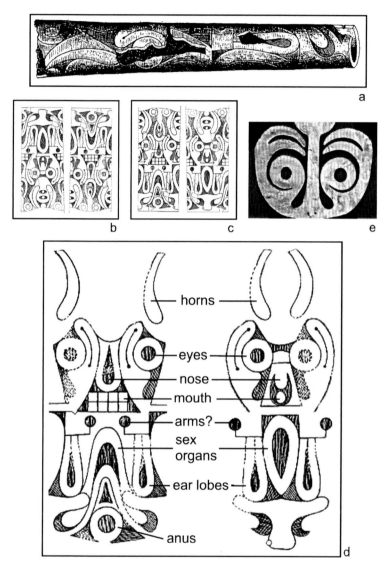

Figure 4.6.   a. Engraved human bone from Turner site. From Willoughby and Hooton 1922:Pl. 2 (h), courtesy of the Peabody Museum, Harvard University. b. Engraved design as illustrated by Willoughby and (1922:Pl. 2 [g, i]). From Willoughby and Hooton 1922: Pl. 2 (g, i), courtesy of the Peabody Museum, Harvard University. c. Willoughby and Hooton figures rotated upside down. From Willoughby and Hooton 1922:Pl. 2 (g, i), courtesy of the Peabody Museum, Harvard University. d. Same illustration as in fig. 4.6c, with the creatures separated. From Willoughby and Hooton 1922:Pl. 2 (g, i), courtesy of the Peabody Museum, Harvard University, annotation added by William Romain. e. Enlarged detail of owl face from Hopewell site piece shown in fig. 4.8d. From Moorehead 1922:Pl. 68(4).

on either side of the head, framing the eyes; (3) the eyes in both creatures are rendered in a similar fashion, using round rather than oval shapes—with the pupils rendered as small center circles; (4) the proportionate size of the pupil to iris diameters for the eyes of both creatures is the same; (5) the size of the eyes in proportion to their respective heads is the same; (6) the noses of both creatures are narrow at the top and wider at the bottom; (7) both creatures have nearly identical teardrop-shaped markings on either side of their noses; and (8) in both creatures, these markings are part of a contrasting field that helps define the shape of the eyes. I will have more to say about the Hopewell site, mound 25 copper piece later in this chapter. For now, the point is that a second occurrence of the monster face supports the interpretation offered for the Turner engraving.

Although it is instructive to examine the Turner creatures individually, it is important to keep in mind that the two monsters are actually part of a single design that wraps around the entire bone. Thus, the edges and elements of each figure not only make up that figure, they also define corresponding parts of the opposite figure. For example, the left horn of the female figure is also the right horn of the male figure; the left eye of the female figure is also the right eye of the male figure; and so on. The result is that as the piece is rotated around its longitudinal axis, the male creature, upon reaching its extreme, merges into and becomes its opposite, which is the female creature. In the same way, upon reaching its extreme state, the female transforms back into the male figure. As will be recalled from chapter 3, a similar three-dimensional transformation technique appears utilized in the Wray figurine.

In the Turner design, we find complementary but opposite male and female figures. The interlocking of mutually shared body parts suggests that at one level, the figures are polarized and separate; at the same time, however, one cannot exist without the other, and together they form One. By unique design, the piece integrates the notion of a holistic One formed through the dualistic and interrelated merging of male and female.

Vertically Layered Universe

In chapter 2 it was proposed that the shamanic cosmos is vertically layered. This belief appears neurologically generated in several mutually reinforcing ways. Lewis-Williams and Pearce propose that belief in a layered cosmos can "be ascribed to the functioning of the human nervous system in a variety of altered states" (2005:69). As Lewis-Williams and Pearce point out, "[a]ll religions have an ecstatic component, and all involve altering human consciousness to some extent by prayer, meditation, chanting and many other techniques" (10;

emphasis in original). Based in studies involving electrical stimulation and mapping of the brain (e.g., Blanke et al. 2002), Lewis-Williams and Pearce (68–69) propose that altered states of consciousness activate areas in our brains that cause illusions of travel to upper and lower worlds. Movement upward is by flight; movement downward is through a vortex or tunnel. According to Blanke et al., the area of the brain responsible for these visual illusions is the right angular gyrus. Since these illusions originate in our brains, they seem real. Since they involve movement along a vertically oriented axis, such illusions provide validity to our notion of a vertically layered universe.

Our notions of a layered cosmos can also be accounted for by our embodiment in the world. Our situation as humans is such that what we "know" about the world derives from our interaction with it. In this interaction, humans maintain an upright body position. As space opens before us, "vertical-horizontal, top-bottom, front-back and left-right are positions and coordinates of the body that are extrapolated onto space" (Tuan 1977:35). By the mere presence of our bodies, therefore, we impose a particular structure to the space around us. The vertical axis of this structure has two poles—high and low, above and below. The cosmic analogue to above and below becomes the upperworld and lowerworld, with the in-between region being the place where we exist.

Expressed another way, according to d'Aquili (1993:52), by function of the dominant-side parieto-occipital area of the brain, we are able to divide space into "coordinate axes." Expanding upon this hypothesis, gravity provides a vertical axis for every individual. By operation of the binary operator, we divide this vertical axis into complementary opposites of up and down. In its simplest iteration, this results in a vertically tiered cosmos consisting of earth-down and sky-up. In Native American belief, this binary division of space is often personified as "Mother Earth" and "Father Sky."

Although we structure the vertical axis into opposites, we are also compelled to mediate or "resolve" the inherent contradictions presented by these opposites. Thus we find that "opposites are often mediated by a third term" (Tuan 1974:16). Roe (1995:61) refers to this concept as triadic dualism (also see Turff and Carr 2005:670; Lévi-Strauss 1963:132–62). In the shamanic universe, triadic dualism results in a vertically structured cosmos made-up of three basic levels. The result, as explained by Eliade is that "the universe in general is conceived as having three levels—sky, earth, and underworld" (1964:259). Often, in shamanic belief, upper and lower worlds are further divided into additional levels. So the upper and lower worlds may, for example, have four, seven, or some other number of levels.

There are many cross-cultural variations on the theme of a vertically layered cosmos. Generally speaking, however, in Native American cosmologies—and across the Eastern Woodlands in particular—the upperworld is inhabited by the sun, moon, and stars, as well as powerful thunderbird spirits and, in some cases, anthropomorphic beings believed to be the creators of the world.

The middle world—earth—is this world of everyday existence and includes people and land animals. Often, the middle world/earth is conceptualized as a flat disk. Spirits and dangerous creatures such as pygmies, flying heads, and cannibal giants are often believed to inhabit special places in the middle world, including secluded forests, mountain passes, and caves.

The lowerworld is located beneath the middle world and is accessible through caves, rivers, springs, and lakes. Of significance is that the lowerworld "is often comprised of mirror and converse images of this one" (Ripinsky-Naxon 1993:120). Typically, the lowerworld is inhabited by fantastical monsters. In the Eastern Woodlands, these monsters are often modeled after the elusive panther, peculiar fishes, frogs, and giant snakes (Dewdney 1975:122–29). In some cases the lowerworld is home to spirits of the dead, as well as giants, dwarfs, and hunchbacks.

In Eastern Woodlands cosmologies, upperworld avian creatures are engaged in a cosmic struggle with lowerworld serpent or reptilian creatures (Morrisseau 1998; Lankford 1987; Smith 1995). In some instances, it may be that Native American tales of upperworld and lowerworld creatures were partially inspired by fossil finds of giant prehistoric flying creatures and serpentlike beasts (Mayor 2005).

The above-noted beliefs concerning Otherworld creatures provide a good example of what Boyer (2001) and Pyysiäinen (2003) describe as counterintuitive representations. Counterintuitive representations, which contradict our expectations of how things should be, are common to religious beliefs. In the case of the cosmological schemes mentioned above, real time and mythic time are collapsed, sun and moon fly without wings, and serpents and panthers move unimpeded through the earth. Normal rules of physics and biology are violated by combining features from different cognitive domains and by denying attributes such as aging, growth, or the need to eat. Essentially, it is the counterintuitiveness of upper- and lowerworld creatures that grabs our attention and makes them superhuman and memorable. As Denise Dennett remarks, "put these two ideas together—a hyperactive agent-seeking bias and a weakness for certain sorts of memorable combos—and you get a kind of fiction-generating contraption" (2006:119–20). We are that fiction-generating contraption.

To summarize thus far, the mind-brain creates a sense of order through its neuropsychological assumption that the world has vertical and horizontal axes. Further, the mind-brain divides the vertical axis into up and down. This results in the notion of a layered universe. Often these levels are inhabited by opposite kinds of beings—that is, birds and serpent or water creatures. Because these beliefs are universal to shamanic cosmologies, including those of the Eastern Woodlands, we can surmise that the Hopewell likewise believed in a vertically layered cosmos and that, in their cosmology, the upperworld and lowerworld were inhabited by avian and serpentlike creatures, respectively. In the next several pages, we will look at Hopewell expressions of these beliefs.

Artifact Designs

The Adena Pipe

In chapter 3, the Adena pipe was briefly discussed. Of interest to the present discussion are the designs found on the front and rear of the beltlike device the dwarf is wearing. Figures 4.7a and 4.7b show close-up photographs of these design elements. I propose that the front design resembles the sinuous form of a serpent, while the rear element represents a feather bustle (Romain 2004b). In this representation, a complementary opposite duality is symbolized, with a serpent on the front and bird element on the rear. The further implication is that, in the Adena-Hopewell worldview, serpent and bird creatures occupied opposite realms. Also, we note that the dwarf is, in effect, situated "betwixt and between" the two opposite design symbols—appropriate to the liminal status of dwarfs in general and perhaps further implying that the dwarf provided access to both realms, possibly by means of the smoking pipe to which he gives form.

While birds and serpents generally represent opposite realms, it appears that on occasion the Hopewell also used different kinds of birds to symbolize the same idea. The next case provides an example.

Mound City Pottery

Art historian David Penny has pointed out that during Middle Woodland times, two different kinds of bird images appear on Hopewell pottery: raptors and ducks. Based in Native American mythology, Penny proposes that raptor images on pottery were associated with the upperworld, while duck designs were associated with the watery lowerworld. Together, "the two designs describe a cohesive universe structure" (1985:184).

Penny's hypothesis is supported by a series of discoveries at Mound City. Several decorated pots were found in mound 2 at Mound City. Figure 4.7c shows one of these pots, found by Squier and Davis (1848:190). Figure 4.7d shows a second vessel found years later by Mills (1922:511) in the same mound. The birds are rendered in the same fashion on both pots. Decorative elements that frame the birds are similar. The manner in which the lips of the pots are decorated are also the same. In these correspondences, it appears that the two pots comprise a complementary set.

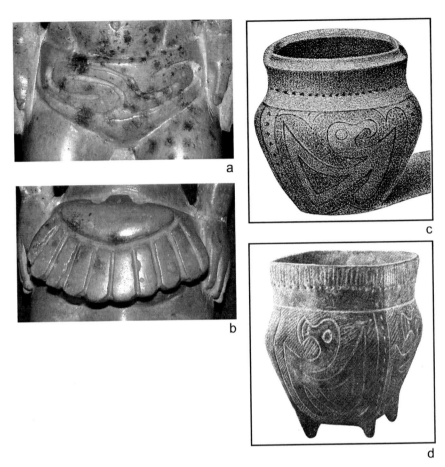

Figure 4.7. a. Close-up front view of Adena pipe loin cloth, showing possible serpent motif. Photo by William Romain, used by permission of the Ohio Historical Society. b. Close-up rear view of Adena pipe loin cloth, showing feather bustle. Photo by William Romain. Used by permission of the Ohio Historical Society. c. Decorated pottery vessel from Mound City, mound 2. From Squier and Davis (1848:Pl. 46). d. Decorated pottery vessel from Mound City, mound 2. From Mills 1922:fig. 40; used with permission of the Ohio Historical Society. Scan provided by Arthur W. McGraw.

Notable, however, is that two very different kinds of birds are shown. While the pot in figure 4.7c shows a raptor, the figure 4.7d pot shows a broad-billed bird, most likely a duck. The raptor bird faces to the right; the duck faces to the left. Moreover, as if to emphasize the opposite nature of what we are looking at, the rim of the raptor pot is a circle, while the rim of the duck pot is more like a square.

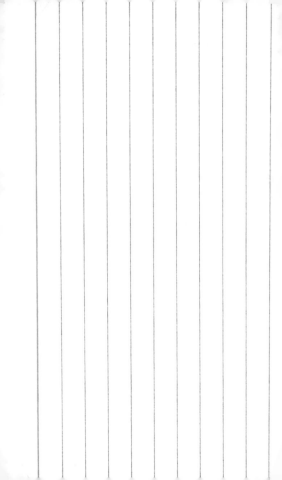

In life, raptors soar at high altitudes as they look for prey. Ducks, on the other hand, are a different kind of bird. Quite the opposite of raptors, ducks spend most of their time on water. Indeed, their specialty is in diving beneath the surface into the watery domain of the lowerworld.

As Penny suggests, the avian designs on these two pottery vessels seem to reflect an intentional pairing of upperworld and lowerworld symbolism—expressed in this instance by opposite kinds of birds. If Penny is correct, then in this symbolism we have graphic expression of a vertically layered cosmos, with raptor birds above and duck birds below.

The Hopewell Site Serpent
As suggested by the Mound City pots, birds can be used as both upperworld and lowerworld symbols. In the next piece, we find the possibility that night creatures might also have been used to express upperworld and lowerworld concepts. Figure 4.8a shows what has often been interpreted as the top view of a snake's head (Willoughby 1916:490; Moorehead 1922:124).[4] Figure 4.8b shows additional copper pieces that have been interpreted as tongue elements intended to accompany the serpent head (Willoughby 1916:490). Figure 4.8c shows the resulting image if one of the tongue elements is placed in association with the serpent head. Both the posited serpent head and tongue elements were found in mound 25 at the Hopewell site.[5]

Two more animals appear in the scroll designs within the serpent's head. Figure 4.8d shows these designs. Based in a number of features, including the shape of the head and facial markings, my interpretation is that these two designs show an upperworld owl and a lowerworld panther.

Willoughby (1916) was the first to suggest that the one design in the serpent head represents an owl. Supportive of this notion is that owls were often depicted by the Hopewell. In his discussion of the Tremper mound effigy pipes, for example, Mills notes that "[m]ore than twelve genera of birds have been recognized, and in one instance—the owls—six individual specimens, representing at least five species were found" (1916:324). The fact that ear tufts are not shown in the mound 25 copper piece suggests that the design might have been modeled after the barred owl (cf. figure 4.8f). The barred owl (*Strix varia*) is common in Ohio.

As to the other creature in the serpent's head, my interpretation is that a panther is represented.[6] Also known as mountain lion, puma, or cougar, the panther (*Felis concolor*) ranged across the Eastern Woodlands during Hopewell times. Panther effigies are also found in sculpted three-dimensional form on Hopewell effigy pipes.

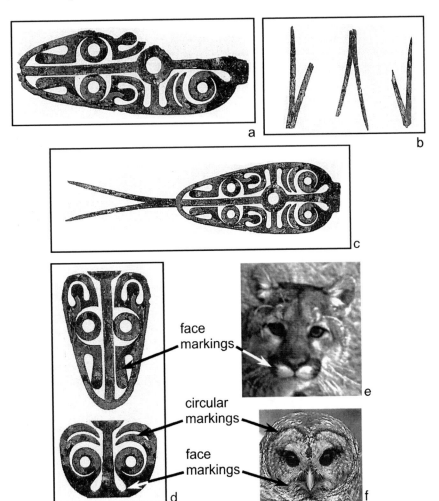

Figure 4.8. a. Copper serpent design from the Hopewell site. From Moorehead 1922: Pl. 68(4). b. Copper serpent tongue elements from the Hopewell site. From Moorehead 1922:Pl. 61(6). c. Reconstructed serpent head and tongue design by the present author. Reconstruction by William Romain from images in figs. 4.8a and 4.8b from Moorehead 1922:Pls. 68(4) and 61(6). d. Panther and owl faces within the serpent's head. Reconstruction by William Romain from images in figs. 4.8a and 4.8b from Moorehead 1922: Pls. 68(4) and 61(6). e. Panther face showing characteristic black markings on snout. From U.S. Fish and Wildlife Service, Digital Library, www.fws.gov/DLS/, accessed February 22, 2008. f. Barred owl. Courtesy of the Illinois Raptor Center.

As to their symbolic associations, as a nocturnal raptor, the owl may represent the nighttime aspect of the upperworld. Panthers, on the other hand, are associated with the lowerworld (Hamell 1998). Indeed, according to some Eastern Woodland beliefs, the Underwater Panther is the chief of the lowerworld. Further, panthers are nocturnal. Like the owl, they are also predators.

In the head of the serpent therefore, we perhaps find nocturnal aspects of the upperworld and lowerworld represented.[7] In the design, the upperworld owl is situated in an opposite position relative to the lowerworld panther. Moreover, the owl is facing in the opposite direction. Thus upperworld and lowerworld are the reverse of each other.

Continuing this line of thought, we note that in the Hopewell copper piece, the owl and panther are separated by a circle and cross design. If the circle and cross are rotated in space so they extend perpendicular to the owl and panther, the result might be interpreted as a horizontal circle that represents the flat circle earth, with the four world quarters delineated by the four arms of the cross. Perpendicular to the horizontal earth circle are the upper and lower worlds, symbolized by the owl and panther, respectively. Figure 4.9 shows the rotated cosmogram.

Consistent with the thesis just offered are the tiny perforations through the "neck" of the serpent piece, just barely visible in figure 4.8c. Fastened

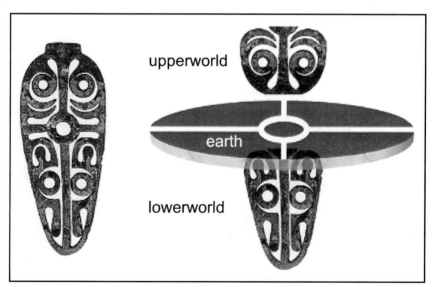

Figure 4.9. **Three-dimensional rendering of the Hopewell cosmos based on the design elements found in the copper piece shown on the left. Shown in the exploded view are the upper and lower worlds, circle earth, and four world directions. In this conception, the owl symbolizes the upperworld; the panther represents the lowerworld. Reconstruction by William Romain from images in fig. 4.8a from Moorehead 1922:Pl. 68(4).**

to clothing or another backing, the serpent head would point downward, in the direction of the lowerworld. In this orientation, the upperworld owl is situated above the lowerworld panther, reminiscent of the vertical structure of the shamanic cosmos.

Copper and Stone Birds and Fish
Several additional pieces suggest that the Hopewell universe was vertically layered. In the next examples, however, the upperworld is represented by bird designs, while fish effigies represent the lowerworld.

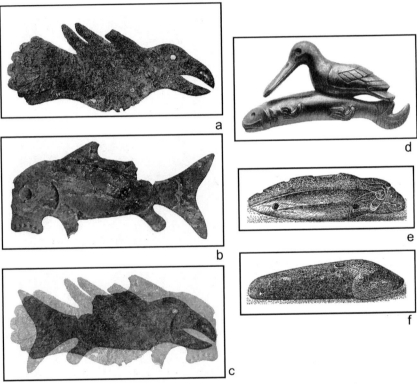

Figure 4.10. a. Copper raven or crow effigy from Hopewell site, mound 25. From Moorehead 1922:Pl. 69(3). b. Copper fish effigy from Hopewell site, mound 25. From Moorehead 1922:Pl. 69(2). c. Bird effigy shown in fig. 4.10a superimposed over fish shown in fig. 4.10b. Image superimposition by William Romain from images in figs. 4.10a and 4.10b. From Moorehead 1922:Pls. 69(3)(2). d. Fish and bird effigy pipe recovered from the Hopewell site, mound 25, altar 2. From Moorehead 1922:Pl. 78(2). e. Stone bird effigy from the Hopewell site. From Moorehead 1922:fig. 37. f. Stone tadpole effigy from the Hopewell site. From Moorehead 1922:fig. 36. Copper effigies are not to same scale as pipe and stone effigies.

Shown in figure 4.10a is one of several copper bird effigies found in mound 25 at the Hopewell site. The design represents a crow or raven. Shown in figure 4.10b is one of four copper fish effigies also found in mound 25 at the Hopewell site. The copper pieces shown are in relatively good condition. Moorehead (1922:127) reported that most of the other fish and birds were in fragmented condition.

In figure 4.10c, the bird and fish images have been superimposed.[8] What this reveals is a series of correspondences between the two designs leading to the suggestion that although each was part of a larger group of fishes and birds, the individual fish and birds were made to complement each other. As shown by figure 4.10c, there are several correspondences between the two figures shown: (1) both are made out of flattened copper sheets; (2) they are very nearly the same size; (3) both creatures are shown in flat profile views; (4) the heads of the bird and fish extend downward at about the same angle; (5) the angle of the dorsal fin on the fish and leading edge of the bird wing extend at the same angle; and (6) the upper part of the fish tail fin and bird tail extend at approximately the same angle.

What this seems to suggest is that the bird and fish were intended as symbols of complementary opposite but interrelated and balanced realms—that is, the upperworld realm of birds and lowerworld realm of fishes. Given their size and design similarities, the images are also evocative of the transformational capability between living forms, discussed in more detail in the next chapter.

Figure 4.10d shows an effigy pipe from the Hopewell site. The pipe shows a water bird seated on the back of a catfish. The catfish is identified by its barbells, or "whiskers," near its mouth. Of interest is that the fins of the fish curve upward, resembling raptor talons in their shape. Perhaps this was intended as a metaphorical equivalent of raptor talons. Catfish fins are well known for their ability to inflict serious, penetrating wounds, exacerbated by protein venom released when the fin spines are torn. In any case, the pipe seems to represent an upperworld bird situated opposite to a lowerworld fish.

Figures 4.10e and 4.10f show a similar set of complementary images. Made out of serpentine stone, both effigies were found at the Hopewell site. Judging from its prominent beak, the creature in figure 4.10e is a bird. Visible on the creature in figure 4.10f are gills. Based on the shape of its head and body and lack of feet, the creature in figure 4.10f resembles a tadpole. In this interpretation, we again find complementary opposite creatures rendered in a stylistically similar fashion, seemingly expressive of a dualistic and vertically layered universe, with birds above and water creatures below.

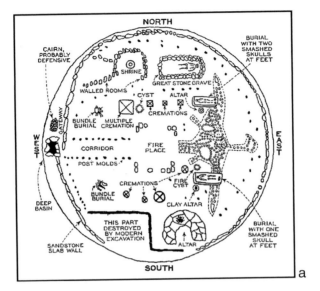

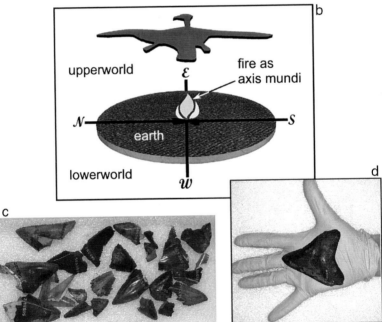

Figure 4.11.   a. North Benton mound, located near the village of North Benton, Ohio. From Magrath 1940:fig. 1. b. Schematic representation of the Hopewell cosmos based on symbolism found in the North Benton mound. Drawing by William Romain. c. Shark teeth from the Hopewell site. Photo by William Romain of objects in the Field Museum (accession #56538). d. Fossil shark tooth from the Hopewell site. Photo by William Romain of object in the Field Museum (accession #56538.2).

The North Benton Mound Effigy

One of the central features of the archetypal shamanic worldview is the idea of soul flight to the upper and lower worlds (Eliade 1964:259). Such journeys can occur through altered states of consciousness or through death. Given that birds are associated with flight, it is not uncommon to find cross-culturally that shamans use birds to cross to the Otherworld. The same principle applies to the deceased soul. An example seems provided in the North Benton mound.

The North Benton mound is a large Hopewell burial mound located in northeast Ohio. One of the remarkable things about the mound is that a large bird mosaic made of stone and clay was found at its base. The wingspan of the bird stretched more than 30 feet (9.1 m) across (Magrath 1945:42) and appears to represent a raptor with hooked beak (figure 4.11a). Resting on each of the raptor's wings was a human burial. One was an extended male; the other, an extended female.

One interpretation of the symbolism involved is that physically placing the deceased on the wings of the giant bird ensured that the souls of the dead would be carried to the Otherworld, or upperworld. As mentioned earlier, in Native American mythology the upperworld was the abode of giant thunderbird beings. Eagles, hawks, and falcons were their smaller brethren. As suggested elsewhere (Romain 2005b), by virtue of the North Benton raptor's tremendous size—larger than any known bird in this world—it may be that the effigy was intended to depict an upperworld thunderbird. Moreover, association of the raptor effigy with the dead suggests the non-ordinary or spirit aspect of the giant bird—appropriate to the non-ordinary reality of the upperworld.

Of course, the giant bird could also represent a clan symbol that gave specific identity to the dead. In either case, the existence of the giant effigy suggests that larger-than-life raptors were part of the Hopewell universe. Figure 4.11b shows a hypothetical sketch of the Hopewell cosmos based in this understanding.

Supportive of this notion is that complementary-opposite larger-than-life lowerworld creatures may also have been part of the Hopewell worldview. Shown in figure 4.11c is a collection of shark teeth recovered from the Hopewell site. The finding of shark teeth in Ohio Hopewell contexts is intriguing. Figure 4.11d, however, is of special interest. Figure 4.11d shows a fossil shark tooth also recovered from the Hopewell site (Moorehead 1922:143). This tooth, however, is not from any ordinary shark. Based on its enormous size and the V-shaped band of enamel just below the root, known as a *bourlette*, it can be identified as the tooth of the extinct great white shark (*Carcharodon megalodon*). These beasts grew to an estimated length of 60 feet

(18.2 m) and may have weighed as much as 70 metric tons. Looking at this tooth, it is easy to imagine how the Hopewell might have believed the watery lowerworld to be the home of monsters equivalent in size and power to their upperworld counterparts.

The Hopewell Lowerworld

A further glimpse into the Hopewell lowerworld may be provided by the contents of altar 1 in mound 4 at the Turner earthwork (Willoughby and Hooton 1922:63). Altar 1 was a rounded square feature made of clay, measuring roughly 6 feet (1.8 m) diagonally from corner to corner and 10 inches (25.4 cm) in thickness. The altar was located in the approximate center of the mound.

Covering the floor of the altar was a layer of black ashes 13 inches (33 cm) deep. On top of the black ashes, a layer of white ashes extended across one side of the floor. On top of this layer, another layer of black ashes was found. Resting on the first black layer of ashes, near the center of the altar, was a large piece of copper weighing more than 3 pounds (1.4 kg). Found near the copper piece were fragments of several terra-cotta human figurines and two unique stone effigies.

The one stone effigy is carved from red slate and represents a fantastical, monster creature (figure 4.12a). About 9 1/2 inches (24.1 cm) in length, the creature has forward-facing horns or stingers, four limbs terminating in claws, and a rattlesnake tail. A pattern suggestive of "reptilian plates" or scales is engraved on top of the head (Willoughby and Hooton 1922:70). Close examination shows that the size and pattern of the effigy head scales resemble those found on two snakes common to southern Ohio—namely, the copperhead (*Agkistrodon contortrix*) and black rat snake (*Elaphe obsoleta obsoleta*; cf. figs. 4.12b and 4.12c). By contrast, most other snakes in Ohio (e.g., timber rattlesnake) have small scales on the top of their head. The copperhead, which is a venomous snake, accounts for more bites than any other snake in North America (Campbell and Lamar 2004:257). The black rat snake is the largest snake in Ohio, sometimes growing to a length of 8 feet (2.4 m). Both snakes, therefore, would have been of potential interest to the Hopewell.

The second effigy is engraved on a smooth, dark stone. The design suggests some sort of aquatic creature (figure 4.12d). The creature has a long snout, four weblike appendages, and a long tail.

Situated on top of these two effigies was a serpent effigy cut out of mica. Covering these deposits were layers of black, gray, and white ashes. Found in the ash layers were a large number of fossils, small copper nuggets, more than two hundred deer and elk astragali bones, dozens of hollow cones made from antler tips, and fragments of worked shell, bone, teeth, and claws. The ash

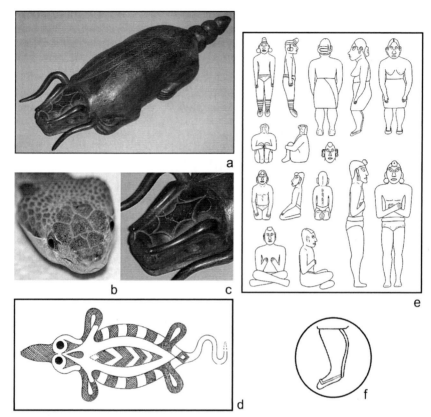

Figure 4.12. a. Horned monster effigy from the Turner site. Photo by William Romain, used by permission of the Peabody Museum, Harvard University. b. Photo of copperhead snake showing resemblance of head scales to engraved design on dorsal aspect of Turner horned monster. Photo by William Romain. c. Close-up view of effigy shown in fig. 4.12a. Photo by William Romain, used by permission of the Peabody Museum, Harvard University. d. Rollout of engraved design on stone from the Turner site. From Willoughby and Hooton 1922:fig. 33, courtesy of the Peabody Museum, Harvard University. e. Outlines of restored clay figurines from the Turner site, altar 1, mound 4. From Willoughby and Hooton, 1922:Pl. 21; courtesy of the Peabody Museum, Harvard University. f. Enlarged detail of woman's foot in figure 4.12e. From Willoughby and Hooton 1922: Pl. 21, courtesy of the Peabody Museum, Harvard University.

layers, in turn, were covered by a layer of worked cannel coal. Covering the cannel coal, as well as the entire altar, was a layer of sand 5 inches (12.7 cm) thick. Overlying the sand layer were three layers of flat stones.

As to the stone effigies, the horned serpent monster (figure 4.12a) does not resemble any creature known in this world. Instead, the creature is a chimera kind of monster with features derived from the rattlesnake, the copperhead or black rat snake, possibly the alligator, and an unidentified creature having forward-pointing horns or stinger-devices.[9] In its conceptually blended anatomy, the effigy resembles later Mississippian and Historic period representations of lowerworld monsters (see e.g., Phillips and Brown 1975, vol. 3:opposite plate 80; Dewdney 1975:fig. 124).

With reference to the second stone effigy (figure 4.12d), the engraving resembles what might be drawn based on the verbal description of an alligator (*Alligator mississippiensis*). Alligators are not found in Ohio; however, alligator teeth have been found at several Hopewell sites including Turner (Willoughby and Hooton 1922:46). As to the mica serpent found in the Turner deposit, based on the rattles shown on its tail (see figure 5.5g), there is no doubt that the cutout is modeled after a rattlesnake.

The discovery in the Turner deposit of copper nuggets, including one nugget weighing more than 3 pounds (1.4 kg), is of interest. A number of Native American groups believed that copper comes from underwater monsters (see, e.g., Halsey 1992 [1983]:1). The occurrence of shell fossils in the ash layers is of interest because they represent bizarre life forms not found in the living Hopewell world.

In summary, what we find in the altar 1 deposit are representations of serpent and alligator-like monsters, in association with exotic materials having lowerworld connotations. The broken human figurines (figure 4.12e) were found at the same level as the stone effigies, and again, all of these items were buried under a series of colored ash layers followed by layers of sand and stone.

The human effigies seem to represent dead persons. I make that suggestion based on a couple of observations. First, several of the body positions exhibited by the figurines are similar to burial positions sometimes used by Historic period Native Americans. Thus the Turner figurines may represent corpse positions during the stasis period prior to cremation. Second, two of the figurines exhibit relaxed foot positions typical to dead bodies. In death, the feet of a corpse usually do not point straight up; rather, as the muscles relax, the feet point at a slight downward angle. In the Turner large female figurine especially, the downward pointing angle of the feet suggest the person is deceased. Figure 4.12f shows a close-up detail of the female's foot position.

Penny suggests that together, "[t]he assembled objects may be interpreted as an evocation of the burial group en route to the Land of the Dead, with the cremated deceased represented by the group of figures and the underworld journey implied by the host of underworld creatures" (1985:185). I would go further and suggest that the deposit is a generalized model of the Hopewell lowerworld. The model suggests a layered aspect to the Hopewell lowerworld. Indeed, the different sand and stone levels found in the deposit are reminiscent of the different levels attributed to the upper and lower worlds by Historic period Eastern Woodland tribes.

Axis Mundi

Our mind-brains have evolved so that we are able to function in an environment that has three spatial dimensions. In a three-dimensional world where the upperworld, this world, and the lowerworld are arranged as horizontal layers, the shortest connecting line is a vector that extends perpendicular to the levels. The cosmic analogue of this perpendicular line or path is referred to as an *axis mundi*.

Cross-culturally, the *axis mundi* is expressed in many different ways. In some cultures the *axis mundi* is symbolized by a "world tree" that links the upper and lower worlds. Other cultures visualize the *axis mundi* as a column or pillar. Yet others describe it as a cosmic mountain. In many cases, the *axis mundi* is symbolized by special temples, cities, and palaces.

Structures that reach up toward the heavens imply the *axis mundi* concept. The concept can also be expressed, however, by passageways, chambers, pits, and tunnels that extend downward. Thus in addition to their vertical aspect, many temples, pyramids, and sacred structures have complementary underground components that extend toward the lowerworld.

Neurobiologically generated cosmology is not without contradictions. The *axis mundi* for an entire culture may be a particular mountain, temple, or city. Additionally, since each individual is at the center of his or her own subjective view of the cosmos, the *axis mundi* is also situated wherever the individual is. In either case, because it connects the upperworld, this world, and the lowerworld, in the shamanic universe the *axis mundi* is the pathway that the souls of shamans and the deceased often use to move between worlds.

An example of an *axis mundi* drawn from the Northeast is provided by the Iroquois. The pine tree was a symbol for the Iroquoian Confederacy. According to ethnologist Carrie Lyford (1989 [1945]:91), however, the pine tree was also referred to as the "world tree," "celestial tree," or "tree of life." Lyford explains that the Iroquois believed the "tree of life" was situated at the center of the world and that its branches supported the sun and moon. The roots of the world tree were said to penetrate into the primal Great Turtle, on whose back the earth was made.

The notion that the Hopewell recognized the concept of an *axis mundi* is suggested by both artifact and earthwork evidence (also see Romain 2000:185, 205).

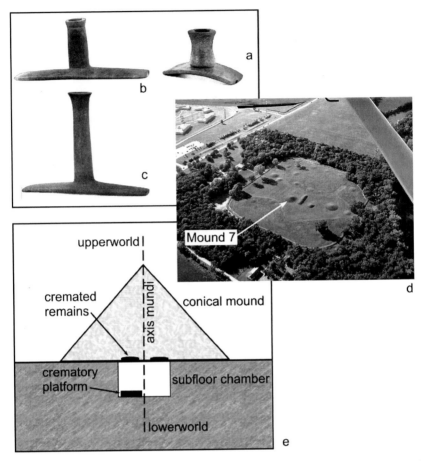

Figure 4.13. a–c. Pipes from the Tremper mound. From Mills 1916:figs. 71, 77, 81; used with permission of the Ohio Historical Society. d. Aerial view of Mound City showing location of mound 7. Photo by William Romain. e. Schematic drawing of Mound City, mound 7 showing *axis mundi*. Drawing by William Romain.

Smoking Pipes

The *axis mundi* concept appears expressed in Hopewell smoking pipes of a particular kind. Hopewell smoking pipes include tube, effigy, platform, and smokestack. Figure 4.13a shows a typical platform pipe. Figures 4.13b and 4.13c show two smokestack pipes. The pipes in figures 4.13a–4.13c are from the Tremper site, where dozens more were found (Mills 1916). Similar platform pipes have also been found at many other Hopewell sites. In chapter 7 we will consider how tube and effigy pipes may have been used. Of present interest are platform and smokestack pipes. What seems emphasized in these pipes is their vertical aspect. In the platform pipes, special decorative emphasis is often given to the pipes' bowls. In the smokestack pipes, the vertical aspect is emphasized by the proportionate size of the bowls compared to their stems.

Pipe smoking was used as a form of communication with the spirit world by virtually all Native American peoples. The smoke was believed to carry the thoughts and prayers of the smoker to the upperworld. Where the vertical aspect of Hopewell platform and smokestack pipes is emphasized, it may be that the *axis mundi* concept was being referenced. In this, the vertical aspect of the pipe bowl reinforced the vertical column of smoke that emanated from the pipe, which was the visual manifestation of the *axis mundi*. In essence, the vertical aspect of these pipes created and reinforced the link between this world and the Otherworld.

Mound City *Axis Mundi*

An impressive example of the *axis mundi* concept is memorialized in a Hopewell burial mound located at Mound City, in Ross County, Ohio. Mound City is a geometric enclosure, shaped like a square with rounded corners (figure 4.13d). At least twenty-four burial mounds were originally situated within the enclosure. Of these, mound 7 was the most impressive. Mound 7 was a cone-shaped burial mound. Squier and Davis (1848:154) give the dimensions of the mound as 17 1/2 feet (5.3 m) in height and 90 feet (27.4 m) in diameter. Based on its size and location, Mills (1922:471) considered mound 7 to be the "great central tumulus" of the Mound City earthwork. Found within mound 7 were thirteen cremated burials. Of the thirteen burials, ten were situated on the ground-level floor; the other three were situated between 3 and 4 feet (0.9—1.2 m) above ground level.

Where things become intriguing is in the discovery of a large underground chamber underneath mound 7, below the ground-level floor (figure 4.13e). Mills described the chamber in the following way:

> Its average depth below the floor of the mound proper was 5 1/2 feet [1.7 m], although in places this depth was close upon 6 feet [1.8 m]. The excavation corresponding to the basement was oval in form, with its longest axis extending northeast and southwest. Its length was approximately 40 feet [12.2 m] and its width 30 feet [9.1]. . . . The floor of the basement was carefully made of puddled clay. (1922:477–78)

The underground chamber was located in the approximate center of mound 7. A graded slope located in the northeast end of the chamber provided access into the underground area. Post molds along both sides of the entranceway suggest that the northeast half of the chamber may have been shielded by a screen or roof.

Excavation of the underground room revealed the presence of a large crematory basin, approximately 6 feet (1.8 m) in length by 4 feet (1.2 m) in width, located near the southwest end. Based on its burned condition and evidence of frequent repairs, Mills (1922:479) surmised that the basin had been used for a long time. As to its use for crematory purposes there is little doubt, as Mills noted that he found calcined bones and ashes still remaining in the basin. Presumably the remains were human, although Mills does not explicitly document that.

The finding of a crematory chamber below ground level suggests—at least in this instance—that a lowerworld context was associated with processing the dead.[10] Also revealing is that the floor of the subterranean room was made from puddled clay, which is clay that has been mixed with water and allowed to set. As mentioned earlier, many Native American peoples believe that rivers, streams, and springs are entrances to the lowerworld. That the floor of the underground room was made of puddled clay perhaps indicates a similar association by the Hopewell between water and the lowerworld.

In reconstructing what might have taken place at mound 7, we can imagine how a column of smoke that issued from the subterranean crematory fire might have been thought of as a link, or *axis mundi*, between worlds—that is, a path for the deceased between the lowerworld represented by the puddled-clay underground chamber; the earth represented by the ground-level geometric enclosure; and the upperworld above. In this interpretation, the *axis mundi* concept was later reinforced by the addition of the conical mound over the underground room. In this view, mound 7 served as an *axis mundi* between worlds. Figure 4.13e illustrates the idea (also see Buikstra et al. 1998:89 for a similar expression in Illinois Hopewell).

An equally explicit example of the *axis mundi* concept seems expressed in the North Benton mound discussed earlier and shown in figure 4.11a. As this figure shows, a "fireplace" was situated in the center of the mound. From the occurrence of similar features found in other Hopewell mounds, it is appears that the North Benton fireplace feature was probably used for cremation purposes—perhaps to process the cremated human remains found flanking the fireplace itself. Relevant to the present discussion is that the crematory fireplace is situated at the intersection of two axes established by the cardinal directions; that is, the fireplace is aligned north-south and east-west, with the center of the fireplace situated at the intersection of these two axes. The result was a centrally located fire feature almost entirely surrounded by human burials. In this intentional positioning, the importance of the fire seems emphasized. From its central location in a liminal mortuary area and given that crematory fires were used by the Hopewell to further the deceased on their journey into the afterlife, it seems reasonable to suppose that the North Benton fireplace served as an *axis mundi* between this world and the Otherworld. The concept is illustrated in figure 4.11b.

Both the Mound City and North Benton cases are conceptually reminiscent of a story told by the Ottawa Indians. After creating the world, Nanabozho tells the people that they should burn the bodies of the deceased and scatter their ashes so "that they might more easily rise to the sky" (Kinietz 1965:298).

Four Directions

Arguably, the binary operator simplifies and reduces spatial relationships to pairs of complementary opposites. When applied to the horizontal aspect of our world, the result is a series of opposites constrained by the three-dimensional nature of space and related to the human body. That is, our mind-brains perceive four basic orientations that conform to the structure of our bodies: front and back, left and right (Tuan 1977:35). The result is a quadripartite division of space in the horizontal plane that, when applied to the surface of the earth, presupposes the four directions.

The four directions establish the trajectory of horizontal space and the four quadrants. The problem, however, is that since our perceptions of front and back and left and right are tied to our body, as we move through space the world's quadrants appear to revolve with the body. Indeed, in some Native American origin stories, the primordial world is said to have continued spinning until the Creator used four serpents as stakes to hold down the corners of the earth (e.g., Miller 2001:169).

For purposes of common reference, therefore, we need to anchor the quadrants. As it happens, the sun provides the necessary reference. Accordingly, we find that many cultures—including those in the Americas—"anchor" the quadrants by reference to solar-derived cardinal or solstice directions. The way in which cardinal and solstice directions can be used to establish the world's quadrants is shown in figures 4.14a–4.14c.

As shown by figure 4.14a, in the cardinal direction system, orthogonal pairs of points establish a quadripartite universe, with north-south and east-west situated at right angles to each other. In this system, the east-west line of the sun's rising and setting at the equinoxes is crossed by an orthogonal north-south line, thereby forming a cross—often used as a symbol for the world's four quarters or directions. In this system, the azimuths of 0°, 90°,

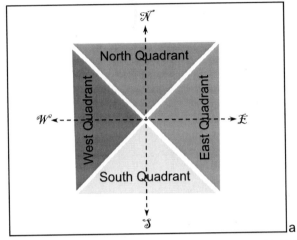

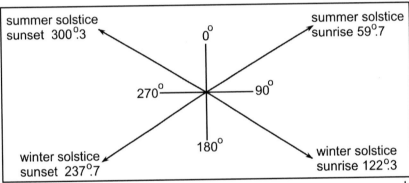

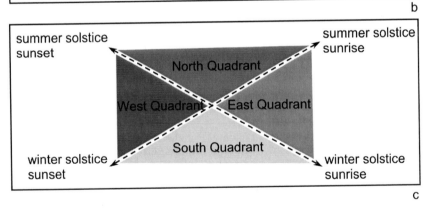

Figure 4.14.   a. Cardinal system of reference with the four quarters defined by the cardinal directions. Drawing by William Romain. b. Solstice directions for central Ohio area. Drawing by William Romain. c. Solstice system of reference, with four quarters defined by the boundary azimuths of the solstices. Drawing by William Romain.

180°, and 270° establish the four directions, while the intercardinal directions establish the boundaries of the world quarters.

Alternatively, in the solstice system of reference, the world quarters and boundaries are established by the sun's solstice azimuths (figure 4.14c)—which, in the region of central and southern Ohio during Hopewell times, occurred at the approximate azimuths of 60°, 122°, 238°, and 300° (figure 4.14b).[11] What both reference systems have in common is that they use the sun to establish their anchor points. And again, both systems of reference divide horizontal space into quadrants.

Relevant to the matter are the comments of archaeologist Thomas Emerson who explains that in North America, the quadripartite division of the cosmos was "quite literally all pervasive" (1995:400). Most Historic period Native American peoples divided space into four quarters and tied the quarters to the cardinal directions. While not as common, other Indian groups such as the Tewa, although cognizant of the cardinal directions, link their world quarters to the solstice directions (see, e.g., Ortiz 1969).

In either case, the practical importance of the world quarters or directions for hunters and gatherers in particular is that the direction from which weather systems approach anticipates the kind of weather that will prevail, which in turn influences the kinds of animals that can be successfully hunted, as well as the seasonal availability of plant foods. An example is provided by the Sandy Lake Cree of Canada, who believe that spirits live in each of the four directions (Stevens 1971:62–63). The North Spirit brings snow and ice, which allow the people to track game. The South Spirit brings warm weather, which allows for the growth of food plants. The West Spirit brings darkness. The East Spirit brings light. Since the spirits of the Four Directions approach as winds, the Four Directions or Four Quarters are also the Four Winds.

From the perspective of the shaman, directional orientation might also be important when traveling between realms and across time and space.

It appears that the Hopewell used both the cardinal and solstice systems of reference to establish a quadripartite division of space.

Earthwork Orientation

The matter of earthwork orientation is discussed in detail elsewhere (Romain 2005a, 2004a, 2000). Briefly summarized, however, analyses show that, out of sixteen major geometrically shaped earthworks whose original orientation could be reliably determined, all were oriented to celestial events (Romain 2005a:table 1). Fourteen were oriented to either the solstice or cardinal directions; two were aligned to the moon. Two examples illustrate these findings.

Mound City

Located in Chillicothe, Ohio, the Mound City earthwork is oriented through its diagonal axis to the summer solstice sunset. The sides of the earthwork are roughly 745 feet (227 m) in length. Its walls are relatively low—about 3 to 4 feet (0.9–1.2 m) in height. The walls of the earthwork have been restored. However, analysis indicates that the restoration was accurate since it relied on existing and contiguous remnants of the original embankment walls found by excavation (see Romain 2000:125–29 for further discussion). Figure 4.15b shows a map of the earthwork made from a combination of ground survey, global positioning system (GPS), and light detection and ranging (LiDAR) data. The map is aligned to true north

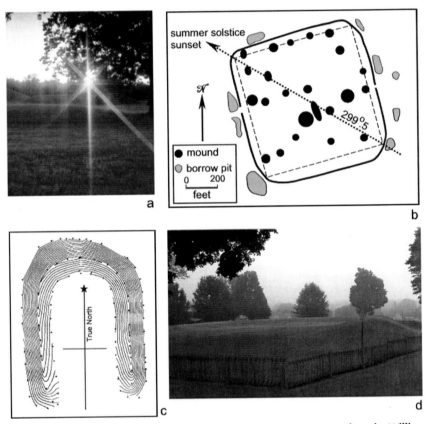

Figure 4.15. a. Summer solstice sunset at Mound City, June 20, 2000. Photo by William Romain. b. Map of Mound City showing summer solstice alignment. Map by William Romain. c. Contour map of the Portsmouth Group B earthwork. Map by William Romain. d. Photo of the Portsmouth Group B earthwork. Photo by William Romain. Figures not to scale.

based on a series of solar observations. As figure 4.15b shows, the diagonal axis of the earthwork extends along an azimuth of about 299°.5. Since the earthwork is not perfectly symmetrical and because its corners are rounded, it is difficult to know exactly what points to use to draw a diagonal sightline across the site. The solution was to draw a square inside the enclosure. This provides two opposite-situated coordinate point locations for the sightline that are not arbitrary, but rather based in their geometric relationship to each other.

From analysis of the relevant USGS topographic map, it is found that the apparent horizon elevation along this sightline is 2°.01. This value is corrected for refraction and lower limb tangency for a final horizon value of 1°.96. Latitude for the site is 39°.38. Using these values it is found by formulae that, at Mound City, in A.D. 250 ± 100, the solstice sunset occurred at an azimuth of 299°.4.

By subtracting the azimuth of the diagonal sightline from the calculated sunset azimuth, it is found that the difference is 0°.1. Given the enclosure's rounded corners, however, there is a window of about ± 1°.0 degree in the proposed sightline. When this is taken into account, the final assessment is that the Mound City enclosure is aligned to the A.D. 250 summer solstice sunset to within 0°.1 ± 1°.0. Figure 4.15a shows a photograph of the actual solstice alignment event.

Other major earthworks oriented to the solstices include Baum, Hopeton, Portsmouth Group A, Hopewell, Marietta, Anderson, Cedar Banks, Dunlap, and Seip (Romain 2004a, 2005a).

Portsmouth Group B, U-shaped Mound
Figure 4.15d shows the Portsmouth Group B, U-shaped mound. The mound is roughly 180 feet (54.9 m) in length and 140 feet (42.7 m) wide. Figure 4.15c shows the results of a total station survey of the mound. Coordinate-point data were oriented to true north by a series of solar observations (Romain 2004a). As figure 4.15c shows, the earthwork is oriented to the cardinal directions.

Another example of an earthwork oriented to the cardinal directions or conceptually related equinoxes is the Seal Township Works (also known as the Barnes Works).

Internal Mound Features   Certain features within a number of Hopewell mounds also appear oriented to the cardinal directions. Mentioned earlier was the North Benton mound and the 30-foot (9.1 m) raptor effigy found at its base. Notably, the raptor is oriented to the cardinal directions. As shown by figure 4.11a, the head of the bird points east, toward the rising sun; the tail points west. One wing tip points north; the other points south. Reinforcing this directional symbolism is the cardinal orientation of the centrally located square "fireplace." So too, the skeletal remains situated on the raptor's wings extend along an east-west axis, their heads to the west in the direction of the setting sun.

Artifact Designs   In addition to earthwork and mound features, many smaller Hopewell objects and designs incorporate the notion of a quadripartite division of space. An example is provided by Hopewell copper plates.[12]

Hopewell copper plates are flat. Most are made from cold-hammered copper, although a rare few are made from meteoric iron or mica. The plates vary in size. Most are 8–10 inches (20.3–25.4 cm) in length and 4–6 inches (10.2–15.2 cm) in width. They vary in thickness from 1/16 to 1/8 inch (0.2– 0.3 cm). Several plates incorporate either embossed or cutout designs. Most, however, are plain. Seeman (1979:316) notes that more than 180 plates have been recovered from fifteen sites located in the Scioto River Valley area. Additional plates are known from Hopewell sites outside of Ohio.

One of the interesting things about the plain copper plates is that, although they vary in size, they are made to similar proportions and generally to the same shape. I know of no technical name for the geometric shape of the plates. Perhaps they can be described as "lobed trapezoids."

Earlier in this chapter I suggested that in Hopewell cosmology, square and rectangle designs were associated with the cardinal directions, four quarters, and a quadripartite division of space. I suspect that in their shape, proportion, and sidedness, the lobed trapezoid plates carry similar meanings. In support of this interpretation, we begin with a discussion of the most explicit of the plates.

Mound City Raptor Plate

Figure 4.16a shows an embossed copper plate found in mound 7 at Mound City. The plate is about 5 1/2 inches (14 cm) in height and 10 inches (25.4 cm) in width. As can be seen, a raptor is located in each of the plate's four corners.

One way of looking at this plate is to consider it as a cosmogram, or a two-dimensional map of the Hopewell cosmos. Figure 4.16b shows the result, however, if the posited cosmogram is rendered in three dimensions. In this three-dimensional conception, north is not "up" (as might be interpreted from looking at the copper plate as presented in figure 4.16a); rather, north and the other directions extend horizontally, as related to the viewer in the center of the drawing. Looking now to the four raptors, we find that in both the copper plate and the three-dimensional rendering, the positions of the raptors establish the world quarters.

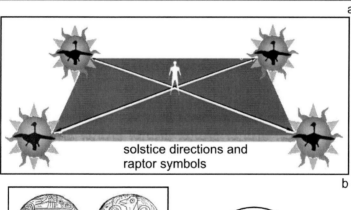

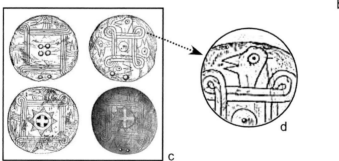

Figure 4.16.   a. Mound City raptor plate with solstice directions template superimposed by the present author. Raptor plate from Mills 1922:fig. 62; used with permission of the Ohio Historical Society. Scan provided by Arthur W. McGraw, annotation added by William Romain. b. Schematic representation of Hopewell cosmos based on Mound City raptor plate. Drawing by William Romain. c. Engraved shell gorgets from Mississippian sites. From Holmes 1883:Pls. 61 and 58. d. Enlarged detail from fig. 4.16c. From Holmes 1883:Pls. 61 and 58.

Earlier in this chapter it was proposed that the Hopewell may have used the owl as a symbol for the upperworld, and in the North Benton mound, we found a large-scale raptor effigy oriented to the cardinal directions. The idea that the raptors in the Mound City plate might embody directional and upperworld associations is therefore consistent with a pattern that is beginning to emerge. Based on the Mound City plate, we can tentatively add the world quarters to the list of phenomena associated with the raptor symbol.

Another piece of information accessible to us in the Mound City, mound 7 plate lies in the possibility that the solstice directions are intentionally incorporated in its symbolism. As noted above, figure 4.14b shows the solstice directions for the latitude of Mound City. When this directional template is superimposed over the Mound City plate, we find that the solstice angles correspond to the angular separation between the beaks of the four birds (Romain 1991b:119). Figure 4.16a shows this correspondence.[13]

Figure 4.16b shows the result if we again rotate the surface of the plate so that it extends horizontally. In this perspective, the viewer is centered in the middle of the flat earth plane, with the sun's solstice positions as indicated on the distant horizon. In figure 4.16b, the spatial relationship between the raptors and the sun is made explicit. The raptors and solstice directions are conceptually and spatially merged.

As discussed earlier, both the cardinal and solstice directions can be used to establish the world quarters. In the Mound City raptor plate, it appears that the solstice directions were used. While more data are needed to firmly establish a direct historic link, the conclusion that raptors symbolize the four quarters finds support from later periods. Figure 4.16c, for example, shows four shell gorgets recovered from several Mississippian sites. In these designs we find the familiar bird motif associated with the cardinal directions, or world quarters. Figure 4.16d shows a detail of one of the cardinal direction birds.

Hopewell Raptor Talon Plate

The Mound City, mound 7 raptor plate is not the only plate that incorporates solstice and raptor symbolism in its quadripartite representation of space. The same idea is expressed in a plate recovered from the Hopewell site. Figure 4.17a shows the Hopewell site plate. Of interest is that instead of bird head images, we find raptor talon designs in each corner (also see Turff and Carr 2005:675). Identification of the scroll designs in each corner as raptor talons is demonstrated by the following exercise. Figure 4.17b shows a bald eagle talon (replica).[14] Figure 4.17c shows the talon superimposed over the scroll designs in the copper plate. As can be seen, the shape and curvature of the eagle talon and copper design elements match. If the raptor talons

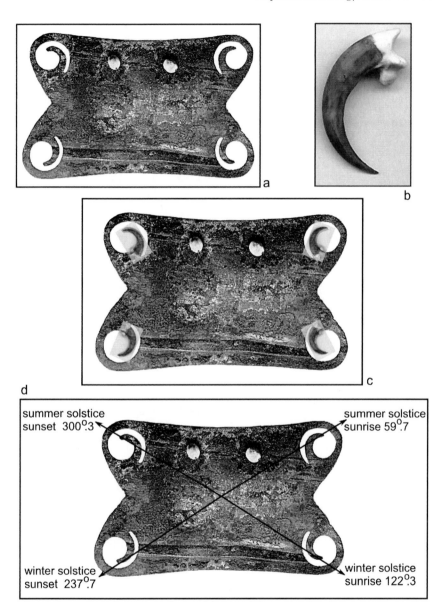

Figure 4.17.   a. Copper plate from the Hopewell site. From Shetrone 1930:fig. 59. b. Bald eagle talon replica. Photo by William Romain. c. Eagle talon superimposed over scroll designs. Not to scale. Plate photo from Shetrone 1930:fig. 59 with talon photo by William Romain superimposed. d. Copper plate with solstice direction template super-imposed. Plate photo from Shetrone 1930:fig. 59 with annotation by William Romain.

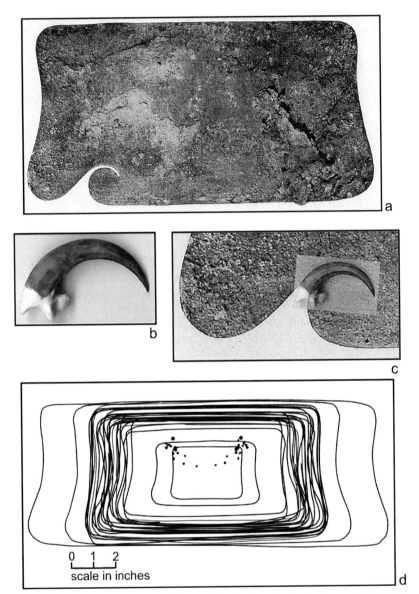

Figure 4.18.   a. Copper plate with scroll design from Seip site. From Mills 1909:
fig. 10; used with permission of the Ohio Historical Society. b. Raptor talon replica.
Photo by William Romain. c. Raptor talon superimposed over enlarged detail of design shown in fig. 4.18a. Not to scale. From Mills 1909:fig. 10. d. Outline sketches of
twenty-nine copper plates from three sites. Drawing by William Romain.

were used as symbols for individual raptors, then, by implication, a raptor is associated with each of the plate's four corners and the world's quarters.

Further, like the Mound City plate, the Hopewell site raptor talon plate incorporates the solstice directions. This correspondence is revealed when the solstice direction template is superimposed over the copper plate. As figure 4.17d shows, the solstice angles correspond to the angular separation between the raptor talons.

In the Hopewell site raptor plate, we have an example of synecdoche, where the talon design is used as symbol for the larger creature. This design technique is found in increasingly simpler forms in the plates discussed next.

Seip Raptor Talon Plate
Figure 4.18a shows a copper plate from the Seip site. In this plate we find an increasingly simpler design, but still, it is a design that incorporates raptor and directional symbolism. Figure 4.18b again shows the eagle talon. Figure 4.18c shows the eagle talon superimposed over the scroll design in the copper plate. The shapes match, implying that the scroll design cut into the plate was intended as a raptor symbol. Since the talon symbol occurs in one corner of the plate, the implication is that the same symbol could be applied to the other lobed corners. In this case, then, as occurs in the Mound City and Hopewell site plates, raptor symbolism is again associated with the world quarters.

Turner Raptor Scrolls
The copper plates discussed to this point have in common some fairly explicit symbolism. These plates, however, are the exception. The majority of Hopewell plates are of a slightly different shape than the plates shown thus far. Moreover, no other plates have embossed raptor images or cutout talon symbols in their corners. Figure 4.18d shows the outlines of twenty-nine plain copper plates. As I will demonstrate, however, these plates also incorporate raptor and directional symbolism. In order to successfully "read" the raptor and directional symbolism in the plain plates, however, we need to digress and first consider a group of four copper scrolls found at the Turner site.

Figure 4.19a shows the four copper scroll designs found at the Turner site. Elsewhere (Romain 2000:fig. 7.2), I proposed that these designs might represent a floral pattern. In retrospect, I think there is a better explanation. Figure 4.19b shows the now-familiar raptor talon. Figures 4.19c and 4.19d show two ways the shape of the raptor talon corresponds to the shape of the copper scrolls.

Figure 4.19e shows one of the scroll designs (not to scale) superimposed over the copper falcon plate from Mound City (discussed earlier and shown

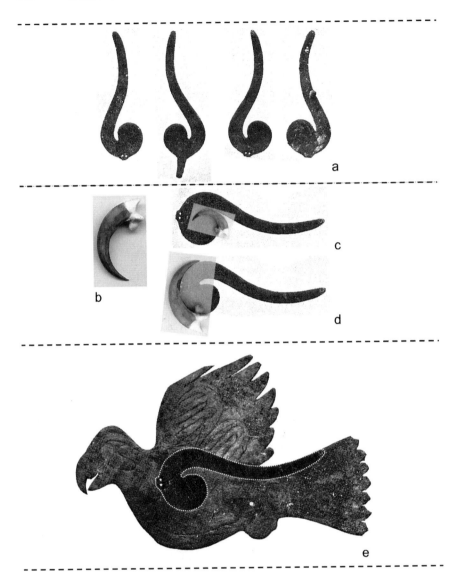

Figure 4.19.   a. Copper scroll designs from the Turner site. From Willoughby and Hooton 1922:Pl. 11, courtesy of the Peabody Museum, Harvard University. b. Replica raptor talon (bald eagle). Photo by William Romain. c and d. Raptor talon superimposed over copper scroll designs. Photo of talon by Romain; scrolls from Willoughby and Hooton 1922:Pl. 11, courtesy of the Peabody Museum, Harvard University. e. Turner scroll design superimposed over Mound City falcon effigy. Falcon image from Mills 1922:Fig. 60, used by permission of Ohio Historical Society, scan provided by Arthur W. McGraw. Scroll from Willoughby and Hooton 1922:Pl. 11, courtesy of the Peabody Museum, Harvard University. Figures not to scale.

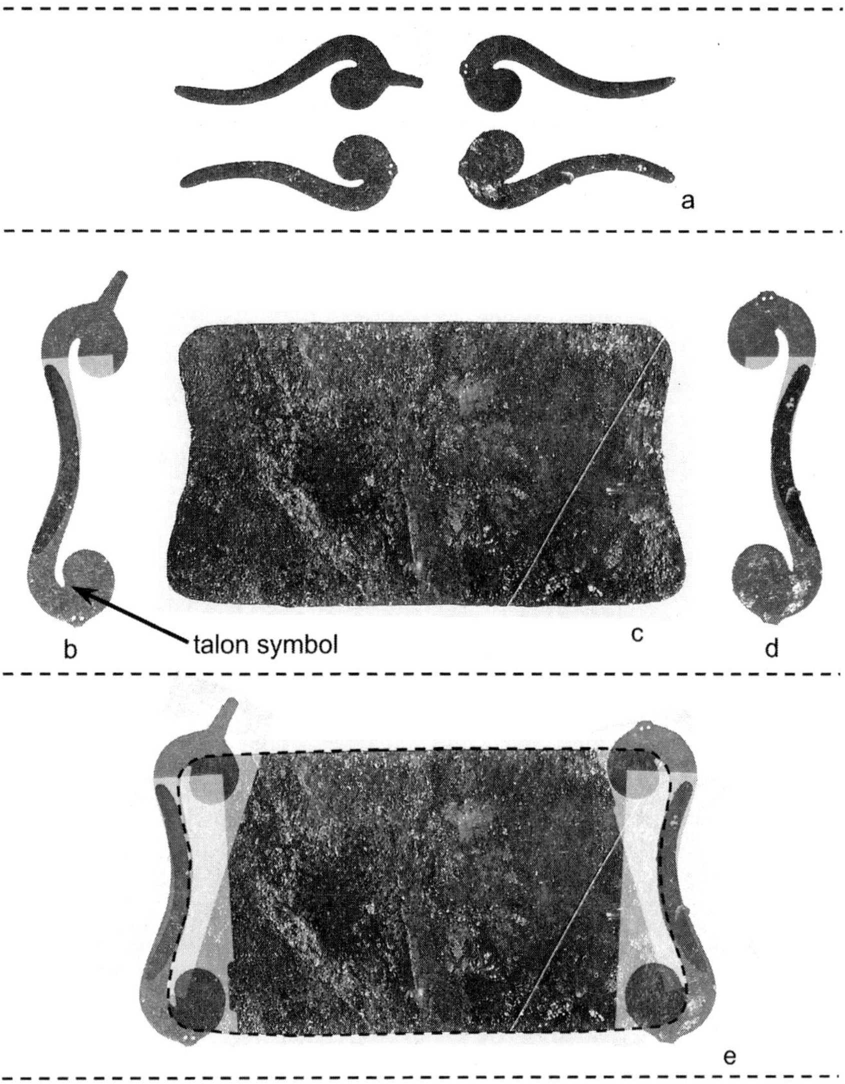

Figure 4.20. a. Copper scroll designs from the Turner site. From Willoughby and Hooton 1922:Pl. 11, courtesy of the Peabody Museum, Harvard University. b. Turner scroll designs superimposed on each other. From Willoughby and Hooton 1922:Pl. 11, courtesy of the Peabody Museum, Harvard University. c. Plain copper plate from the Hopewell site. From Moorehead 1922:Pl. 55(1). d. Other Turner scroll designs superimposed on each other. From Willoughby and Hooton 1922:Pl. 11, courtesy of the Peabody Museum, Harvard University. e. Copper scroll designs superimposed over copper plate shown in figure 4.20c. Scrolls from Willoughby and Hooton 1922:Pl. 11; copper plate from Moorehead 1922:Pl. 55(1). Figures not to scale.

in figure 4.5b). As can be seen, the Turner scroll matches the shape of the bird's back. The bulbous end of the scroll design generally corresponds to the copper bird's hood, and the talon visible in the negative space of the scroll design reinforces the raptor symbolism of both pieces.

From these correspondences we can infer as a working hypothesis that the Turner scroll designs are raptor symbols. Also of possible significance is that four copper scrolls were found. This number corresponds to the number of world quarters, as well as the number of talons found on real raptor feet.

Hopewell Plain Copper Plate
Presuming that the Turner scroll designs are raptor symbols, we can use this information to help interpret the plain copper plates. Figure 4.20a again shows the Turner scroll designs. Figure 4.20c shows a plain copper plate from the Hopewell site (Moorehead 1922:Pl. 55). Shown alongside the plate in figures 4.20b and 4.20d are the four Turner scrolls, except in this instance I have superimposed the scroll designs onto each other. What results are two double scroll designs.

If the double scrolls are superimposed over the plain copper plate (again, not to scale), the result is that the inside edges of the double scroll designs match the peculiar curved sides of the Hopewell plate. These correspondences are shown in figure 4.20e. In this interpretation, then, and as figure 4.20e shows, a raptor talon is implied for each of the plate's four corners. Thus we find in the plain Hopewell site plate that each rounded lobe represents a raptor—and one of the world's quarters.

Lastly, it should be noted that if the double scroll designs are rotated ever so slightly, the the lower lobes of the plate are slightly further apart than the upper lobes. It may be that the wider girth of the lower lobes represent larger female falcons, while the more narrowly spaced upper lobes represent male falcons—the result being two sets of male and female raptors represented.

In the next set of illustrations, in figures 4.21a–4.21c, the same design protocol appears to have been used to establish the shape of several additional plain copper plates from Harness, Seip, and the Hopewell sites. Again, the double scroll designs closely match the plates' sides. In these cases, however, close inspection reveals that the correspondences are not quite perfect. What this tells us is that the copper plates were not stamped-out copies based on a single template; rather, each was handcrafted to a slightly different size and proportion, while at the same time maintaining the integrity of the key raptor and directional symbolism.

In looking at the corpus of Hopewell plates, it appears that more than one design protocol was used. Although not illustrated here, a second set of copper

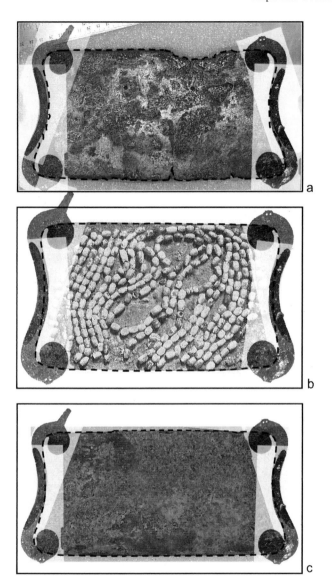

Figure 4.21.   a. Turner copper scroll designs from fig. 4.20 superimposed over copper plate from Harness mound. Scrolls from Willoughby and Hooton 1922:Pl. 11, courtesy of the Peabody Museum, Harvard University; photo of plate by William Romain, used by permission of Ohio Historical Society. b. Copper plate from Seip with Turner scrolls superimposed. Plate from Mills 1909:fig. 12; scroll designs from Willoughby and Hooton 1922:Pl. 11, courtesy of the Peabody Museum, Harvard University. c. Copper plate from Hopewell site with Turner scrolls superimposed. Scroll designs from Willoughby and Hooton 1922:Pl. 11, courtesy of the Peabody Museum, Harvard University; photo of plate by William Romain by permission of Ohio Historical Society. Figures not to scale.

scrolls was found at the Hopewell site (Shetrone 1926:186). Following the same procedure as was done for the Turner scrolls, we can overlap those scrolls and place the resulting designs over various plates; again we find that the composite designs closely match the shapes of several additional plain plates.

Other Designs in Copper

Still, there are other lobed trapezoidal plates that the copper scrolls do *not* perfectly match up with. And it is the case that due to their differing proportions, not all copper plates describe the solstice directions. In these cases, I propose that precise template matches were simply not required. Once it was generally understood how raptor talons were analogically incorporated into any quadrangular plate by virtue of its lobes, the precise curvature of the plate's sides, as well as the overall proportions of a plate, were of less importance. Precise template matches would simply not have been necessary to communicate the idea of raptor and directional symbolism. For people already in the know, almost any plate having concave sides—thereby creating four talon-lobes roughly pointing to the solstice directions or world quarters—would successfully communicate the intended concepts.

Indeed, as with all things Hopewell, there is no reason to assume, a priori, that one procedure or protocol should account for every design. What different protocols succeed in doing is make the point that the concepts of interest could be communicated in multiple ways. Figures 4.22a–4.23c provide further cases in point.

In these designs, raptor symbolism and the cardinal and solstice directions are combined, resulting in one-of-a-kind pieces. In looking at these figures, as was the case for the lobed copper plates, we need to keep in mind that the designs are two-dimensional cosmograms showing a three-dimensional Hopewell universe. Accordingly, it bears repeating that the directions shown in the figures are not intended to reflect Western notions of north at the top of the design, south at the bottom, and so on. Rather, when the Hopewell designs are rotated, the result is that the directional elements extend horizontally.

Center

The term *center* has several meanings. For example, one of the fascinating things about human consciousness is that each of us feel as though we are at the center of things. Seemingly, each of us is at the center of sensory experience, as well as at the center of time, balanced between anticipation of future events and memories of the past. The very essence of being an individual

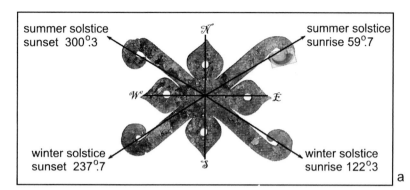

summer solstice sunset 300°.3
summer solstice sunrise 59°.7
winter solstice sunset 237°.7
winter solstice sunrise 122°.3

a

summer solstice sunset 300°.3
summer solstice sunrise 59°.7
winter solstice sunset 237°.7
winter solstice sunrise 122°.3

b

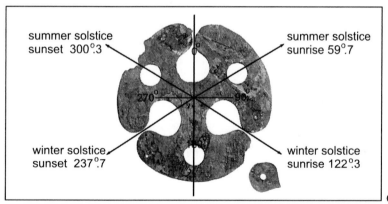

summer solstice sunset 300°.3
summer solstice sunrise 59°.7
winter solstice sunset 237°.7
winter solstice sunrise 122°.3

c

Figure 4.22. a. Hopewell site copper piece with solstice directions and raptor talon superimposed. Copper piece from Moorehead 1922:Pl. 65; raptor talon photo and annotation by William Romain. b. Turner site copper piece with solstice directions and raptor talon superimposed. Copper piece from Willoughby and Hooton 1922:Pl. 10, courtesy of the Peabody Museum, Harvard University; raptor talon photo and annotation by William Romain. c. Hopewell site copper piece with solstice directions superimposed. From Moorehead 1922:Pl. 65.

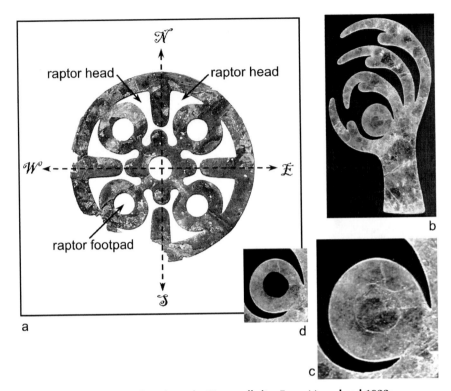

Figure 4.23. a. Copper piece from the Hopewell site. From Moorehead 1922: Pl. 65. b. Mica raptor foot from the Hopewell site. Ohio Historical Society image #A283/000292.001, used with permission. c. Enlarged detail of fig. 4.23b raptor foot showing footpad. Detail from Ohio Historical Society image #A283/000292.001, used with permission. d. Footpad from fig. 4.23c with inner circle darkened and equalized in scale to copper piece to show the resemblance. Detail from Ohio Historical Society image #A283/000292.001, used with permission. Figures not to scale.

requires that we apprehend the world from this first-person perspective. Historian Arnold Toynbee provides an explanation of why this might be:

> [S]elf-centredness is evidently the essence of Terrestrial Life. A living creature might, indeed, be defined as a minor and subordinate piece of the Universe which, by tour de force, has partially disengaged itself from the rest and set itself up as an autonomous power that strives, up to the limits of its capacity, to make the rest of the Universe minister to its selfish purposes. . . . For every living creature, this self-centredness is one of the necessities of life, because it is indispensable for the creature's existence. A complete renunciation of self-centredness would bring with it, for any living creature, a complete extinction of that particular local and temporary vehicle of Life. (1979:2)

Alternatively, we can consider center from the perspective of spherical geometry. In a three-dimensional world, center can be referenced to a vertical axis. If we are at the center of the earth, we are equidistant from the surface whether we proceed up or down. Center can also be referenced to a horizontal axis. For a person standing on the surface of the earth, center is where the directions of left-right and front-back intersect. Accordingly, center mediates opposite directions.

From a cosmological perspective, center is the place where vectors intersect and through which the *axis mundi* passes. Center is equidistant in all directions and in all planes.

Center is also a point of origin. It is the place from which the directions and *axis mundi* originate. It is that understanding that gives rise to the belief that cities, temples, and palaces are at the center of the world or of the cosmos (Eliade 1954:12).

For the Lakota, the intersection of the Four Directions establishes the center, which is the dwelling place for *Wakan-Tanka*, the Great Spirit (Brown 1975 [1953]:24). Among certain shamanic cultures, such as the Beaver Indians of British Columbia, since center is at the intersection of the four world directions and at the intersection between the upper and lower worlds, center is also a place of entrance into the Otherworld (Ridington and Ridington 1975 [1970]:199).

Consideration of Hopewell earthwork geometry suggests that the Hopewell intentionally utilized the concept of center (Romain 2004a:134–135). In this section, we look at several Hopewell expressions of that idea.

Earthworks

A dramatic example of how the Hopewell employed the concept of center is found at the Fort Ancient earthwork. Located in southwestern Ohio, Fort Ancient is a hilltop enclosure (Connolly and Lepper 2004). Figure 4.24a shows a map of Fort Ancient, made from a GPS survey. The map shows the crest of the perimeter embankment walls, as well as gateways through the walls. Also shown are four mounds in the North Fort area and several circle features located in the Middle Fort area.

Of interest is the feature designated on the map as "center stone ring." A photograph of this feature is shown in figure 4.24b. What makes this feature special is that the center of the stone ring marks the center of the nearly mile-long site to within 60 feet (18.3 m). The longitudinal axis of the site is established by a line that extends through the center of the North Fort Square and the center stone circle to the north and south perimeter walls.[15] As indicated on the map, the GPS-measured distance along this line from

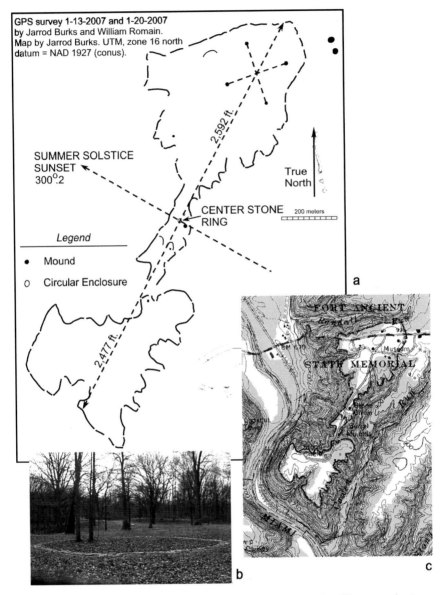

Figure 4.24. a. Map of Fort Ancient. Survey by Jarrod Burks and William Romain. Base map by Jarrod Burks from GPS survey. Astronomic and measurement data added by William Romain. b. Fort Ancient center stone ring. Photo by William Romain. c. Fort Ancient embankment walls per GPS survey superimposed over USGS 7.5 minute series map section. U.S. Geological Services.

the center of the center stone ring to the crest of the north perimeter wall is 2,592 feet (790.0 m). The GPS-measured distance going the other way along the line, from the center of the center stone ring to the crest of the south perimeter wall is 2,477 feet (754.9 m). Thus the center of the center stone ring defines the center of the site to within 1 percent. Also shown by figure 4.24a, the minor axis of the site is oriented to the summer solstice to within about 1 degree (Romain 2004c).

In summary, as shown by figure 4.24c, the earthwork walls follow the contour of the promontory that the earthwork is situated on. The longitudinal axis of the earthwork therefore extends parallel to the lay of the land and is in alignment with the topography of the earth at that location. The solstice azimuth is derived from the sun. Therefore, the stone circle that marks the intersection of the solstice azimuth and longitudinal site axis not only locates the center of the site, but also, in symbolic terms, marks a place of intersection between earth and sky. At Fort Ancient, center is situated at a cosmological nexus of earth and sky.

Other examples of how the Hopewell expressed the notion of center are found in the occurrence of circle-shaped earthworks with mounds in their centers. Earthworks configured in this manner are found at Marietta, Seip, Circleville, Portsmouth, and Newark. Several are shown in figures 4.25a–4.25c. Notably at Seip, Marietta, and Circleville, the mounds at the centers of the circle-shaped enclosures were found to contain human burials. Reminiscent of the way center provides an entrance into the Otherworld for the Beaver Indians mentioned earlier, it may be that the centrally located burial mounds inside these Hopewell circle earthworks functioned in a similar way. Moreover, this idea would be consistent with the earlier discussed *axis mundi* concept, wherein centrally situated crematory fires perhaps served as portals or entranceways for spirits of the deceased to transition to the Otherworld.

Artifacts

Several Hopewell artifacts also demonstrate reference to the concept of center. Figure 4.25d shows a copper design from the Hopewell site. The piece is distinguished by its quadripartite division of space. It also has a very specific design element that indicates its center. Figure 4.25e shows another design—this one a copper earspool, also from the Hopewell site. Like the copper quadrant piece, the earspool design divides space into quarters and has a clearly defined center. It may be that both designs are so similar because they were meant as cosmograms along the design principles already discussed, which include an understanding of center as a meeting point for the cosmic world quarters in the horizontal plane and upper and lower worlds along the vertical.

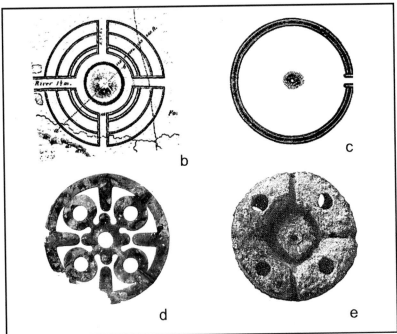

Figure 4.25. a. Marietta Conus Mound. From Squier and Davis 1848:Pl. 45. b. Portsmouth Group C Circle. From Squier and Davis 1848:Pl. 28. c. Circleville Circle. From Squier and Davis 1848:fig. 10. d. Copper piece from the Hopewell site. From Moorehead 1922:Pl. 65. e. Copper earspool from the Hopewell site. From Moorehead 1922:Pl. 56. Figures not to scale.

Cyclic Time

As far as we know, only humans have the ability to recognize and mentally manipulate precise increments of time and space. Newberg, d'Aquili, and Rause (2001:49) attribute this ability to the mind-brain's quantitative operator. As d'Aquili and Newberg explain, it is the quantitative operator that "permits the abstraction of quantity from the perception of various elements" (1999:55). According to d'Aquili and Newberg (55), the quantitative operator is associated with the inferior parietal lobe.

Our ability to quantify has allowed us to formulate concepts of infinity and eternity. Arguably, it is the quantitative operator that allows us to apprehend temporal periodicities or cycles.[16] Among the cycles of which we have direct awareness are breathing and heart rhythms, wake and sleep cycles, digestive activity, and menstrual cycles.[17] On a different scale, we recognize temporal periodicities in the alternations between night and day, the monthly phases of the moon, and the seasonal cycles of winter and summer or wet and dry.

Observations of these and other phenomena give rise to the idea that the cosmos and living things within it proceed in a cyclic manner involving creation, exhaustion, destruction, and renewal. As explained by Eliade:

> The death of the individual and the death of humanity are alike necessary for their regeneration. Any form whatever, by the mere fact that it exists as such and endures, necessarily loses vigor and becomes worn; to recover vigor, it must be reabsorbed into the formless if only for an instant; it must be restored to the primordial unity from which it issued. (1954:88)

From this it follows that "[t]his periodic regeneration presupposes that every re-creation is a repetition of the first act of genesis or becoming" (Aveni 2002:57).

Cosmologies that emphasize this perspective are said to incorporate a cyclic view of time. This is usually contrasted with certain Western notions of time that are more linear. A linear notion of time posits that the universe was created at a specific point, or singularity, and will end at a unique time in the future.

The shamanic universe is cyclic in that it is characterized by recurring celestial events and life cycles. This is not to say that time is experienced any differently by people in shamanic cultures as compared to Western cultures; rather, the difference is in the interpretation of the underlying experience. With reference to the Osage, for example, Garrick Bailey tells us:

They further noticed that this same pattern of birth, maturity, old age, and death was repeated over and over. They observed it daily in the succession from sunrise to midday, sunset, and night. The cosmos was in constant motion and consisted of unending, varied cycles of birth, maturity, old age, death, and rebirth. (1995:30)

Like other shamanic cultures, Hopewell groups recognized the cyclic nature of the cosmos (Romain 2000:199–200, 2004a:135–36). In the case of Hopewell structures, recognition of the cyclic nature of the cosmos is indicated in two different ways: (1) by internal earthwork features and (2) by earthwork orientation.

Earthwork Features

Archaeologist N'omi Greber (1996:164–65) has suggested that evidence for Ohio Hopewell recognition of a "long term calendric cycle" is found in mound and earthwork stratigraphy. Greber points out that several large burial mounds—such as the Harness and Seip-Pricer mounds—were constructed by covering over smaller, conjoined primary burial mounds with a unifying layer of earth. In such cases, more than one episode of construction is indicated. Citing the work of Lepper (1996), Riordan (1996), and Shane (1971), Greber also points out that "some enclosure walls show evidence of cyclic rebuilding. Two stages have been identified at Newark and possibly also at Pollock and High Bank" (165).

On a smaller scale, Greber (1996:165) proposes that superimposed wooden structures at Mound City, superimposed floors within the Capitolium mound at Marietta and superimposed basins, or "altars," at Turner also suggest a cyclic aspect to mound activities.

Looking to Illinois Hopewell, Buikstra et al. find archaeological evidence for "proscribed sequences of ceremonial events that imply decision-making and control of a complex, multi-community ritual calendar" (1998:83). Among the evidence they provide are instances of burned areas in mortuary contexts. As Buikstra and her colleagues point out, "As the ritual renewal of fire is widely associated with the sun and rebirth among eastern North American Indians, it is not unreasonable to associate the presence of fired areas with similar beliefs" (82).

Of course, the question that begs to be answered is: To what events were these cyclic mound activities or ritual calendars tied to? A possible answer is offered below.

Earthwork Orientation

Celestial events such as solstices, heliacal risings, and lunar standstills are recurring phenomena that, for indigenous peoples, provide visual proof that cosmic time is punctuated by cyclic events. Detailed archaeoastronomical analyses of the Hopewell geometric earthworks have been presented elsewhere (Romain 2005a, 2004a; Hively and Horn 1984, 1982). What these analyses reveal is that every major geometric enclosure that can be accurately assessed is aligned with a significant celestial event. Most are aligned with the winter or summer solstices, although alignments with the moon and the cardinal directions or equinoxes also occur. Solstitial alignments as a group are generally accurate to within plus or minus 1°, although we need to keep in mind that if earthworks were aligned to celestial events for symbolic reasons, then absolute precision in the Western sense may not have been a requirement. In any event, these alignments tell us that for the Hopewell, cyclic events involving celestial entities were of sufficient importance that large-scale earthworks were designed and built with those events taken into account.

The Sacra Via alignment provides an example of such an alignment still visible today. Located in Marietta, Ohio, the Sacra Via originally consisted of a graded or sloped avenue cut into the ground. The avenue was flanked on both sides by earthen walls. The Sacra Via feature led from the Marietta Large Square earthwork, down to the Muskingum River—a distance of about 1,400 feet (426.7 m). Today, the graded way is still visible and preserved in a city park.

The sun has changed very little in its rising and setting positions since Hopewell times (see Romain [2004a:80] for further details). As a consequence, what we see today in terms of sunrise and sunset is, for all practical purposes, the same as what the Hopewell would have seen. As figures 4.26a and 4.26b show, the Sacra Via is directly aligned to the winter solstice sunset. (Viewed from the intersection of Sacra Via and Third Street, after correcting for refraction and lower limb tangency and using a date of A.D. 250, the alignment is accurate to within 0°.1 ± 0.5 [Romain 2000:135–41]).

It is difficult to know what Hopewell people thought about the winter solstice. What we can comment upon, however, are the physical characteristics of that event likely perceived by the Hopewell. For example, at the moment of the winter solstice sunset, the sun is at its most southern position in the sky. It is also at its weakest strength. From the instant of the winter solstice sunset onward, however, the sun progressively moves northward, gains in its vertical height and intensity, and provides for longer days. In a metaphorical sense, the winter solstice sunset anticipates the beginning of the sun's next cycle of regeneration or renewal, as winter turns to spring. Based on this, and on archaeological evidence consisting of superimposed layers containing burned floral remains found within the

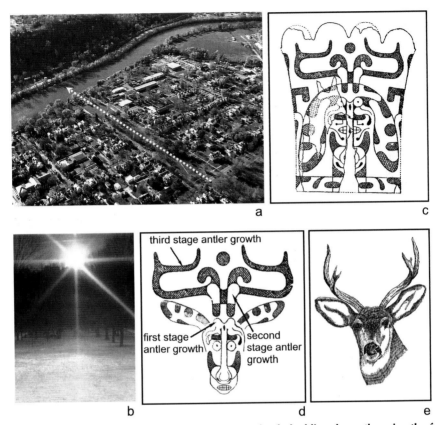

Figure 4.26. a. Aerial view of the Marietta Sacra Via; dashed line shows the azimuth of the winter solstice sunset. Photo by William Romain. b. Winter solstice sunset in alignment with the Sacra Via, December 21, 1996. Photo by William Romain. c. Engraved design on human bone from the Hopewell site. From Moorehead 1922:fig. 20. d. Deer design found in figure 4.26c. Drawing by William Romain. e. Drawing of male deer showing fully developed antlers. From U.S. Fish and Wildlife Service, Digital Library, www.fws.gov/DLS/, accessed February 22, 2008.

associated Capitolium mound, it may be that the alignment of the Sacra Via—and indeed, the entire Marietta complex—was tied to the cyclic renewal of plant and animal resources. Arguably, this was no small matter. For hunters and gatherers and incipient horticulturalists like the Hopewell, it was crucial that they adapt their behaviors to the seasonal cycles of the plants and animals they needed for survival. In such societies, periodic ceremonies such as solstice rituals not only serve as markers of time, they also serve to connect the world of humans to the seasonal rhythms of plants and animals.

Artifacts

The Hopewell Deer

Hopewell interest in the cyclic aspect of the cosmos is also demonstrated by certain artifact designs. One of the most intriguing is a piece of engraved human femur bone, found with burial 278 in mound 25 at the Hopewell site. Figure 4.26c shows the engraved design as represented by Willoughby (1916:Pl. 6b).

Various interpretations have been offered for the design. Most often it is proposed that the engraving represents some sort of composite creature. All agree that deer antlers are shown. From there, interpretations variously include deer or rabbit ears, a roseate spoonbill beak, a masked figure, and even caiman tooth holes (see, e.g., Willoughby 1916:495; Moorehead 1922; Greber and Ruhl 1989; Carr and Case 2005b:202).

My interpretation is that a white-tailed deer is found in the mix of body parts. Figure 4.26d shows the creature that emerges once the face elements are appropriately scaled and reassembled. In figure 4.26d, all the design elements—including the creature's eyes, ears, nose, mouth, and antlers—are found in the original engraving. To bring out the image, I rearranged and/or resized the various pieces, as was done earlier for the Turner turtle. The only lines I added were to the lower jaw and lower nose, where the original engraving had been damaged. Comparison of figure 4.26d with figure 4.26e shows the resemblance of the engraved deer to a real deer. If my interpretation is correct, then what we are looking at is a deer showing several stages of antler growth.

It was actually Willoughby (cited in Greber and Ruhl 2000:194–99) who first recognized that the engraving shows stages of antler growth. Specifically, Willoughby recognized two growth stages: the button stage and full-growth antlers. Elaborating on Willoughby's interpretation, I find that three stages of antler growth are indicated.

Antler growth is a cyclic phenomenon. White-tailed deer grow an entirely new set of antlers every year. During the winter, their old antlers drop off, and in the spring, a new set grow from bony structures known as pedicles, also called "button antlers." Pedicles look like bony stumps and are about 1 inch (2.5 cm) in length. In the Hopewell deer engraving shown in figure 4.26d, the animal's button antlers are represented by the two raised bumps that partially define the outline of the animal's skull. The posited second phase of growth is represented by the small set of antlers having somewhat bulbous ends. Lastly, a fully developed set of antlers, with its characteristic points, is shown.

Interpretation of this engraving as a deer is supported by the cervid head-dresses found at the Hopewell and Mound City sites, discussed in chapter 3.

As pointed out by Willoughby (quoted in Greber and Ruhl 2000:199) and illustrated in figures 3.1b and 3.1d, these headdresses show stages of antler growth that include both mature and button antlers. Clearly, the Hopewell were familiar with these growth stages. As to the deer engraving, I would propose that the significance of the piece is in its representation of an annual or cyclic phenomenon, expressed in this case not by reference to celestial events, but rather to phenomena associated with the world of animals.

Summary

In this chapter, evidence was presented that strengthens the hypothesis that the Hopewell thought of the cosmos as a holistic entity comprised of interrelated complementary opposites and/or mirror-image components expressive of cosmic dualism. Among the data considered were Hopewell geometric earthworks, with their linked circle and square elements, as well as smaller designs in copper, mica, and bone. What stands out is that the Hopewell frequently expressed the dualistic nature of the universe through linked male and female opposites. Multiple examples were provided suggesting Hopewell interest in male-female pairs. In chapter 6 we will find that male-female duality was further linked to concepts of renewal.

The hypothesis that the Hopewell understood their cosmos as vertically layered is accounted for by neuropsychological principles and supported by converging lines of evidence, including ethnographic data from the Eastern Woodlands, the positioning of buried deposits, and design symbolism.

More than twenty years ago, Penny (1985) recognized the vertically layered aspect of the Hopewell cosmos and described how the Hopewell upperworld was associated with avian imagery while the lowerworld was associated with serpent imagery. The data presented here strengthen that notion.

Associated with a vertically tiered cosmos is the idea of an *axis mundi*. In Hopewell, we find that concept expressed in the structure of their burial mounds (Romain 2000:185–86). In fact, if each Hopewell burial mound were to be considered as its own *axis mundi* for the movement of the deceased to the Otherworld, then, given the hundreds of Hopewell burial mounds scattered across southern Ohio, we might conclude that the *axis mundi* concept is rather strongly expressed. Support for the *axis mundi* concept was also found on a smaller scale in the form of Hopewell platform and smokestack pipes.

Considered at some length was the idea that the Hopewell viewed the cosmos as quadripartite in the horizontal dimension. The quadripartite division of space as expressed in Hopewell artifacts has long been recognized (e.g., Willoughby 1916; Penny 1985). The findings discussed here support that recognition, and the present work contributes evidence that for the Hopewell, raptors, solstice directions, cardinal directions, and the world quarters comprised an interrelated analogical symbolic system.

Notably, it is the repeated occurrence of raptor imagery in association with the solstice and cardinal directions that lends credibility to the interpretations offered. Importantly, this association is consistent with and anticipates later ethnographic association of the Four Quarters and Four Winds with thunderbird beings. In other words, what we may be looking at in the raptor images and symbols found in Hopewell are some of the earliest Eastern Woodlands symbols of upperworld thunderbird beings.

In connection with the shamanic worldview notion of center, it was proposed that a significant number of Hopewell earthworks incorporate physical expression of that idea. Mounds placed in the center of circle earthworks are evidence for centricity. Physical demarcation of the center of Fort Ancient by a stone circle and association of that point with a solstice alignment further indicates that the concept of center had cosmological significance.

Lastly, evidence that Hopewell cosmology incorporated a cyclic view of the cosmos is strong. Several lines of evidence—including earthwork orientation, internal mound features, and artifact symbolism—support that hypothesis. Of course, the idea that the Hopewell might think of the cosmos as moving in a cyclic fashion is not surprising, given that they were crucially dependent on the annual renewal of plant and animal resources.

CHAPTER FIVE

Hopewell Cosmology: Part II

In the preceding chapter, it was shown how Hopewell earthworks and small objects incorporate shamanic beliefs about the structure of the cosmos. The present chapter continues that assessment, with reference, however, to the more qualitative aspects of the shamanic worldview model.

Hidden Dimensions

At the most fundamental level, human beings are both predators and prey. In this world of eat or be eaten, stealth plays an important role. As predators, humans often use stealth to approach their prey. At the same time, humans and other animals use stealth to avoid becoming prey.

Stealth involves deception. For the predator, the objective is to cause the prey to believe that danger is not present. For the prey, one strategy is to cause the predator to believe the prey does not exist. In both cases, the deception is often effected by blending in with the surrounding environment. For all practical purposes, the ability to blend in with the environment—whether by color, patterns or structure—is equivalent to becoming invisible (Guthrie 1993).

Invisibility and the knowledge that there are unseen entities that can act upon us is part of our cognitive evolutionary reality. To survive in this kind of world, the mind-brain's causal operator compels us to seek causes for what we see or otherwise sense (Newberg, d'Aquili, and Rause 2001:50; d'Aquili and Newberg 1999:52). Where there is no visible explanation for what we see, we conclude that what we have witnessed is the result of an invisible cause (Barrett 1997). Since there are a multitude of invisible causes, it seems logical to conclude that there is, in effect, a hidden world. We can call this invisible world the spirit world, Otherworld, or realm of quantum entanglements. Whatever the case, we proceed in the assumption that these unseen dimensions truly exist.

In the shamanic universe, the ordinary world is intertwined with the invisible world. Entities that exist in this hidden reality include spirits, souls, ghosts, demons, and gods. The shaman is able to see and interact with this invisible world and its beings through altered states of consciousness.

In the case of the Hopewell, the question becomes: How might we identify intangible beliefs in invisible entities and hidden dimensions presumably held by people who died two thousand years ago? What sort of archaeological evidence might inform us in this regard?

Ghost and Spirit Barriers

One possibility lies in the existence of ghost and spirit barriers. In a search of the electronic Human Relations Area Files (eHRAF) Probability Sample database, I found that of the sixty represented traditional cultures, a belief in ghosts was mentioned in the reports for forty-eight. Of the remaining twelve cultures, a belief in spirits was mentioned for all but one culture.

Native American concepts of the soul are often complex. In most Native American religions, a person is believed to have more than one soul (Hultzkrantz 1953). Many believe that a person has several souls. In its simplest version, one soul leaves the body at death and continues to the Otherworld, or Realm of the Dead; the second soul lingers with the body as a grave ghost, usually until the bones totally disintegrate (25). There are many variations on this theme. The important point is that either soul—that is, the free soul, if it is lost, lonely, under the control of a sorcerer, or simply not willing to cross over; or the second soul as a grave ghost—is capable of causing all sorts of mischief and harm to the living. Some ghost souls are carnivorous; others cause illness. Some are able to enter the body of living persons. Especially feared are the ghosts of powerful shamans. Because of the harm ghosts can cause, great efforts were made by many Native American peoples to ensure that the deceased person's soul(s) or ghost did the right thing—either moving on to the Otherworld or staying in its grave.

According to Native American accounts, there are many ways a ghost can be kept in its grave: removal of the corpse's head, face-down burial, spells and incantations, containment devices, and barriers. In connection with the Hopewell, archaeologist Robert Hall (1976) has proposed that moats or ditches surrounding various Adena and Hopewell earthworks served as ghost barriers. His thesis is based in the widespread Native American belief that ghosts are not able to cross water (e.g., Fletcher and La Fleshe 1911:591; Hewitt 1894:114–15). Hall proposes that the potential of water to stop ghosts is found in its ability to reflect, or capture, the image of a person—the image being identified with the person's soul.

In the same article, Hall mentions the protective efficacy of magic circles, as well as "ashes and other substances with special properties or associations that may substitute for water" (1976:362). In total, Hall identifies moats, ditches, ashes, red soil, and circles as potential ghost barriers. Expanding on Hall's ideas, other researchers (e.g., Bacon 1993; Romain 2000; Carr and Case 2005a) have proposed that other forms of Hopewell ghost and spirit barriers might have included water-borne soils and muck; water-associated substances, including river-worn cobbles and shells; reflective materials such as mica; sand and gravel layers; stone and earthen walls; wooden screens or "palisades"; labyrinth entrances at hilltop enclosures; blocking mounds at geometric enclosure entrances; and geometric shapes in addition to circles. For the Hopewell, the decision as to what kind of barrier to use may have depended on the nature of the targeted ghost or spirit (Bacon 1993:259–60).

We do not have space here to pursue the question of how each device may have functioned and the ethnographic data in that regard. (Also worth noting is that there are differences between ghosts and spirits.) But in reference, for example, to labyrinth entrances at hilltop enclosures and analogous blocking mounds at geometric enclosure entrances, when these devices are viewed on the ground today, what becomes apparent is that even in their original state, they would not have been very effective in keeping out people or animals. Where labyrinth entrances occur, one could easily walk across the adjacent walls; where blocking mounds occur, one only has to walk an angled course to enter the earthwork.

On the other hand, although ghosts and spirits are believed to have special powers, they are also, in many cases, amazingly easy to thwart in their movement. As already mentioned, many ghosts are not able to cross water. In still other cases—in Western folklore, for example—the movement of a ghost or spirit can be stopped by something as simple as a cross, a clove of garlic, or the sprinkling of holy water. In some belief systems, ghosts and spirits are not able to move in zigzag paths. In the case of the Hopewell, labyrinth entrances and blocking mounds might have been intended to take advantage of this inability to move in zigzag paths.

Review of the Hopewell data suggest that if these varied devices were used as ghost or spirit barriers, then, as suggested by their ubiquity, belief in ghosts and spirits must have been a powerful influence. Ditches and other water features, for example, essentially surround many of the major earthworks such as Fort Ancient and the Newark Great Circle. Where water features are not contiguous—as in the case of the surrounding deep pits at Mound City (see, e.g., figure 4.15b)—by "connecting the dots" between pit features, a symbolic barrier is constructed. Other ghost barriers may have included low walls of stone sometimes found at the base of burial mounds. And layers of sand and gravel found in Hopewell mounds—whether they physically extend all the way across a mound surface or not—establish an element of separation between the living and the dead.

Geometric shapes seem to have intrinsic magical properties associated with their form. Perhaps in giving their large earthen enclosures geometric shapes, the Hopewell utilized those seemingly magical properties to keep in or keep out ghosts and spirits, in a manner similar to the use of protective pentagrams and circles by magicians of other cultures.

Alternative explanations for each of these features can be imagined. If, however, most or even some of these features served as ghost barriers, then we can conclude that for the Hopewell, ghosts and spirits were all around and that, in their existence, these entities represented a normally unseen or hidden aspect of the cosmos. What also appears to be the case is that, by using what are essentially containment devices, the Hopewell apparently believed that they had the means to control the movement of these unseen forces, spirits, or ghosts.

Artifact Designs

In preceding chapters we caught a glimpse of some of the beings that inhabited the Hopewell universe. What we found was that the uniqueness of Hopewell is not in their repertoire of Otherworld creatures, but rather the way in which they represented the hidden world in which these beings live. What I mean is this: It often happens that the animal or monster in a Hopewell or Adena piece remains hidden until the object is manipulated in just the right way. Sometimes the only manipulation required is that the object be rotated. To see the Gaitskill salamander, for example, we only need to rotate the Gaitskill tablet so that its central design is recognized. For the Hopewell site copper serpent, the panther and owl faces come into view when we rotate the snake's head first in one direction, then the other.

In other instances, to see the hidden figure we have to completely dissect and then reassemble the design. Examples of this include the Hopewell deer, the Turner turtle, and the Cincinnati wolf (discussed later). A more complicated example is provided by the Turner male and female monsters, which become visible once we rotate and disentangle the creatures.

In each of these instances, the creatures within the pieces are brought into our consciousness, and into our subjective world, when the piece is correctly manipulated—that is, when the viewer has changed his or her perspective. What seems indicated by this technique is that for the Hopewell, things were not always as they first appear, and that beneath surface appearances there was another reality.

Another way the idea of a hidden reality might be expressed relates to the earlier-mentioned belief, found in many shamanic cultures, that things in the Otherworld are the reverse of how they appear or function in this world. In fact, this belief accounts for many examples of reversed actions and symbolism among shamans. Viewed from the Otherworld, the mortal world might appear as upside down, inside out, back-to-front, or a mirror image.

In Hopewell and Adena designs, where we find normal and reversed imagery in the same piece (e.g., in certain of the Adena tablets and Hopewell copper plates), it may be that several meanings are being simultaneously referenced—including the notion that this world and the Otherworld are the reverse of each other.

In summary, possible ghost barriers and artifact designs suggest that ghosts and spirits were an important part of the Hopewell universe. As an everyday matter, Hopewell people moved about in a world that was subject to the influences of these entities. For the Hopewell, the everyday world was a place of spirit and material form, a place of both visible and invisible realities.

Animism

According to anthropologist Stewart Guthrie (1993:61), human beings have a built-in perceptual strategy that results in animism and anthropomorphism. Animism means the attribution of life to things and events that are lifeless; anthropomorphism means the attribution of humanlike characteristics to things and events. According to Guthrie, humans and animals both "display the common denominator of religions: seeing more organization in things and events than these things and events really have. Like us, other animals appear to attribute characteristics of life and agency to the inanimate world" (2002:38–39).

At the heart of this perceptual strategy is that our attention is drawn to movement. Boyer (2001:218) explains that movement across our visual field activates the mind-brain's animacy system. This system, in turn, generates inferences and expectations about the thing we have seen move. In its most essential aspect, motion suggests life. In other words, we interpret movement as the result of intentional agency—that is, something that moves in pursuit of its own subjective goals.[1] The evolutionary value of the animacy system is that it helps us to identify potential predators and prey.

As to the tendency to anthropomorphize, Guthrie (1993:62) explains that in our search for organization and significance in the world, we look for things that concern us most. The things that concern us most are distinguished by highly organized patterns and include living things and other humans in particular. Often, we animate and anthropomorphize at the same time. Guthrie explains:

> We animate and anthropomorphize because, when we see something as alive we can, for example, stalk it or flee. If we see it as humanlike, we can try to establish a social relationship. If it turns out not to be alive or humanlike, we usually lose little by having thought that it was. This practice thus yields more in occasional big successes than it costs in frequent little failures. (1993:5)

An informative example of our tendency to anthropomorphize is provided by a seminal experiment conducted by psychologists Fritz Heider and Marianne Simmel. Heider and Simmer showed a movie to thirty-four people. The movie showed three geometric shapes—a large triangle, a small triangle, and a circle—moving in various ways in relation to each other. Asked to describe what they saw, all but one person "interpreted the picture in terms of actions of animated beings, chiefly persons" (1944:259). In fact, all but one person described the geometric shapes as having specific goals, feelings, and gender, and interpreted the movements as having a coherent story line.

In the archetypal shamanic worldview—which is neuropsychologically generated along the lines just discussed—the entire cosmos is animate and often anthropomorphized. All things are alive in the sense that they possess a life force, spirit, or soul. Moreover, in the shamanic worldview, most things are thought to have humanlike attributes such as the ability to think, feel, and communicate. As Tremlin points out, "We know of only one kind of mind—a human mind—and it's this sort that we attribute to other agents" (2006:101). Indeed, we go so far as to attribute humanlike social behavior and emotions to nonhuman spirits and gods.

In the shamanic worldview, among the things that are often believed to possess a life force or spirit are human and animal figurines, masks, body parts, teeth, bones, crystals, feathers, fossils, smoking pipes, weapons, the sun, the moon, winds, flint, and even stories and myths (Driver 1969:425; Quimby 1960:141; Swentzell 1997:188; Hallowell 1964 [1960]:56). Several lines of evidence suggest that the Hopewell worldview incorporated the notion of animism.

Faces in the Gaitskill Stone Tablet

Several researchers have suggested that humans are pre-disposed to look for and recognize human faces in visual data. According to E. H. Gombrich, for example,

> [W]e respond with particular readiness to certain configurations of biological significance to our survival. The recognition of the human face, on this argument, is not wholly learned. It is based on some kind of inborn disposition. . . . Whenever anything remotely facelike enters our field of vision, we are alerted and respond. (quoted in Guthrie 1993:103)

Evidence for the belief that nonhuman entities possess an animating spirit, life force, or soul is perhaps suggested by the occurrence of small faces in certain of the Adena tablets. The Gaitskill stone tablet was shown in figure 4.2b. Found within the salamander design are two humanlike faces. The attribution of humanlike faces to a nonhuman salamander implies an anthropomorphic characterization of the creature. From this it follows that if the salamander has a human face, it might also have a soul—or even multiple souls, as represented by the two faces.

Ritually Killed Artifacts

Evidence that the Hopewell believed all things to possess a life force may also be indicated by artifacts that have been ritually terminated or killed (in the sense of Hubert and Mauss 1964 [1899]). A considerable number of Hopewell artifacts appear to have been intentionally damaged or destroyed before being buried. Among the best known are the Hopewell effigy pipes. At Tremper, 145 pipes were found in two caches (Mills 1916:288–89). The large cache contained 136 pipes; the smaller cache contained 9 pipes. All the pipes in the large cache had been broken.

At Mound City, a cache of approximately two hundred pipes was discovered in mound 8 (Squier and Davis 1848:152). All of these pipes were broken. Also found in mound 8 were sixteen copper pieces that included plates, earspools, and pendants. According to Mills (1922:433), the pieces had been destroyed by hammering them together.

Found in mound 13 at Mound City was a deposit that included five thousand shell beads. From the mold of the clay surrounding the mass of beads, it appeared that the beads were contained in a bag, possibly made of animal skin. According to Mills, "A further feature of this deposit was that before being placed where found, it had been subjected to the 'killing' ceremony. This was effected by placing the bag of beads upon a hard surface, and repeatedly striking them with a stone hammer, the result being that the greater parts of the contents were crushed and broken" (1922:454).

Many more examples of destroyed items could be cited. The problem, of course, is the question of motive. There are a number of reasons why objects might be intentionally destroyed prior to discard or burial. They might be broken as part of a social display of disposable wealth. They might be broken to negate their value and deter theft. They might be broken to signify that their use was ended, or so their power could not be used again. Objects can be broken in the theory that since things are reversed in the Otherworld, breaking the object will cause it to manifest intact in the spirit world. Objects might also be broken, or "killed," to release their souls. Often associated with this is the belief that "killed" objects (but also intact objects) interred with the dead make the transition to the Otherworld with the deceased, and once there will be of use to the deceased. Cross-culturally, this belief often accounts for the funeral sacrifice of people and animals as well as the provisioning of the deceased with food, drink, and assorted valuables. Although the reasons for the intentional destruction of precious things are many, two large caches may provide insight into Hopewell beliefs.

The first case involves the Sunkle cache. Discovered in Newark, Ohio, the cache contained 551 artifacts including 157 diagnostic Hopewell cores and core fragments, 150 blades and bladelets, and 22 projectile points (Lepper 1998:128). In her analysis of these artifacts, archaeologist Barbara Harkness (1982) reported that many of the artifacts were broken. The cache was not associated with a habitation area, nor was it situated in a mound or earthwork. Its discovery was made quite by accident when a homeowner decided to dig in her backyard.

In this case, there was no need for the Hopewell to break the pieces in order to discourage them from being taken. Except for a bit of luck, the cache would never have been discovered. Since the cache did not accompany a burial, ostensibly the objects were not intended for use by a specific person in the afterlife. Perhaps the individual use of each piece had come to its end. But if that was the case, why save each piece for later burial as a group?

A second case is provided by the Harness cache (Holzapfel 1994). This cache consisted of 16 pounds (7.3 kg) of broken blades made from white Burlington, Illinois, flint. The cache was discovered as a result of plowing. It was located at the edge of a river terrace, roughly 150 feet (45.7 m) from the Liberty Large Circle earthwork. The blades had been burned, then broken, then buried.

As with the Sunkle cache, there seems little reason to have so thoroughly destroyed the blades in order to prevent them from being taken. Burial alone would have been quite sufficient. Indeed, the cache went undiscovered for almost two thousand years. That their potential use life ended seems unlikely. Out of 16 pounds (7.3 kg) of blades, many could have been refashioned into useful tools, as was often done by the Hopewell in other instances. Again, the cache did not accompany a burial, so the idea that they were broken in order to provision the deceased seems unlikely.

Perhaps it was the case that in their destruction and disposal, the cache objects provided some measure of social standing for the depositors. That social result, however, may be related to another motivation. Based in multiple examples in the ethnographic literature of offerings made by Native Americans to spirit entities of the Otherworld, it may be that the Sunkle and Harness caches were offerings—in these instances, to lower-world chiefs. Analogous offerings noted in the ethnographic literature include tobacco consigned to the fire, dogs tossed into lakes, and food offerings left in special places. With reference to the posited Hopewell offerings, as mentioned earlier, most Native Americans traditionally believed that all things have a spirit or soul. This includes blades, weapons, and tools. Certainly, the breaking of an animate object would kill it. If the Hopewell believed something similar, then breaking these objects might have had two intended results: (1) the objects would be dispatched to the Otherworld by ending their participation in this realm and (2) once broken and their spirits released, the pieces would appear as whole objects in the reversed Otherworld, presumably to the satisfaction of the lowerworld chiefs.

The same beliefs may also be expressed in the observation that Hopewell burial mounds were typically "capped" with a final layer of soil, effectively ending their use life. Similarly, Hopewell charnel houses—or, as I prefer to call them, Spirit Houses—within these mounds were typically dismantled and burned, thereby ending their use. We can refer to these events—whether they involve copper or flint objects, smoking pipes, Spirit Houses, burial mounds, or human figurines—as termination rituals. In these rituals, the physical form of these objects was dramatically manipulated, destroyed, and essentially removed from active engagement with this world. By removal from participation in this world, their use life was terminated. The notion of a use life that can be intentionally ended, in turn, implies a belief that the destroyed objects possess an essence, a life force, spirit, or power that can in fact be ended, consigned, or otherwise manipulated.

Transformation and Metamorphosis

By *transformation* I mean a change in form or appearance. Transformation is a property of nature. Inorganic things change as they boil, evaporate, dissolve, melt, and freeze. Biological transformations are ubiquitous as plants and animals change their appearance from infancy through old age. Transformation implies a vital force or spirit within. Perhaps for that reason, transformation is a central feature of the shamanic worldview (Pasztory 1982:7; Furst 1977:16; Ripinsky-Naxon 1993:109–11).

In many cultures, the ability to change from human to animal form is an earmark of shamanic power. Archaeological evidence suggests that people have long believed that special persons are able to make such transformations (Furst 1968; Miller and Taube 1993:102–104; VanPool 2003).

On the face of it, for most Western peoples, the notion that humans can change into other-than-human creatures seems naive. Still, the notion that such things are possible fascinates us and provides an endless source of inspiration for horror films and books. We might ask, however: On what grounds can a belief in human to nonhuman transformation be sustained?

Two cognitive theories may hold the answer. The first is conceptual blending. Consider the bear shaman, represented by the Wray figurine (figure 3.1a). In this instance, one input space is represented by the bearskin and a second input space is represented by the human. Cross-space mapping connects the bear and human. The bear and human are projected into the "blend" space, where they are fused. The resulting creature is the bear shaman. And even though the hybrid creature defies biological reality, the bear shaman makes intuitive sense because we have created it in our minds. It is not a foreign or alien concept. Moreover, the resulting creature has emergent properties or powers. Needless to say, the were-bear is also memorable.

A second cognitive theory that helps explain human-animal transformation involves perspective switching. Premack and Woodruff (1978), Barrett (1999), and others have pointed out that, as humans, we possess the ability to visualize the world through the perspectives of others. Generally attributed to the functioning of the frontal lobes (Goldberg 2001), our ability to form a Theory of Mind concerning the beliefs, desires, and possible actions of others exceeds any comparable ability in the animal world. The origin of this ability is explained by H. Clark Barrett:

> [H]umans have a single predator-prey behavior prediction system, or causal inference system if you prefer, that represents predator and prey behavior as mutually interdependent, and that incorporates a design feature of perspective switching, allowing humans to adopt the perspective of either predator or prey

as the situation dictates, in order to generate useful, context-specific predictions of opponent behavior. (1999:46)

The evolutionary advantage provided by perspective switching is obvious.

As discussed earlier, in the shamanic worldview, all living things are qualitatively equal. All things possess a life force, spirit, and even sentience. As A. Irving Hallowell explains with reference to the Ojibway, "vital personal attributes such as sentience, volition, memory, speech are not dependent upon outward appearance but upon the inner essence of being" (1964 [1960]:72).

In the case of the shaman, when perspective switching is combined with qualitative equality, the result is the ability to visualize the world from the perspective of nonhuman entities, including the perspective of the animal whose guise the shaman assumes.

Transformational themes are common in the beliefs and practices of Native Americans. Many stories, for example, tell of coyote, wolf, rabbit, bear, and others changing their outward appearance (e.g., Pijoan 1992). As Susan Martin explains with reference to Indians who lived in the vicinity of Lake Superior, "everything transformed: water, copper, people, animals, islands, vegetation, manitous. Nothing was as it seemed, and it was imprudent to assume that the face of anything was its totality" (1999:201). The same basic idea seems to have been the case for the Hopewell.

Human-Animal Transformations

In chapter 3 it was suggested that Hopewell human-to-animal transformations involved deer, bears, canids, felines, and birds. Supportive evidence included Hopewell regalia that incorporated symbolically charged animal parts. Hopewell expression of transformation themes is found, however, not only in shamanic accouterments and costumes, but also in artifact designs.

Mica Hand and Bird Claw

Figures 5.1a and 5.1b show a human effigy hand and a four-talon raptor effigy foot cut out of mica. As mentioned in chapter 3, these pieces were found with two individuals who were buried side by side in mound 25 at the Hopewell site (Shetrone 1926:95). The mica hand was situated between the skulls of the two individuals; the mica raptor foot was found on the chest of the north burial. A second mica raptor foot (having three talons and not pictured here) was found on the chest of the south burial. Also found on the chest of the south burial was the actual "head of a small raptorial (bird), presumably a hawk" (95).

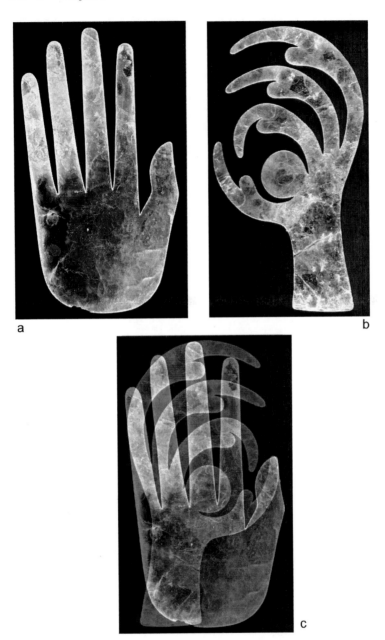

Figure 5.1.   a. Mica hand effigy from the Hopewell site. Ohio Historical Society image #A0283/000294, used with permission. b. Mica raptor foot from the Hopewell site. Ohio Historical Society image #A283/000292.001, used with permission. c. Raptor foot in figure 5.1b flipped and superimposed over hand in figure 5.1a. Ohio Historical Society images #A0283/000294 and #A283/000292.001.

The two mica raptor feet differ from each other in size. Of considerable interest, however, is that the four-talon raptor foot shown here and the human mica hand are nearly the same size. Penny (1985:203) gives the length of the four-talon raptor foot as 28 cm and the length of the mica hand as 29 cm.

We cannot be certain how the Hopewell intended these images to be viewed. However, figure 5.1c shows the result when the raptor foot is flipped along its vertical axis—so it faces the same direction as the mica hand—and then superimposed over the hand effigy. When this is done, some interesting correspondences result. First, the length-to-width proportions of the pieces match. Second, the overall curvature of the raptor foot seems related to the lengths of the human fingers. Third, there is a correspondence in the positions of the bird's rear talon and the human thumb. Indeed, this latter correspondence draws attention to the fact that humans and raptors have equivalent opposing digits. Used to facilitate grasping, in humans this opposing digit is the thumb; in raptors it is the rear talon.

At least part of the symbolic message expressed here seems to be that the raptor foot and human hand are related in the sense that they are made of the same substance, and, further, that they are equivalent in terms of essential form. The significance of this symbolism is that it supports the notion that the Hopewell recognized an equivalency among certain life forms. This recognition, in turn, lays the foundation for human-to-animal transformations, including human-to-bird transformations, as discussed in the next section. That is to say, it becomes easier to accept the concept of human-to-animal transformation once we understand that all living things have in common the same life essence.

The Cincinnati Tablet Transformation

Of considerable interest is that combined human and animal body parts suggestive of conceptual blending and shamanic transformations are found in Adena tablet designs. Figure 5.2a, for example, shows the Cincinnati tablet. Carved into this tablet is a strange little creature. What may be the creature's eyes, nose, and mouth are indicated in figure 5.2b. The face gives the impression of a feline, with its cleft upper lip, small nose, and possible cuspid teeth. The creature has four identical paws, so it is not a bird. Neither are the creature's hands and feet human. Rather, in their mirror-image and tri-lobed aspect, as well as possible claw elements, they resemble feline legs and paws.

The creature's ears are of special interest. In the front-facing view of the head, what could be ears are represented by vertical lines. Additionally,

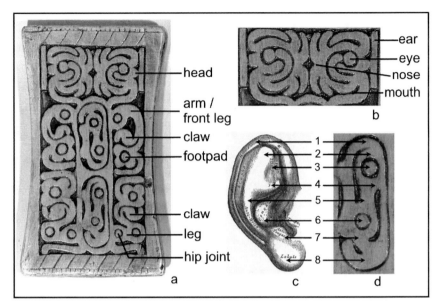

Figure 5.2. a. Cincinnati tablet. Photo courtesy of the Cincinnati Museum Center, Cincinnati Historical Society Library. b. Enlarged detail of Cincinnati tablet. Photo courtesy of the Cincinnati Museum Center, Cincinnati Historical Society Library. c. Human ear. From online edition of the 20th U.S. edition of *Gray's Anatomy of the Human Body*, originally published in 1918. Online edition provided by Bartleby.com, accessed February 23, 2008. d. Enlarged detail of Cincinnati tablet. Photo courtesy of the Cincinnati Museum Center, Cincinnati Historical Society Library.

though, situated within the body are two mirror-image designs. Of interest is that these designs have human ear attributes.[2] As figures 5.2c and 5.2d show, there are a minimum of eight matching identification points between the proposed Cincinnati tablet ears and real human ears.

Two things are of further interest. First, if we accept that the creature represents some variety of feline, then it may be relevant that cats are nocturnal hunters who rely heavily on hearing to locate their prey. Felines can hear sound at further distances and higher frequencies than humans can. In this piece, then, it could be that the cat's exceptional sense of hearing is being conceptually cross-matched to human hearing by placing human ears in the center of the feline design.

Second, whatever the creature is, the design tells us that in Adena-Hopewell belief, attributes from ordinarily separate categories of entities could be combined so that a hybrid creature results. In this, transformational processes are implicated.

Gaitskill Clay and Lakin A Tablets

Creatures that combine human and nonhuman features are also found in other Adena tablets. Hybrid human-bird creatures have long been recognized in the Gaitskill Clay and Lakin A tablets (see, e.g., Webb and Baby 1957:91). Figures 5.3a and 5.3b show the Gaitskill Clay tablet. Measuring roughly 4 1/2 (11.4 cm) by 3 1/2 inches (8.9 cm), this tablet was found in an Adena mound in Montgomery County, Kentucky (Webb and Funkhouser 1932:305–308). In this case, too, an anomalous front-facing creature is shown. The creature's head, eyes, nose, and mouth seem fairly evident. Hands and feet are emphasized by their enlarged size. Figure 5.3c shows the Gaitskill creature's hands. The hands appear human. However, by virtue of the streamerlike appendages emanating from the bottom of the hands—similar to the opposing rear talon of a raptor—the hands are beginning to take on an avian appearance.

Figure 5.3d shows one of the Gaitskill creature's feet compared to the Hopewell site mica raptor foot. Of interest is that both the mica cutout and the Gaitskill tablet feet have three talons situated above their respective footpads. The Gaitskill tablet feet, however, have an extra rear talon below each footpad. In life, raptors have four talons: three in front and one to the rear; humans have five digits. In the Gaitskill tablet design, therefore, we seem to have bird feet that are beginning to take on the attributes of human hands.

A bird tail may be indicated in the Gaitskill tablet by the scalloped feather design found along the bottom of the tablet. Thus the upper half of the tablet has human features, while the bottom half has bird features. What seems indicated is a part-human, part-bird creature, perhaps in the act of transformation.

In many respects, the design found in the Gaitskill Clay tablet resembles the design in yet another tablet, known as the Lakin A tablet (figure 5.4a). Found in an Adena mound in Lakin, West Virginia, the Lakin A creature is a bit more difficult to recognize. As noted by Webb and Baby (1957:91–92), however, careful examination reveals the creature's hands, feet, and presumed tail, all situated in a corresponding manner to the Gaitskill Clay tablet creature. The area where the Lakin A creature's head should be, however, is not the same. In the case of the Lakin A tablet, the head is not situated where we would expect it to be. Perhaps the design represents a decapitation. Supportive of this interpretation is that there is a small head situated in the upper left corner of the Lakin A tablet. The head could be human or bird, depending on which way it is turned. In figure 5.4b, the head shows a human face. When rotated, as in figure 5.4c, the design changes into a bird head, similar to the bird head found in the Berlin tablet (figure 5.4d). In this case,

Figure 5.3. a. Photo of the Gaitskill Clay tablet. From Webb and Funkhouser 1932:fig. 46. Courtesy of the William S. Webb Museum of Anthropology, University of Kentucky. b. Drawing of Gaitskill Clay tablet. From Webb and Baby 1957:fig. 40, used with permission of the Ohio Historical Society. c. Enlarged detail of Gaitskill Clay tablet hands. From Webb and Baby 1957:fig. 40, used with permission of the Ohio Historical Society. d. Enlarged detail of Gaitskill Clay tablet foot compared to mica bird foot from the Hopewell site. Mica bird foot from Shetrone 1930:fig. 62; detail of tablet design from Webb and Baby 1957:fig. 40. Figures not to scale.

therefore, by physical manipulation of the piece, the viewer can control the human-to-bird transformation.

In any event, worth noting is how quickly we are able to recognize faces in the Adena tablet designs once they have been pointed out. As Gombrich notes, "if there is one psychological disposition about which one can afford

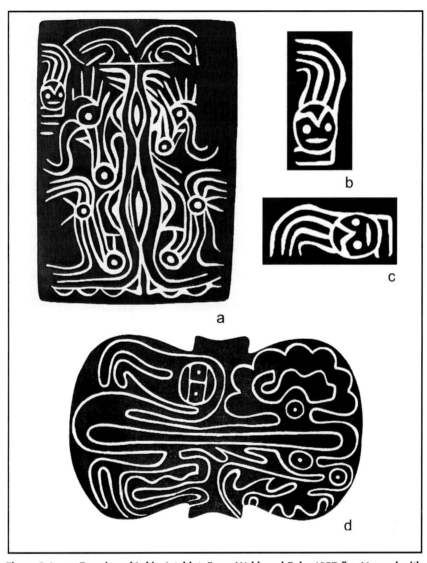

Figure 5.4.   a. Drawing of Lakin A tablet. From Webb and Baby 1957:fig. 41, used with
permission of the Ohio Historical Society. b. Enlarged detail of Lakin A tablet design.
From Webb and Baby 1957:fig. 41, used with permission of the Ohio Historical Society.
c. Rotated detail from Lakin A tablet design. Detail from Webb and Baby 1957:fig. 41,
used with permission of the Ohio Historical Society. d. Drawing of Berlin tablet. From
Webb and Baby 1957:fig. 33, used with permission of the Ohio Historical Society.
Figures not to scale.

to be dogmatic it is our readiness to see faces in any configuration which remotely suggests the presence of eyes and corresponding features" (1979:264). Possibly, this predilection relates in part to our innate ability as infants to search out and recognize the human faces we depend upon for survival and comfort (Morton and Johnson 1991; Pascalis et al. 1995).

Whatever the case, the interpretative process does not end with simple face recognition. Once we have identified possible facial features in a design, we continue to search for additional clues that support our interpretation. In the case of the Adena tablets, these additional clues take the form of recognizable arms and legs.

Predation

I think cultural anthropologist Ernest Becker accurately summarized the situation when he observed that

> [e]xistence, for all organismic life, is a constant struggle to feed—a struggle to incorporate whatever other organisms they can fit into their mouths and press down their gullets without choking. Seen in these stark terms, life on this planet is a gory spectacle, a science-fiction nightmare in which digestive tracts fitted with teeth at one end are tearing away at whatever flesh they can reach, and at the other end are piling up the fuming waste excrement as they move along in search of more flesh. (1975:1)

It was in the world Becker describes that shamanic concepts evolved; a world where the rule was eat or be eaten. As creatures that survived in large measure by hunting, while at the same time needing to avoid becoming prey themselves, the relationships between hunter and hunted have always been of vital interest.

Of the two categories—hunter and prey—the creatures that gain our immediate attention are predators, the power animals that pose a significant threat to our existence. Creatures that posed a threat to us in our evolutionary past included large felines, bears, wolves, snakes, crocodilians, other humans, and possibly large raptors when we were considerably smaller. Indeed, it seems that before we are consciously aware of such creatures, our brains have already detected their presence and caused our bodies to react. As explained by Joseph Giovannoli:

> [S]ensory information is received by the thalamus, organized and sent to the amygdala and hippocampus. The amygdale and hippocampus assign an emotional value to that information that results in a defensive flight or fight

reaction. Information moves from the thalamus to the amygdala at a very fast rate—i.e., in about 12 milliseconds. (1999:128)

Hopewell recognition of, and concern with, the predatory aspect of their world is indicated by two kinds of evidence: (1) the subject matter of their designs and (2) their collections of body parts.

Predator Designs

Shown in figures 5.5a–5.5h are Hopewell representations of various predators. Easily recognized are a falcon, raptor talons, bear effigies, a serpent, and what appears to be a crocodilian head (Hall 2006). The crocodilian design is made out of copper and was found in a Hopewell mound located in Illinois; the other pieces are from Ohio sites. The falcon is recognized by its eye markings. As distinguished by their humps, the three prone bears are brown or grizzly bears (*Ursus arctos* or *U. arctos horribilis*). Brown bears have a large visible hump over their shoulders; black bears do not. From the indications of rattles on its tail, the serpent is a rattlesnake. Figure 5.5f is of special interest. Known as the Esch pipe, the carved pipestone creature is sometimes identified as a frog. Arguing against this interpretation is that frogs have only weak maxillary teeth used to grind food; they do not have teeth in their lower jaw. In contrast, the creature shown in figure 5.5f has rather formidable teeth, including teeth in its lower jaw. Based on this and other features, the Esch pipe creature might be modeled after an alligator.

Another predator design is found in figure 5.6a. This design occurs on an engraved human arm bone found in a mound in Cincinnati (Willoughby 1916:Pl. 7). Willoughby does not specify the arm bone involved, and he only identifies the design as representing a "highly conventionalized carnivorous animal" (Pl. 7 caption). Willoughby's rollout drawing of the design is shown in figure 5.6b.

The design most likely shows a wolf. To see the wolf, it is necessary to first separate the design elements. Once this has been done, the parts can be reassembled in the more familiar form of a wolf as we are accustomed to seeing it. Figure 5.6c shows the resulting image.

Although it is vaguely possible that the rearticulated beast could represent a coyote, fox, or dog, I am inclined to think the animal is a wolf based on the prominence of its canine teeth, its distinctive broad head, and emphasis on the creature's large paws and powerful forelimbs.

Predator behavior is also represented in a number of Hopewell effigy pipes. When we consider what living organisms do with their time, it turns out they are mostly engaged in hunting, foraging, eating, sleeping, mate-seeking,

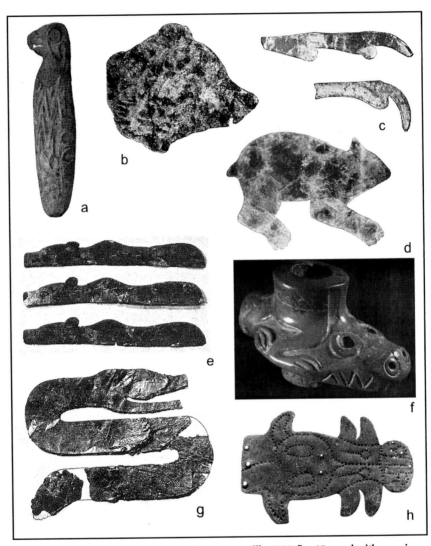

Figure 5.5. a. Copper falcon, Mound City. From Mills 1922:fig. 65, used with permission of the Ohio Historical Society. b. Copper bear head, Hopewell site. From Moorehead 1922:Pl. 72. c. Mica raptor claws, Seip site. From Mills 1909:fig. 40, used with permission of the Ohio Historical Society. d. Mica bear cutout, Tremper site. From Mills 1916:fig. 121, used with permission of the Ohio Historical Society. e. Mica bear cutouts, Turner site. From Willoughby and Hooton 1922:Pl. 15, courtesy of the Peabody Museum, Harvard University. f. Esch alligator pipe. Ohio Historical Society image #A1176-129, used with permission. g. Mica serpent cutout, Turner site. From Willoughby and Hooton 1922:fig. 30, courtesy of the Peabody Museum, Harvard University. h. Crocodilian design in copper. From Perino 2006:fig. 2.10, used with permission of the Illinois Transportation Archaeological Research Program, University of Illinois. Figures not to scale.

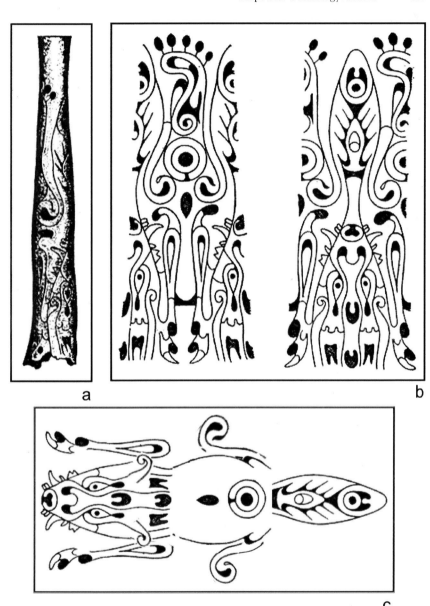

a

b

c

Figure 5.6.   a. Engraved human bone. From Willoughby 1916:Pl. 7. b. Roll-out of engraved design 7. From Willoughby 1916:Pl. 7. c. Wolf design found in figure 5.6b. Image created by William Romain.

or reproductive behavior. Looking at the Hopewell effigy pipes, of the life activities just mentioned, the most common behavior is eating. Of the pipes recovered from the Tremper large cache, for example, sixty were effigy pipes (Mills 1916:289). Of these sixty pipes, fifty show no overt behavior. Ten pipes show activity. Five show otters eating fish. One shows a heron eating a fish. One shows a crane searching for food. One shows a raccoon digging. One shows a canid howling. One shows a bird listening. Of the pipes showing physical activity, the majority show animals engaged in feeding behavior.

Teeth, Claws, and Jaws

Studies by psychologist Richard Coss (2003:90–98) reveal that human interest is aroused by sharp, pointed, and zigzag shapes. Compared to blunt, rounded contours, pointed shapes engender measurable and statistically significant pupil dilation. In another study, Coss and Moore (1990) found that out of a group of 320 slides showing different subjects, the most arousing image, as determined by measurement of pupillary dilation, was a close-up image of baboon canine teeth.

Coss (2003:90) suggests that these reactions have their origin in our evolutionary past, where canine teeth, horns, and other sharp things threatened injury. Because sharp, pointed, and zigzag shapes are potentially dangerous, our attention is immediately directed toward them.

Sharp, pointed, and zigzag shapes also appear related to social hierarchy. As Coss explains, "Canine teeth and sharpness play an important role in acquiring and maintaining dominance rank in primates where fighting ability determines rank" (2003:90).

As symbols, therefore, sharp, pointed, and serrated designs have aggressive connotations that imply power—useful in the shamanic world for deterring evil-intentioned humans, malevolent spirits, as well as symbolizing social dominance. Claws and teeth are especially expressive of these ideas. Thus, while additional meanings might be associated with such items, it is clear that at the most basic level, a statement of power over life is expressed by the display of teeth and/or claws taken from powerful predators—including, in some cases, human predators.

A significant number of Hopewell mounds, caches, and burials include animal teeth, claws, and jaws. According to Carr: "Out of 854 Hopewellian burials in 35 sites across Ohio, 79 have animal power parts (e.g., jaws, teeth, talons, claws). . . . Of the 35 sites, 11 have burials with animal power parts" (2005a:331). Teeth include those of the bear, alligator, shark, raccoon, opossum, panther, fox, wolf, elk, dog, lynx, and deer. Animal claws include bear and wolf, as well as raptor talons. Animal jaws, in order of prevalence, are wolf, bear, panther, and bobcat (Seeman 2007:175). Other cut and/or polished jaws include beaver, fox, barracuda, and human.

Bear canines are among the most commonly found power animal body part. Warren Moorehead (1922:150), for example, reported approximately five hundred cut and perforated bear teeth found at the Hopewell site. At the Harness mound, twenty cut and polished bear canine teeth were found with one burial (Mills 1907:168). Most bear teeth have been intentionally modified by some combination of polishing, grinding, perforation, or cutting. Many have one or more pearls inset in countersunk drilled holes.

A number of the bear teeth found at Seip, Hopewell, and Harness were hollowed out. With reference to this trait, William Mills comments:

> The [bear] canine tooth shown . . . besides being set with a pearl is cut into two parts and perforated with holes in order that the two parts might be fastened together. Invariably one-half of the tooth is hollowed out and the cavity very often filled with a pigment or small piece of quartz or highly colored pieces of flint. (1909:311–12)

In addition to actual bear teeth, effigy bear teeth are also found. Typically, the effigy teeth are made from limestone, bone, or deer antler. Occasionally, some are made out of wood and covered with copper. The craftsmanship of the effigy teeth is such that it is often difficult to distinguish the effigies from real teeth.

As mentioned, other predator teeth are also found in Hopewell contexts. With reference to Mound City, Mills notes that "necklaces of the canine teeth of the wolf, bear, and mountain lion were much in evidence" (1922:556). Perhaps most surprising is that dozens of alligator teeth are reported including those from the Hopewell, Seip, Mound City, and Turner sites (Mills 1909:312, 1922:446; Willoughby and Hooton 1922:46). More intriguing yet are the several fragments of barracuda jaws found at the Hopewell site. One jaw fragment still had twenty-six teeth remaining (Shetrone 1926:84, 164).

Among the many underwater predators, certainly one of the fiercest is the shark. Numerous shark teeth have been found in Hopewell contexts, including the Seip, Liberty, Hopewell, Mound City, and Turner sites. Sometimes the teeth are perforated for suspension; other times they are not.

Other teeth found in Hopewell contexts include the discovery in the Harness mound of "necklaces made of perforated canine teeth of the raccoon and opossum . . . several hundred of these teeth were secured" (Mills 1907:169). Further, Mills (1907:169) reported a necklace made of gray wolf claws from the same mound. At the Hopewell site, burial 207 in mound 27 was found to be wearing a necklace comprised of 506 "pierced wolf and fox teeth" (Moorehead 1922:98). What may be the largest recorded cache of teeth was found at the Turner site, on the central altar of mound 3. According to Willoughby and Hooton, the altar contained "2,000 canine teeth of small mammals, perforated for suspension" (1922:47).

Human jaws found in Hopewell contexts are worthy of note. Like animal jaws, most have been cut, drilled, and otherwise modified. Seeman makes the point that "human jaws were modified after the fashion of predatory animal jaws" (2007:178). Further, as Seeman explains, "cut human jaws, like predator jaws, appear to have been intended to be worn and seen" (179).

Discussion

From the preceding it is apparent that predators were of considerable interest to the Hopewell. The majority of Hopewell animal designs represent predators. Looking to the corpus of Hopewell animal designs and body parts, predators from all three realms are represented. Land predators include the bear, panther, snake, and wolf. Water predators include the turtle, alligator, shark, and barracuda. Sky predators include the eagle, falcon, and owl.

If predators are emphasized in Hopewell designs, then the opposite is also the case. Few, if any, representations in copper or mica are found showing prey animals such as rabbits, elk, chipmunks, woodchucks, skunks, beavers, muskrats, weasels, rats, or mice. Elk teeth have been found with a few Hopewell burials, but they are rare. Only one engraved deer design is known—that I am aware of—which is significant given the considerable economic importance of that animal for the Hopewell.[3] The few examples of prey animals that are found occur on effigy pipes, and in that context likely represent spirit helpers valued for their species-specific capabilities.

Continuing the discussion, there seems to have been an emphasis on two aspects of predator anatomy: killing implements and sensory organs. Of the hard body parts, including bones, that might have been collected, made into necklaces, or otherwise used to adorn clothing or the human body, there was a clear selection for teeth and claws. So too, in Hopewell copper and mica designs, claws, talons, and beaks are emphasized. What claws, talons, beaks, and teeth have in common is that they are specialized parts for killing.

At the same time, there also seems to have been a strong interest in sense organs. Figure 5.2 shows two representations of human ears. Other images of human ears are also known. Eyes are emphasized in the Rutledge salamanders (figure 4.2a). Eyes are also emphasized in the panther and owl designs found in the Hopewell site copper serpent head (figure 4.8c). In this case, emphasis on the eyes may be related to the fact that owls and panthers both have a reflective layer behind the retinas of their eyes called the *tapetum lucidum*. As mentioned, this layer provides for enhanced night vision. At night, as light is reflected off the *tapetum lucidum*, the creatures' eyes appear to glow. Surely, if witnessed at night deep in the woods, that phenomenon would be memorable. Of interest, too, is that raptor claw designs in both positive and negative form comprise part of the panther and owl designs situated within the Hopewell site serpent head (figure 4.8c; also see Greber and Ruhl 2000:99), perhaps symbolizing those creatures' status as predators.

Unique to the Hopewell site serpent head is the depiction of that creature's tongue. Of possible significance is that for the snake, the tongue serves as a highly specialized sensory organ. The snake's flickering tongue collects traces of substances from the air and ground and transfers them to the vomeronasal organ, a special chemical receptor site in the roof of the mouth.

What all of these sensory organs have in common is that they are, in effect, targeting mechanisms used by predators to locate prey. That the Hopewell might be interested in targeting mechanisms and killing devices is appropriate for a people who survived in large measure by hunting. Two of the most essential aspects of hunting include the tracking of prey (by sight, sound, and smell) and the killing of prey using weapons that cut and penetrate.

As to the occurrence of teeth and claw necklaces in association with individual burials, it is instructive to consider the observations of Roe (1998:177–79). Among the reasons for the wearing of body parts that Roe identifies are (1) aesthetic, (2) emulative, (3) performative, (4) protective or talismanic, and (5) demonstrative or corroborative.

In the case of the Hopewell, it seems likely that, to some extent, all these reasons accounted for the wearing of teeth and claw necklaces.[4] Additionally, as suggested by Thomas, Carr, and Keller (2005:339), it is possible that in some cases, the display of animal body parts identified a person's clan membership.

In any case, from the ferocious nature of the animals predominantly represented, it is clear that power was important. The bear, panther, wolf, falcon, eagle, shark, alligator, and barracuda are all "power" animals at the top of their respective food chains. In the shamanic world, if properly assimilated, the power of these animals can be used for killing or curing as well as spiritual protection. As Becker observes,

> [F]or the primitives, power resided in the qualities of living things and in the organs that embodied those qualities: teeth equaled biting and tearing power, with their uncanny smoothness and white luster and their terrible destructiveness to living beings. (1975:77)

Bloch (1992:4–5) makes a related point, suggesting that in rituals involving the killing of living beings, ritual participants gain a certain "vitality" from the killed and consumed animal, plant, or human. Elaborating on Bloch's thesis, it may be the case that in some instances, the intrinsic vitality or other attribute of the source animal was further enhanced and turned to specific purposes by the addition of specially charged substances. A case in point may be the hollowed-out Hopewell bear teeth mentioned earlier. As noted, the hollowed-out cavities were filled with colored pigments, quartz, or colored flint. Once the tooth was closed, these substances would not have added to the visual impact or symbolic information communicated by the piece. Combined with the intrinsic power of the bear's tooth, however, it may be that the intended result was a more potent charm.

One additional comment is in order. It seems that the Hopewell recognized falcons, eagles, and owls as belonging to one kind of avian group or taxon, namely, raptors. Further, they placed this category of bird in structural opposition to earth animals such as the bear and panther (see, e.g. figures 4.8d, 6.1b, and 6.1c). They also placed raptors in structural opposition to fish (e.g., figures 4.10a–4.10f). And they placed raptors in structural opposition to serpents and water birds (e.g., figures 4.7a–4.7d). All of this is consistent with the posited Hopewellian worldview of a vertically layered cosmos, with upper and lower worlds inhabited by opposite kinds of creatures. (Also see DeBoer [1997:236–38] who posits a somewhat different—i.e., "tripolar"—structural relationship among Hopewell creatures.)

Summary

In this chapter, qualitative attributes of the shamanic cosmos were considered. Multiple lines of evidence support the idea that the Hopewell universe included hidden dimensions inhabited by ghosts, spirits, and Otherworld monsters. Among the archaeological evidence for such beliefs were possible ghost barriers and artifact designs. Neuropsychological and ethnographic data were used to help interpret these material remains.

Next considered was the idea that the Hopewell worldview included the belief that the cosmos is animate. Support for this idea was found in independent data sets that include anthropomorphic faces in Adena tablet designs and what may be instances of ritually killed artifacts.

Considerable evidence was identified indicating Hopewell interest in transformation, especially between birds and humans, with special emphasis on raptors. The most obvious attribute of birds, of course, is their ability to fly. In this corpus of symbols, therefore, we find two themes—animal metamorphosis and magical flight—both of which are associated with sha-manic trance and soul travel to the Otherworld.

As to the matter of predation, the evidence strongly supports the notion that the Hopewell viewed their world as a place where predation plays a cen-tral role. It was suggested that power was assimilated from the animal world through the wearing of power animal teeth, claws, and jaws. Lastly, the evi-dence suggests that the Hopewell thought about animals in terms of opposed structural relationships, as might be appropriate to a shamanic universe that includes upper- and lowerworld spirit entities.

From these multiple lines of evidence, a picture of the Hopewell uni-verse begins to emerge. The significance of this picture is that, it was the structure and nature of the Hopewell universe that shaped and influenced crucial aspects of Hopewell life to include the timing of important events, the source of political power, and the nature of social hierarchy to include the relationships between humans and nonhumans; in short, all those things that give expression and meaning to human life. Having arrived at some understanding of the world the Hopewell created, we next consider the roles the Hopewell shamans played.

CHAPTER SIX

Roles of the Hopewell Shaman

In this chapter we consider material evidence that speaks to the roles of Hopewell shamans. In this regard, it is important to note that not all shamanic roles will be visible in the archaeological record. It would be difficult, for example, to find direct evidence that Hopewell shamans concocted love potions, found lost objects, cured snake bites, or were able to bring rain. Several shamanic roles that can be identified for the Hopewell, however, include healer, mediator of plant and animal resources, psychopomp, and diviner. Before considering those roles, however, it is instructive to look at how social intelligence shapes human interaction with the spirit world.

In the 1930s, Edward L. Thorndike defined social intelligence as the ability to understand others. More recently, anthropologist Esther Goody has proposed that "social intelligence seeks to reach goals and solve problems by modeling the ways in which our actions are contingent on others' responses" (1995: 207). Goody refers to this as the "dyadic premise"; and "Others" can include Grandma, the paperboy, the IRS, or God.

Goody suggests that the dyadic premise is so deeply embedded in our mind-brains that we are inclined to posit an Other when attempting to deal with difficult problems such as illness, natural catastrophes, famine, and death. Goody explains that "it is because of the dyadic premise of social intelligence that we find explanations based on chance difficult to accept" (1995:208). Instead, we attempt to establish communications with the Other. Goody explains that communication with the God "Other" occurs through prayer. In addition to prayer, I would propose that the shaman has a number of techniques for communicating with the Other. In any case, as Goody explains, the result is that "when we try to model strategies for solving grave problems we construct ancestral spirits, ghosts, and gods to fill the 'social Other' slot" (208). As social beings, we then attempt to negotiate with the Other. As I will show in this chapter, virtually all aspects of Hopewell shamanic behavior involve this sort of dialogue and negotiation with the Other—Other, in this case, meaning spirits, souls, and ghosts.

Hopewell Shamans as Healers

Common to all life forms is the will to persist, to continue one's existence. Fundamental to this driving force is the harmonious functioning of our physiological systems, or, simply put, the maintenance of good health. Nothing assumes greater importance for most people than their physical state of being, especially when there is a debilitating or painful deviation from the norm. Since we are biological beings susceptible to illness, injury, and aging, it is inevitable that a breakdown in optimal functioning will occur. In the case of simple injuries or minor ailments, standard remedies suffice. In the case of serious or unusual illness, however, it is the shaman who has the ability to mitigate or even cure suffering and illness.

According to Eliade (1964:300) and Furst (1994a:20–21), in the shamanic worldview, illness occurs in two principal ways: (1) by the introduction of malevolent objects, projectiles, or spirits into the body; and (2) by soul loss. Causes of illness range from sorcery and soul theft to sudden fright, malevolent actions by ghosts, and taboo violations. Among the many different techniques used by shamans to address these causes of illness are sucking, blowing of liquids and smoke on to the patient, herbal brewing, bloodletting, chanting, fire manipulation, sweats, and soul retrieval. Of these methods, the best evidence in the Hopewell material record is for the use of sucking and blowing tubes.

Object Intrusion, Sucking and Blowing Tubes

Object or spirit intrusion is often cited as a cause of illness among shamanic cultures generally and among Native Americans in particular. Father Allouez, for example, observed of early historic Iroquoian beliefs that

> [b]esides this general cause of sickness there are certain particular ones, namely certain little manitous, malevolent by nature, who manage to get in of themselves, or who by some enemy are put into those parts of the body which are sick the most. (quoted in Verwyst 2008 [1958]:50)

Similarly, Grace Rajnovich notes that among the Ojibway, "healers believed that some diseases were caused by foreign objects or spirits invading the sick person" (1994:28).

Harmful objects or spirits can be projected into the victim's body by evil-minded shamans, witches, and sorcerers.[1] Among the harmful things witches and sorcerers can project are pebbles, insects, and even small animals. Treatment for this kind of illness requires magical extraction of the offending spirit or object. Prayers, incantations, or exorcisms are typically used to remove the spirit or object. Often these techniques are used in conjunction with physical suction. Sometimes the shaman sucks the skin directly; other times, he or she uses a sucking tube made of stone, bone, or wood.

Both stone and bone tubes are found in Hopewell contexts. At Tremper, for example, two stones tubes were found (Mills 1916:285). And although stone tubes are often assumed to have been used for smoking, they can also be used for suction, or for blowing liquids, powders, or smoke in healing ceremonies. As von Gernet explains,

> The first identifiable smoking implements in eastern North America are tubular in form and date to the Late Archaic. . . . I suggest that the resemblance of these implements to shaman's sucking tubes is not fortuitous . . . and that they were once symbolically and functionally equivalent. It is not difficult to imagine an ideational homology between sucking and blowing "medicine," and the inhaling and exhalation of smoke, since both practices involve the transfer of spiritual power. (1992b:178)

Also found in Hopewell contexts are bone tubes, several of which are known to have been engraved. Two cut and engraved bone tubes were found, for example, in the Harness mound at the Liberty earthwork. Mills (1907:170) identified the bones as bear and noted that the marrow cavities had been greatly enlarged. The two bones have identical designs carved on them in bas-relief. Based on a drawing of the designs (Converse 1994), it appears the engravings show the profile of a raven's head, neck, and part of a wing.

Cut and engraved bone tubes have also been found at the Hopewell site (Moorehead 1922:111–12). One of the most interesting of these is a cut and engraved human femur found with burial 281 in mound 25.

Figure 6.1a shows a close-up view of the burial 281 bone tube. Figures 6.1b and 6.1c show rollouts of the design found on the piece. Looking at figure 6.1b, we can identify a bear paw to include five claws and footpad. Raptor symbolism appears in the opposite side of the rollout design, shown in figure 6.1c. The clue to recognition of the raptor design is in the scroll element discussed in chapter 4 and shown in figures 4.19c, 4.19d, and 6.1d. As will be recalled, the scroll design was suggested as a raptor symbol. Looking at figure 6.1c, the same raptor scroll element is found in the burial 281 bone engraving.

Further support for interpretation of this half of the engraving as incorporating raptor symbolism is found in the center design element. Specifically, the center element appears to show the eye of a raptor—perhaps a peregrine falcon, with its characteristic mustache markings (see figures 6.1e and 6.1f).

In summary, what seems to be represented in this piece is an upperworld raptor situated in a complementary opposite fashion to an earth or lowerworld bear. In both cases, characteristic features of each creature are presented. In the raptor design, the bird's talons and keen eyesight are emphasized. In the bear design, the creature's powerful claws are emphasized. As in other Hopewell designs, although two opposite kinds of creatures are represented, they are at the same time linked or interwoven in such a way as to suggest their interrelatedness. Certainly other interpretive possibilities exist; however, by referencing these two creatures in the design of the bone tube, the intent may have been to draw upon the combined powers of the earth-bear and sky-raptor spirits to help effect cures.

Adena Exodontist

In shamanic belief, sucking is one way of dealing with intrusive malevolent spirits. Yet another way, however, may be indicated by a unique discovery made in an Adena mound, located in Fayette County, Kentucky (Webb and Haag 1947:58). Found in the Fisher mound was an individual who had been buried with four human mandibles and a large piece of human humerus, all of which had been painted with red ocher. Also accompanying this individual was a bowl made from the calvaria of a human skull. Found within the skull bowl was a mass of red ocher that encased a collection of twenty-three human teeth. The teeth had been variously drilled, notched, or grooved, apparently for suspension. Of special interest is that one of the teeth (a left lower canine tooth) fit into a human mandible also recovered from the site (Webb and Baby 1957:fig. 5). Examination of this particular mandible revealed that a drilled hole had been started in the area immediately next to the removed canine tooth. Further, the bone in that area was abscessed. From these observations, Webb and Baby (25) concluded that the individual who was buried with the collection of teeth may have been a shaman who specialized in the removal of teeth. Accounting for why the twenty-three teeth had been drilled and otherwise modified, it may be that the exodontist-shaman wore the teeth—perhaps as a necklace—as a symbol of his or her expertise.

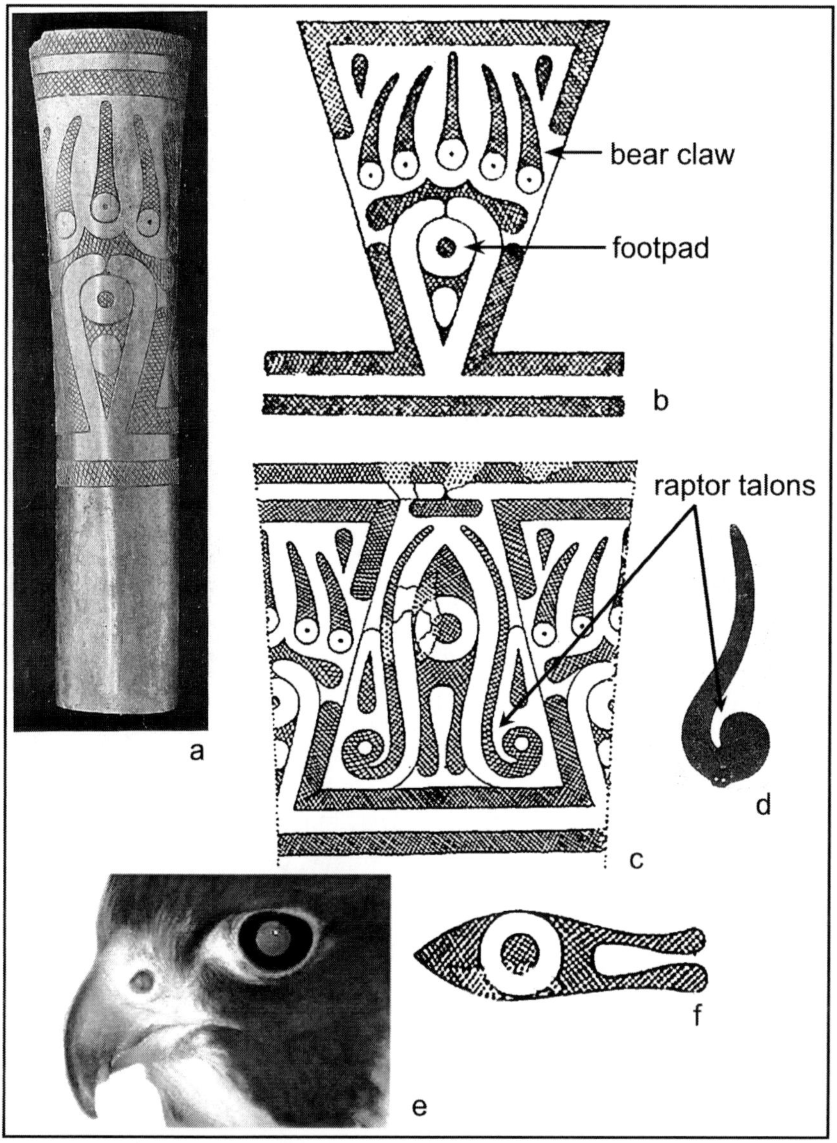

Figure 6.1. a. Engraved human femur from Hopewell site, mound 25, burial #281. From Moorehead 1922:Pl. 82. b. Half of engraved design on bone shown in fig. 6.1a. From Shetrone 1930:fig. 77. c. Other half of engraved design shown in fig. 6.1a. From Shetrone 1930:fig. 77. d. Copper scroll design from Turner site. From Willoughby and Hooton 1922:Pl. 11, courtesy of the Peabody Museum, Harvard University. e. Detail showing falcon eye. Photo by William Romain. f. Enlarged detail from design shown in figure 6.1c. From Shetrone 1930:fig. 77. Figures not to scale.

Hopewell Sorcery

Shamanic power can be used for helpful or harmful purposes. While most historically known shamans publicly use their powers for good, shamans are also known to use their powers to harm and even kill enemies over long distances—sometimes in connection with intergroup warfare (e.g., Schlesier 1987:41; Lyon 1998:93); sometimes for more individually oriented purposes. As Winkelman points out, based in extensive cross-cultural survey: "All societies have magico-religious practitioners involved in malevolent acts" (1990:347). Very often, *sorcery* is the term used to describe shamanic practices used for malevolent purposes. In this regard, the record would not be complete if we failed to consider that Hopewell shamans may have engaged in such acts. The evidence in this regard is very sketchy. However, it is clear—based on their smoking pipe effigies and other designs—that Hopewell shamans were well aware of toxic substances in their environment that could have been used as poisons, including rattlesnake venom, toad parotid and salamander skin secretions, and catfish fin venom. Broken human figurines, as found in the Turner site altar 1, mound 4 deposit, if broken intentionally, could represent sorcery. So-called Hopewell trophy skulls and modified human mandibles and maxillae may also be implicated in such activities, although other explanations are also possible (see, e.g., Seeman 1988). Also worth considering are instances of severed body parts represented in two- and three-dimensional form, including human torsos with severed limbs (figures 6.3a and 6.3b), as well as bodiless leather ears, copper hands and noses, and a unique stone finger carved from cannel coal. A smoking pipe from Seip that shows a dog eating a human head and another from Mound City showing a bird pecking at a human hand also offer intriguing, if uncertain, possibilities.

Hopewell Shamans as Mediators of Animal and Plant Resources

Vitebsky has stated that "shamanism is a hunter's religion, concerned with the necessity of taking life in order to live oneself" (2001 [1995]:11). For humans, the reality is that in order to survive, we need to eat. Our bodies require the nutrients and proteins provided by plants and animals. For humans, therefore, all living things are potential food sources—bags of concentrated food energy, waiting to be stalked, killed, and eaten.

In the shamanic world, however, where it is typically believed that all things have a soul and where the relationship to one's food involves a social component, things are more complicated than simply going into the forest and killing something for dinner. In the shamanic world, the taking of a life needs to be acknowledged, reciprocated, negotiated, or paid for, in order to maintain equilibrium with the nonhuman world. In the shamanic worldview, it is often believed that the souls of animals and plants are under the protection of animal or plant masters directly responsible for their abundance and fertility in this world.

In the Eastern Woodlands, plant and animal masters such as the Underwater Panther and Great Horned Serpent are situated in the lowerworld, where they are chiefs. It falls upon the shaman-hunter to negotiate with these chiefs in order to assure an abundance of game and plants. Since the shaman engages with the lowerworld chiefs, it is the shaman who possesses the knowledge as to the most auspicious times for hunting and planting, as well as where to find game. It is also the shaman who leads communal world renewal ceremonies, which are vitally concerned with plant and animal abundance and renewal.

Hopewell concern with—and efforts to influence—plant and animal renewal through shamanic means is suggested by their artifact designs, evidence for world renewal rituals, and large cache offerings.

Artifact Designs

Motifs that represent male and female pairs are common in Hopewell designs. Such pairs suggest the notion of cosmic duality. However, they also indicate an interest in matters of mating, procreation, and renewal of animal life through subsequent generations. Among the Hopewell designs discussed thus far and likely to represent male and female pairs are the Rutledge copper piece showing two salamanders (figure 4.2a), the two sets of copper vulture cutouts from Mound City (figure 4.3a), the male and female copper falcons from Mound City (figures 4.5a and 4.5b), the engraved male and female monsters from Turner (figure 4.6d), and the two sets of eagles embossed in the copper plate from Mound City (figure 4.16a).

Another example of possible mating pairs is found on an engraved smoking pipe recovered from altar 2 in mound 25 at the Hopewell site. Carved out of black stone, the pipe is shown in figure 6.2a. Figure 6.2b shows the engraved design rotated so that the bird heads are right side up.[2]

Moorehead (1922:140) proposed that roseate spoonbills (*Platalea ajaja*) are represented in the engraved design. Alternatively, given the relatively short necks of the engraved birds, it may be that they were modeled after the northern shoveler duck (*Anas clypeata*). In either case, it is noted that a line is shown connecting the individuals that make up each pair. In life, both the roseate spoonbill and northern shoveler duck establish strong

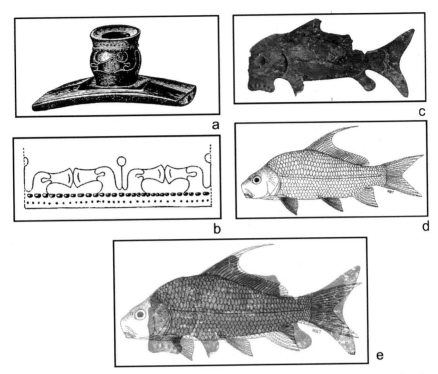

Figure 6.2. a. Smoking pipe from Hopewell site, mound 25, altar 2. From Moorehead 1922:Pl. 78. b. Design found on pipe shown in figure 6.2a, rotated so bird heads are right side up. From Willoughby 1916:Pl. 10(e). c. One of four copper fish recovered from Hopewell site. From Moorehead 1922:Pl. 69. d. Drawing of the Central quillback carpsucker (*Carpiodes cyprinus hinei*). From Trautman 1981:fig.90, used with permission from Ohio State University Press. e. Drawing of the Central quillback carpsucker superimposed over the Hopewell site copper effigy. From Trautman 1981:fig.90, used with permission from Ohio State University Press; copper piece from Moorehead 1922: Pl. 69. Figures not to scale.

pair bonds. Roseate spoonbills are monogamous during their breeding season, with the male and female taking turns sitting on the eggs and both parents feeding the chicks. The northern shoveler duck is unusual in that the male and female remain together during the twenty-eight-day incubation period of their eggs. In the case of most other duck species, the male leaves as soon as incubation begins. Based on these observations, the engraved line that connects the birds perhaps represents a pair bonding connection.

Mating pairs may also be represented in a set of copper fish effigies found at the Hopewell site. Figure 6.2c shows one of four copper fish. The effigy shown in figure 6.2c is the most intact of the group; the others were found in fragmented condition. Moorehead (1922:125) notes that the four fish differed somewhat from each other in size and shape of their body, fins, and mouth. Willoughby's examination of the raised portions of the eyes and mouths of the fish (quoted in Greber and Ruhl 2000:84) led him to conclude that two of the fish faced to the right, while the other two faced left.

The most obvious feature of the effigy fish shown in figure 6.2c is that the fish's mouth is located on the underside of its head. This indicates that the fish belongs to the Catostomidae, or sucker fish family. There are more than eighty species of fish in this family. Based on the blunt nose, hunchback shape of the body, and elongated dorsal fin on the copper effigy, however, it appears that the effigy was modeled after the central quillback carpsucker (*Carpiodes cyprinus hinei*).

Figure 6.2d provides an illustration of the central quillback carpsucker. Figure 6.2e shows the drawing of the carpsucker superimposed over the copper effigy. Worth noting are the matching humpbacked shape of the upper bodies, matching shape and angle of the dorsal fins, and corresponding length-to-width ratio of the two bodies. According to Trautman (1981:419), the central quillback carpsucker was once the most common species of carpsucker in the waterways of southern Ohio, including the Scioto River. Like other sucker fish, the carpsucker is a prolific breeder and spawns during the spring.

I think it is possible that the four copper effigies were intended to represent two mating pairs of fish. In addition to the fact that the "school" of copper fish is made up of two pairs of complementary opposite-facing—presumably male and female—fish, a second observation that supports this thesis is that tubercles are shown on the head of the intact copper fish.

Tubercles are small, raised nodules made up of keratinized epidermal cells found on the snout, head, body, and fins of certain fish, including carpsuckers. Tubercles are believed to aid in maintaining contact between spawning individuals and assist in species recognition (Wiley and Collette 1970). Tubercles appear shortly before spawning season, reach their maximum size during spawning season, and thereafter diminish in size; hence they are often referred to as breeding or nuptial tubercles. Close examination of the copper fish in figure 6.2c shows what appear to be tubercles on the snout of the fish, near its mouth.

From this, it may be that a theme of spring spawning and annual renewal is being expressed. Earlier, I proposed that a similar theme is found in the representation of the two copper falcon pieces from Mound City. In that case, the renewal of avian resources was implied. In the case of the copper fish, the renewal of aquatic resources seems implied.

World Renewal Rituals

Rituals, whether intended to influence the weather or the outcome of war or to promote crop fertility, have in common a fundamental way of thinking that we share with other creatures. The following explains what I mean.

In 1948 behavioral psychologist B. F. Skinner conducted a revealing experiment. Pigeons were placed in a cage that had a mechanically timed hopper that presented food pellets at regular intervals, with no consideration given to what the bird was doing when the food pellet was presented. What happened in short order was that prior to the food presentation, most of the pigeons developed a unique dance or ritual. Two of the pigeons would swing their upper bodies in a pendulum fashion; another developed a bobbing movement with its head. Another would spin around two or three times in a counterclockwise direction. As Skinner explains, "[T]he experiment might be said to demonstrate a sort of superstition. The bird behaves as though there were a casual relation between its behavior and the presentation of food, although such a relation is lacking" (1948:171).

Arguably, in the same way that the pigeons mistakenly attribute the appearance of food pellets to their ritualistic dances, so too, humans attribute natural outcomes to their ritual activities. Special dances, for example, are believed to bring rain; certain incantations are thought to bring hunting success. Special rituals, known as *world renewal rituals*, are believed to renew plant and animal resources. World renewal rituals are of interest because they suggest a public, theatrical display, likely to have been presided over or coordinated by ritual experts or shamans, since it is they who have the ability to communicate directly with the "Other"—synonymous in this case to the plant and animal masters.

Eliade (1962) points out that the need to periodically renew the world is found in all indigenous societies. Over time, the world is "worn down by beings of flesh and blood" (146–47). Thus world renewal rituals serve to repair and return the world to a condition of health and stability, as it was at the beginning. Speaking to New Year events, Eliade captures the essence of such rituals when he explains that

> this annual expulsion of sins, diseases, and demons is basically an attempt to restore—if only momentarily—mythical and primordial time, "pure" time, the moment of the "instant" of the Creation. Every New Year is a resumption of time from the beginning. (1954:54)

World renewal rituals therefore occur in a paradoxical state in which profane time is linked to mythical time at the beginning.[3] By linking the present to the mythical beginning, the world is renewed.

World renewal rituals are well documented for many Native American peoples. Among the Iroquois, for example, Elisabeth Tooker notes that "[o]f all these ceremonies, Midwinter, which both concludes the old year and begins the new, is the longest and most important. The theme is renewal" (1978:269).

Among Southeastern Indians, including the Creek, Seminole, Natchez, Yuchi, and Chickasaw, the Green Corn Ceremony similarly marked the beginning of the New Year and was a time of renewal (Howard 1968). Family and ceremonial dwellings were swept clean, the sacred fire was rekindled, and a series of dances were held in honor of various animal species. Primarily, though, the Green Corn Ceremony was concerned with plant fertility, and its main purpose was to celebrate the ripening of the corn.

Several writers (Birmingham and Eisenberg 2000:109; Buikstra and Charles 1999:221; Byers 1996:183, 2004, 2005; Hall 1993:51, 1997:18; Mallam 1982:61; Romain 1994:41, 1996:208, 2000:218–25; Sunderhaus and Blosser 2006) have proposed that Woodland period earthworks were used for world renewal ceremonies. One of the earliest suggestions along these lines was made by Squier and Davis, who observed that thin layers of charred organic matter are found in many of the mounds located within the geometric enclosures. Squier and Davis noted: "It has been suggested that sacrifices or offerings of vegetables or 'the first fruits' of the year were sometimes made, of which these traces alone remain" (1848:181).

One of the most suggestive pieces of evidence for Hopewell world renewal rituals comes from the Ginther mound, located near Chillicothe, Ohio. Shetrone (1925) described the mound as 10 feet (3 m) high and roughly 100 feet (30 m) in diameter. The only burial found in the mound was an intrusive interment from a later time. Of interest is that the entire floor of the mound was covered with a layer of sand. Found within the sand layer were diagnostic Hopewell flint bladelets and mica. Just beneath the sand floor Shetrone (1925:161) found a round pit containing what appeared to be a "food offering." The pit was 3 feet (0.9 m) in diameter and 18 inches (45.7 cm) deep, and contained "half a bushel" of hickory nuts (161). The edge of the pit was surrounded by a ring of mussel shells. Situated on top of this deposit, in the center, was a pottery vessel containing deer bones.

A similar discovery was made in Porter mound 15, at Frankfort, Ohio. Among the features discovered in this mound was an ash bed measuring 7 feet (2.1 m) wide, 10 feet (3.0 m) long, and 2 feet (0.6 m) thick. Within the ash bed, Moorehead found more than two dozen flint points, a polished celt, five circular pieces of mica, "together with great quantities of the calcined bones of various animals and birds. . . . nearly half a bushel of charred hickory nuts . . . [and] hundreds of fragments of pottery" (1892:130–31). According to Moorehead, however,

> The most interesting find was that of fourteen earthenware pots, each of a capacity of about two quarts. They had been placed in the ash-bed, most of them with the mouth turned downward. (131)

One can only guess what was in the pots. It certainly seems possible, however, that the combination of animals, birds, and hickory nuts was a food offering, as might be presented at a world renewal ritual.

What suggests that the Ginther and Porter mound deposits were offerings rather than just accumulated food debris is the ritualistic positioning of the mussel shells at Ginther and the ritualistic positioning of the pottery at Porter.

Additional evidence suggestive of world renewal rituals comes from the Capitolium mound, located within the Marietta Large Square earthwork. Excavations in that mound revealed two clusters of pottery fragments "that together accounted for two-thirds of the nearly 600 recovered ceramics" (Pickard 1996:280). The fact that the pottery fragments were found in discrete clusters indicates their intentional and possibly ritual deposition. What indicates that offerings made at the Capitolium mound were related to world renewal ceremonies is that, in addition to the pottery deposits, excavation revealed the remains of at least fifteen different kinds of wood that had been deposited and burned on at least two superimposed prepared mound floors. As paleoethnobotanist Dee Anne Wymer (1996:46) points out, Hopewell habitation sites typically average far less diversity in the number of wood species represented. Of considerable interest is that the different kinds of wood were collected from different environments, some of which are not typical to the immediate area. Moreover, a significant percentage of the recovered wood charcoal was from nut-producing species, including hickory, black walnut, and hazelnut. As Wymer explains, the implication is "that a wide variety of species from a wide variety of environments had been deliberately collected and utilized during as yet unspecified ceremonial activities" (1996:47).

These ceremonies may well have been intended to renew nut-producing resources, as well as the other species represented. What seems especially appropriate is that such ceremonies would take place at Marietta, where the two major geometric earthwork enclosures, as well as the Capitolium and Quadranaou mounds, are aligned to the winter solstice sunset. As discussed earlier, it is the winter solstice that marks the beginning of the sun's annual return, bringing with it renewed life.

Cache Offerings

Among the religious rituals that humans engage in are offerings and sacrifices. We can distinguish between offerings and sacrifice using the criteria articulated by Jan van Baal: "[A]n offering [is] any act of presenting something to a supernatural being, a sacrifice [is] an offering accompanied by the ritual killing of the object of the offering" (2003 [1976]:277). In the case of both, the usual objective is to cause a favorable outcome by the gifting of a precious substance. The expectation is that our gift will be reciprocated by the spirit entities of the Otherworld. Other times, offerings are made as presents, in thanks to spirit entities for things already received.

What is fascinating about this exchange is that we typically imagine that spirit entities think and act like humans, which would include an obligation to accept our gift and reciprocate. Indeed, underlying this belief are assumptions that spirit entities have an interest in what people do in this world and that they can be influenced by human behavior, including prayers, offerings, incantations, exorcisms, and other means. For someone not cognizant of spirit entities, this might seem to be a peculiar set of assumptions. As Tremlin points out, however, "religious concepts take their form, function, and plausibility from mental capacities that people already have by virtue of their evolutionary development." As a result, "because we have social minds we also have social gods" and "we naturally think of gods as human-like social beings" (2006:120–21).

One of the ways the Hopewell entered into communication with the Otherworld and maintained balance and equilibrium in their world may have been through a system of reciprocal exchange with the nonhuman entities of their universe. Ethnologist George Hamell explains the concept. According to Hamell (1987:77), the world of the Northeastern Woodland Indians was one of social relations between humans and other-than-human beings. Reciprocal exchange between humans and other-than-human beings was an obligatory responsibility that maintained social order and balance. Human-to-human exchange was occasioned by gift giving, feasting, and passing of the pipe between individuals. Exchange between humans and animals included prayers, rituals, and token offerings for taking the life of an animal. Reciprocal exchange with nonhuman beings of the Otherworld included offerings of precious substances in return for good fortune, abundant game, and plant fertility.

To understand this cycle, it is important to recall that, in general, Eastern Woodlands Native Americans traditionally believed that upperworld thunderbirds controlled the weather, wind, thunderstorms, and rain. Thunderbirds were generally helpful to humans and were often called upon for success in war and hunting.

Conversely, the lowerworld Great Horned Serpent and Underwater Panther chiefs controlled bodies of water, game animals, and plant fertility. While the lowerworld chiefs could bring about an abundance of game and plants, they also had the power to bring death and misfortune to individuals and communities. Many stories tell of Underwater Panthers and Great Serpents causing the deaths of humans, especially by drowning. Thus, relations with the lowerworld could be dangerous.

In the Eastern Woodlands, the lowerworld chiefs controlled not only game and plant abundance, they were also the source of copper, mica, shell, quartz, and similar substances. Copper scales, for example, were said to cover the body of the Great Horned Serpent, and they were believed to comprise the creature's horns (Smith 1995:111; Howard 1965:105; Radin and Reagan 1928:145). With their origins in the lowerworld, copper, shell, quartz, and mica had the power to bring long life, health, and good fortune. Sometimes these substances could be obtained by killing a lowerworld creature, such as a Cherokee Uktena serpent; more often, they were obtained by journeying to a special source area, sometimes located at the geographical limits of the known world, or by exchange with peoples who lived on the periphery of the known world. Other times such substances might be obtained as gifts from the lowerworld entities. George Lankford explains: "The metaphorical conception is that the Great Serpent bestows power as gifts of his own body. The three major forms the gifts take are horns, bones, and scales (which were considered manifest in the Middle World as shells or copper)" (2007:119).

As these substances, or "medicines," possess intrinsic power, it was appropriate to offer these same substances back to the lowerworld chiefs as a way of giving thanks for good health, animal abundance, plant fertility, and continued life. According to Hamell,

> In the Great Lakes Region the under(water) world and its horned or antlered serpent, panther, and dragon man-being chiefs were the traditionally ascribed source of metallic substances such as red copper, and of "white stones" and white shells. These substances were also appropriate gifts to these grandfathers . . . . Real human man-beings offered such gifts in rituals of sacrifice exchange at the thresholds of the under(water) world grandfathers—at the waters-edge, at waterfalls and whirlpools, and at the entrance into animal medicine society lodges. (1987:79)

Thus a system of reciprocal gift exchange between the people of this world and the chiefs of the lowerworld served to establish contact with the Otherworld, helped situate the Hopewell in their cosmos, provided for their participatory role in the scheme of things (in the sense of van Baal 2003 [1976]), and maintained the status quo of human life.

Looking to Hopewell, large deposits of copper, flint, mica, shell, and other precious lowerworld substances are often found.[4] Examples include a deposit of more than 8,000 flint disks found in mound 2 at the Hopewell site (Moorehead 1922:96). A similar deposit of several thousand flint bifaces was found in the GE mound in Indiana (Seeman 1995). A deposit of 120 copper items covering a 3-foot (0.9 m) by 2-foot (0.6 m) area was found in mound 25 at the Hopewell site (Moorehead 1922:109). In mound 17 at the Hopewell site, more than 3,000 sheets of mica were found (92).

Other deposits include a cache of almost 300 pounds (136 kg) of obsidian found in mound 11 at the Hopewell site. At Mound City, a cache of nearly 200 smoking pipes was discovered in mound 8 (Squier and Davis 1848:152). Found in mound 13 at Mound City were 25 pounds (11.3 kg) of galena, as well as a deposit of 5,000 smashed shell beads, apparently contained in an animal skin bag (Mills 1922:449, 453). At Seip, a deposit of 12 copper plates was found in mound 1, with no associated burials (Greber 1979:32). At Fort Ancient, a cache containing 59 copper pieces, including embossed plates and ear spools, 44 pieces of galena, and 8 pendant fragments, all covered by more than 100 sheets of mica, was found without associated burials (Morgan 1946:38–39).

By collecting these substances and often rendering them into man-made designs, the objective was not the accumulation of wealth for what it could "buy," in Western economic terms; rather, the point was the gathering of the power in these substances—power to be used for the benefit of the community—to ensure good health, abundant crops, successful hunting, and so on. To provide continued good fortune and as a way of giving thanks, at some point these substances were offered back to the lowerworld chiefs, in what amounts to a reciprocal exchange. As Hamell explains, "Such goods were being returned to the Under(water) World and to the Under(water) World Grandfathers from whence they were ultimately derived and from whom more such goods would be received in this grand cyclic exchange between this and the 'other' world" (1983:28).

Based in the above, most large Hopewell caches may represent gifts or expressions of thanks,[5] reflective of the belief that the gifts of animal and plant life provided by the chiefs, grandfathers, and masters of the lowerworld needed to be reciprocated. Likely, too, is that large cache deposits involved ceremonial or theatrical presentations, presided over by Hopewell shamans, who, through their ability to soul travel, were in direct contact with the lowerworld chiefs.

Hopewell Shamans as Soul Guides

Human beings eat together, sleep together, and hunt and forage together. Throughout our evolutionary history, our survival has always been contingent on being part of a small group. The solitary human stranded in the wilderness has a problem. A band of humans, however, is a synergistic force multiplier, capable of not only long-term survival, but mastery of the environment. Thus natural selection has shaped us into social animals. Indeed, one of the worst punishments we can inflict upon a miscreant is to place him outside the social group—in exile or solitary confinement. So strong is the need for human contact that when such contact is absent, we imagine or hallucinate other human beings (e.g., Slocum 1999 [1899]:39–42; Lindbergh 1953:389).

Given our preference to negotiate life in the company of others, it comes as no surprise to find that humans might wish to have the company of others during the transition from life into the afterlife.[6] Ideally, this other person or spirit would act as a guide through the death experience. In fact, that is the definition of a psychopomp—an escort, or guide of recently deceased souls to the Otherworld. A psychopomp can be a spirit, deity, angel, or demon. In many indigenous cultures, however, it is the shaman who guides or escorts the deceased to the Otherworld. In some cases, a psychopomp is needed to escort the deceased because the soul is not willing to leave its worldly existence. Sometimes, the psychopomp delivers the souls of sacrificed animals to deceased ancestors, or other spirits. Typically it is the psychopomp shaman who retrieves captured and lost souls and escorts them back to this world or on to the Land of the Dead.

While it is not possible to show that Hopewell shamans escorted deceased souls back and forth to the Otherworld, there is indirect evidence that Hopewell shamans presided over the physical treatment of the Hopewell dead and, at least in that sense, accompanied or furthered the movement of the dead from this world to next.

The way in which Hopewell dead were disposed of varied considerably. Some individuals were interred by themselves as extended burials. In other cases, multiple individuals are found in the same grave. Very often, burials are found in small primary mounds that, in turn, are covered over by larger mounds. In these cases it may have been believed that transition of the dead to the Otherworld occurred as a group. Certain individuals were accompanied by massive amounts of grave goods; others were buried with nothing, or only one or two items. Most Hopewell people appear to have been cremated.[7]

As Miller explains, "[I]n Native America death was viewed as a process, analogous to that of living. It was a sequence of events rather than one or more isolated events" (1988:85).[8] An example is provided by the Cheyenne. The Cheyenne believe that people have a *hematassoma*, or immortal soul, and an *omotome*, or breath soul (Schlesier 1987:10). When physical death occurs, the immortal soul departs from the body. Disengagement of the breath soul from the body is a two-stage process. Disengagement begins with the first burial of the body. The process is not complete, however, until a second burial is concluded. It is the second burial that results in the departure of the breath soul.

Evidence that the Hopewell thought of death in a similar way as described by Miller and Schlesier is found in their burial practices—particularly in their cremations. Although a great deal of variation occurs, there does seem to be a loose pattern, at least for the Scioto Hopewell. For individuals who were cremated, the process generally seems to have proceeded in the following manner: First, the body was dismembered and sometimes de-fleshed.[9] Next, the body was cremated in a special basin. The ashes were then gathered and transported to another location for burial.

To better understand the psychopomp role of the Hopewell shaman, however, we need to take a more detailed look at the Hopewell cremation process. And we need to keep in mind that Hopewell burial sites are in essence liminal areas. As explained by Wendy Ashmore and Pamela Geller, burial sites breach the "boundaries of time at the edge of human life, as well as boundaries of space between earthly and supernatural realms" (2005:84).

Having said that, we can piece together the following picture of the Hopewell cremation process:

1. The dead body was cut into pieces according to a proscribed pattern. The ritualized nature of the dismemberment process invoked symbolic meanings that were manipulated by the person carrying out the procedure.
2. The dismembered torso and other parts were burned in a fire situated within a special area. Physical movement within the special cremation area appears to have been limited. This is suggested by the fact that Hopewell cremation spaces appear to have been either screened-off areas or roomed structures sufficient to accommodate relatively small numbers of people.
3. The cremated remains were then gathered up and moved to yet another location, again requiring movement across liminal space.
4. The final grave was prepared at the direction of a person who was presumably knowledgeable in the proper way to ritually consecrate the grave.

5. Selected grave goods were placed in symbolically significant locations, requiring intimate knowledge of the symbolism of the grave goods and their preferred placement.

6. Next, the grave was covered with selected soil, sand, gravel, or mica layers—also requiring knowledge of the ritual requirements involved in the proper selection and sequencing of materials.

7. Lastly, the deceased was incorporated into the community of ancestors by finally capping the larger burial mound. This event was timed to coincide with cosmological considerations.

In the Hopewell world, the person best suited for these tasks would have been a ritual expert having intimate knowledge of the requisite procedures needed to properly negotiate the boundaries between worlds. Accordingly, in most cases it was probably a shaman who presided over the mortuary process, and in that sense served as a psychopomp—that is, one who accompanied and furthered the deceased through his or her transformation into the world of spirit.

At Mound City, the individual identified as burial 12 in mound 7 may have been a psychopomp-shaman. I make this suggestion based in the observation that in addition to the copper effigy horn found with this individual, discussed earlier, a second copper effigy headdress was found. This second headdress is shown in figure 6.3a. As can be seen, it represents a partially dismembered human. Except for the legs, the pattern of dismemberment exhibited by the headdress follows the pattern of dismemberment described for actual Hopewell bodies (Baby 1954; also see figure 6.3b).[10] The curvature of the copper piece is the same as that of other effigy headdresses. When worn as a headdress, therefore, this particular copper piece may have identified the wearer as a psychopomp-shaman.

Hopewell Shamans as Diviners

Pratt defines divination as "the act of consulting the beings, or wisdom, of the spirit world to gain information about the past, present, or future in order to facilitate problem solving" (2007:144). In an uncertain world where drought, famine, flood, war, and disease can wipe out an entire community, it is of vital importance that humans be able to gain information about the causes of events and what the future holds. By understanding the causes of events, we can take appropriate steps to alter their course. By anticipating the future, we can take steps to avert disaster. Our ability in the latter regard is impressive, and appears to have originated in our cognitive evolutionary development, specifically as related to "our ability to view intentional agents as having purposes" (Kelemen

 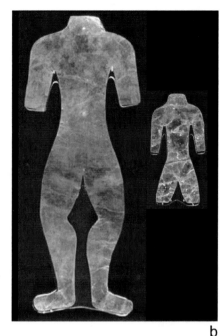

a   b

Figure 6.3. a. Copper effigy from Mound City, mound 7. From Mills 1922:fig. 67, used with permission from the Ohio Historical Society; scan provided by Arthur W. McGraw. b. Effigy figures cut from mica from the Hopewell site, mound 25. Ohio Historical Society images #A283/000242A and #A283/000242B, used with permission. Copper and mica figures not to same scale.

1999:287). That is, we seek to know the teleological purpose and future behavior of human and non-human agents. Elkhonon Goldberg explains:

> Our success in life critically depends on two abilities: the capacity for insight into our own mental world and that of other people. These abilities are closely interrelated and both are under frontal lobe control. The ability to imagine ourselves in the place of other creatures gives us a unique survival advantage. Through this ability we are able to predict what course of action other creatures are likely to take in relation to ourselves. Thus, if we can anticipate the likely movement of prey, we stand a good chance of having it for dinner. So too, if we can empathetically imagine and predict the movements of a predatory creature stalking us, we can take appropriate evasive action and avoid being someone else's dinner. (2001:135)

The teleological reasoning or predictive ability that Kelemen and Goldberg refer to provides us with the means of anticipating future events, far in advance of other creatures. Still, it is not enough. As creatures who rely in large measure on information, we are in constant need of more and increasingly detailed data.

In the shamanic worldview, since Otherworld entities possess superhuman powers, it follows that their understanding of the causes of events and knowledge of the future is superior to that of humans. Since counterintuitive Otherworld agents operate in a realm not subject to the laws of this world, they are able to move freely across time and space, the result being that they have access to information that ordinary humans do not (Whitehouse 2007:221). And so it becomes the job of the shaman, who has the ability to directly communicate with Otherworld spirits, to learn from them what the future holds, as well as the reasons for events in this world, such as illness. Divination is therefore used to diagnose the cause of illness, to understand the meaning of events, to find game, and for other tasks.

In other cases, clues to future events and causes are found in omens, the casting of lots, augury of entrails, astrology, and numerology. In these instances, in much the same way that we are able to anticipate the location of an animal by studying its tracks, future events and causes are believed to be reflected in the signs and patterns studied by the diviner, or reader of signs. As Anthony F. C. Wallace explains, "The logical structure of this belief [divination] is that one aspect of nature will, when appropriate power is invoked by the rite, act as an index to the phenomenon of interest" (1966:108). At least that is the assumption implicit in the shaman's efforts to divine such things as who will live or die, animal whereabouts, the outcome of war, and the weather.

Evidence that Hopewell shamans engaged in divination is suggested by earthwork alignments and certain paraphernalia.

Earthwork Alignments
As mentioned earlier, virtually all of the major Hopewell geometric earthworks are aligned to celestial events (Romain 2005a, 2004a; Hively and Horn 1984, 1982). Most appear aligned to either the summer or winter solstices. Fewer are aligned to the sun's equinox positions, the cardinal directions, and the moon's standstill positions.

For the Hopewell, celestial alignments brought the earthworks into a harmonious relationship with the heavens. At the same time, however, if one knows how to correctly read the information encoded in an earthwork, it becomes possible to accurately predict the movements of the sun and moon. In an uncertain world, that sort of predictive ability is worth having. As a practical matter, such predictive ability would have enabled Hopewell shamans to establish, for example, a celestially anchored date for world renewal and other ceremonies crucial to the success of the community.

Perhaps equally important, the ability to predict the movement of the sun, moon, and stars gives one the power to anticipate and set the most auspicious times for planting and harvesting plant foods. In many indigenous cultures, it is the shaman or shaman-priest who decides the timing of such events, based in celestial positions and alignments.

Divination Paraphernalia

There are a number of Hopewell pieces that are enigmatic in that we do not know what they were used for. Such items include deer astragali, stone "marbles," quartz crystals, mica mirrors, an elk antler with circular holes cut through it, and similar copper plates. Based in ethnographic and ethnohistoric accounts that describe the use of similar objects for divination, it is possible that some of these items were used for that purpose.

Astragali

Astragali are basically anklebones. Of interest is that 284 deer and elk astragali were found mixed in with other items on altar 1 in mound 4 at the Turner site (Willoughby and Hooton 1922:64). Figure 6.4a shows the recovered bones.

Astragalus bones were used by Native Americans for ring-and-pin games, whirligigs, and as components of fire-drill sets. More common cross-culturally and among Native Americans in particular, however, is the use of astragali as dice, for gaming and divination (Gabriel 1996:160–62; Koerper and Whitney-Desautels 1999). What makes astragali well suited for such purposes is that they have relatively flat sides, fit comfortably in the hand, and roll easily. McGee (quoted in Culin 1975 [1907]:148) explains the use of astragali in a game called *tanwan*, played by the Pima Indians. In this game, the player retains control of the bone as long as the "pitted side" turns up. The player with the highest count of pitted-side throws wins.

From the photograph in figure 6.4a it appears that the Turner astragali are not perforated. Thus it is not likely that they were used for ring-and-pin games or as whirligigs. One alternative is that they were used for gaming in a manner similar to that described above.

Games of chance and divination are related in that both are based in the belief that superhuman forces determine outcomes. In their use for divination, throwing two or more astragali that have sides with assigned numeric values will result in a particular configuration. Each possible configuration has an associated meaning. Through this mechanism, the opinions of spirit beings or forces can become known, since it is they who presumably control the outcome of the roll.

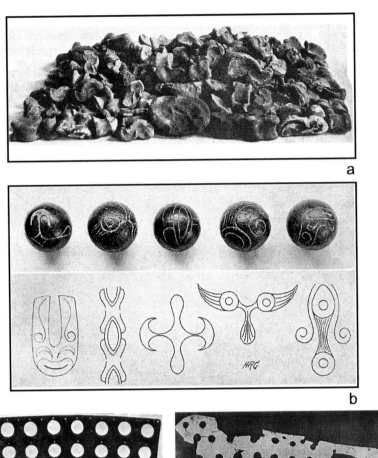

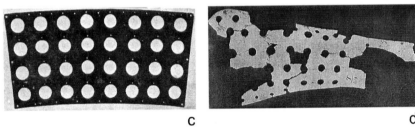

Figure 6.4.   a. Deer and elk astragali from Turner site, mound 4, altar 1. From Wil-loughby and Hooton 1922:Pl. 17(e), courtesy of the Peabody Museum, Harvard Univer-sity. b. Engraved stone balls from Seip mound. From Shetrone 1930:fig. 51. c. Copper plate from Turner site. From Willoughby and Hooton 1922:Pl. 10(g), courtesy of the Peabody Museum, Harvard University. d. Elk horn with holes from Liberty site, Harness mound. From Mills 1907:fig. 53; used with permission from the Ohio Historical Society. Figures not to scale.

What makes interpretation of the Turner bones problematic is that, if they were used for gaming, we might expect to find similar discoveries of as-tragali bones in ceremonial contexts at other Hopewell sites. As pointed out by

Thomas, Carr, and Keller (2005:359), however, the Turner collection appears to represent a one-of-a-kind occurrence. On the other hand, the large number of astragali bones found in this one deposit suggests that perhaps bones belonging to a number of individual persons were gathered together for a collective offering, similar in concept to cache burials of pipes and earspools. In this scenario, dozens of people could have had sets of gaming or divination bones.

Marbles

Evidence that the Hopewell had an interest in matters of chance may be indicated by a collection of engraved stone balls recovered from the Seip site (Shetrone 1930:103). Shown in figure 6.4b, each object is about the size of a large marble. Each is engraved with a different design. Raptor symbols can be recognized on several. The engraved balls were found with the remains of a child, approximately nine or ten years of age. This suggests that the balls might have been components of some kind of game. Since different symbols are found on each ball, it may be that the posited game relied on chance outcomes. What is peculiar is that, again, the marbles in this collection represent a one-time occurrence. Similar collections are not found in other Hopewell contexts.

Number Sequences

Figure 6.4c shows one of two nearly identical copper plates found on the central altar of mound 3 at the Turner site. The plate shown is about 9 inches (22.9 cm) in length and 4 1/2 inches (11.4 cm) in width. A number of equal-sized and equally spaced circle holes have been cut through the object. Smaller perforations are found along the edge of the piece and also adjacent to each large circle. The large circles are situated to form eight vertical rows, with four circles in each row. Thus the number 4 is repeated 8 times, for a total of 32 large circles. The same number sequence is repeated in the second plate.

Figure 6.4d shows a similar object. This piece was found in the Harness mound at the Liberty earthwork. Mills (1907:170) identified the object as made from elk horn. It is roughly 7 3/8 inches (18.7 cm) in length, which makes it close to the same size as the Turner copper pieces. Although it is broken, the pattern again seems to consist of multiple groups of four large holes.

Where a particular number or series of numbers is repeated, it is reasonable to think that special significance was attached to that number or number sequence. In the case of the Turner site copper plates, the significance of the number 32 is not known. Perhaps a cyclic phenomenon is being referenced. Equally plausible is that significance was found in the itera-tion of the number 4, for example, 4 x 4 + 4 x 4 = 32. In any event, given that both the Turner and Harness mound devices have repeated number sequences, it is possible that they were used for an activity that involved the random selection of one or more holes. If that was the case, divination purposes may be indicated.

Mica Mirrors

Mica is a silicate mineral. One of its unique properties is that it splits into thin, flexible sheets. Mica sheets can be transparent, opalescent, or matte. Generally, mica is valued for its sparkling, light-reflecting properties. Ac-cording to Seeman (1979:333), the source for Hopewell mica was probably the southern Appalachian area.

Mica is found in significant quantities at many Hopewell sites. Review of the literature shows that it is found in several different contexts: (1) as cache deposits; (2) as "mirrors" accompanying individual burials; (3) as beds or coverings for human remains; and (4) as cutouts in the shape of animals, plants, and geometric forms.

One of the largest deposits of mica was found in mound 17 at the Hopewell site. This deposit consisted of roughly three thousand mica sheets, each measuring approximately 8 inches (20.3 cm) by 10 inches (25.4 cm; Moorehead 1922:92). In cases such as this, where a deposit is not directly associated with a burial (although burials were found in other areas of the mound), it may be that, as discussed earlier, the deposit was intended as an offering to lowerworld chiefs.

So-called mica mirrors are usually found with individual burials. A typical mirror measures 8 to 10 inches (20.3–25.4 cm) in diameter and is roughly circular in shape, although edge sections are often straight. Although these objects are called mirrors, they are nowhere near as reflective as mirrors used today for cosmetic purposes. Of the mica mirrors I have personally examined, none provide more than a very murky reflection (see, e.g., figure 6.5a). Most would be of doubtful utility if intended for cosmetic purposes. By far, polished copper would have made more effective mirrors.

According to MacDonald et al. (1989:45), however, Hopewell mica mirrors may have been used for divination. Many ethnographic examples are found wherein reflective or semireflective surfaces, including obsidian, pyrite, slate, copper, and bronze, are used for divination purposes. Used in this fashion, reflective surfaces provide a means of focusing thought, a way to directly contact spirit beings, or portal to the Otherworld. Anthropologist Harvey Feit explains:

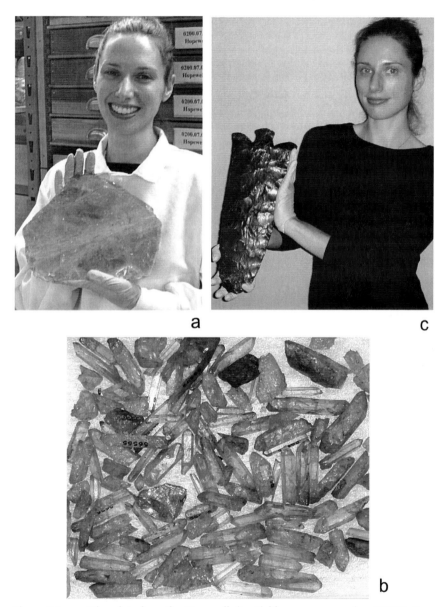

Figure 6.5. a. Mica plate from the Hopewell site. Field museum accession #56581.G.
b. Quartz crystals from the Hopewell site. Field museum accession #56555. c. Obsidian
biface from the Hopewell site. Field museum accession #56808. All photos by William
Romain.

"Seeing" and "visions" are the most general metaphors for the special experiences by which spirit beings are experienced by humans. Many of the specialized techniques for experiencing spirit beings involve actions whose symbolism directly refers to seeing. Looking into water reflections, playing with the eyes of animals such as the otter, looking into mirrors, or just "having visions" are examples of these. (1994:292)

Presumably, through contact with spirit beings as aided by reflective surfaces, or by means of visions seen in such devices, the shaman is able to learn the causes and future outcome of events.

Alternatively, Hopewell mica mirrors may have been included with burials either to contain the soul of the deceased within the grave or to ward off evil spirits. Both uses are documented in the ethnographic literature. In China and Mongolia, especially, mirrors were included with the dead to frighten away evil spirits that might disturb the resting soul (Heissig 2000:19). Similarly, metal mirrors (known as *toli*) were worn by shamans in China and Siberia as protections from evil spirits and invisible missiles (19).

As mentioned, in some instances mica sheets were used by the Hopewell as beds or coverings for human remains. At Newark, for example, Squier and Davis documented the use of fifteen to twenty bushels of cut mica used to cover a group of fourteen skeletons. According to Squier and Davis (1848:72), the mica sheets were "eight and ten inches long by four and five wide" and had been "carefully and regularly" placed. At Mound City, in mound 13, a large area measuring 7 feet (2.1 m) by 6 1/2 feet (1.9 m) was found lined with mica sheets (Mills 1922:270). In this case, four cremated burials were placed on top of the mica bed.

Used in this fashion, mica could have provided a portal to the Otherworld for the deceased. Certainly, graves are at threshold locations between this world and the Otherworld, and, as mentioned, reflective surfaces are sometimes believed to provide access between realms. Along these lines, the reversed and murky images seen in mica are consistent with Native American and Eurasian beliefs about the Otherworld, where things are believed to be the reverse of this world (e.g., Kalweit 1988:59; Fogelson and Bell 1983).

Alternatively, as mentioned earlier with reference to smaller mica mirrors, mica beds and coverings could have been used to keep the soul or skeleton ghost of the deceased in its grave,[11] or perhaps to ward off evil spirits who might disturb the dead.

As also noted earlier, mica was used by the Hopewell to make cutout figures. Mica cutouts typically depict animals, animal body parts, or geometric shapes. Possibly attached to shaman costumes, Hopewell cutouts are reminiscent of animal and other symbols cut out of metal and attached to Siberian shaman costumes. In the case of Tungus shaman costumes, Shirokogoroff explains that "[t]he animals [symbols] are manifestations of spirits which can be assumed by the shaman during the performance" (1935:289).

Alternatively, Hopewell mica cutouts could have been attached to textiles or leather and simply hung in the vicinity of shamanic performances. In either case, it would be consistent with many ethnographic accounts that such images were used to acquire or provide a locus for spirit helpers, in the case of animal and plant cutouts (e.g., Speck 1977:197), or as power attractors in the case of geometric forms.

For the Hopewell, mica was used in different ways, and may have incorporated multiple meanings. The common denominator, however—whether offered as a gift to lowerworld spirits, used for divination, used as a covering or bed for the deceased, or used to make symbolic cutouts—seems to be that mica was used to bridge levels of reality and, in various ways, manipulate life forces. In this, mica was special.

Crystals

Human beings—but also many other creatures—are attracted to bright, shiny things. Whether in the form of mirrors, metallic paint, copper plates, or crystal rocks, if it sparkles and reflects light, it attracts our attention and we are drawn to it. Often we attribute special properties to reflective materials, especially metals and crystals. Perhaps as a consequence, the use of crystals for shamanic purposes is nearly universal. As Ripinsky-Naxon notes,

> [R]ock crystals are shamanistic, transformational, power objects and spirit helpers, valued most highly for their potency and regarded as vitally essential among peoples throughout the globe, ranging from the rain forests of South America to the arid regions of Australia. (1993:123)

Among the cross-cultural shamanic uses for crystals identified by anthropologist E. A. Okladnikova (1989:346) are to "call" as well as "stop" storms, rain, cold weather, flood, drought, and illness. In the Americas, rock crystals and quartz crystals in particular were often used for divination and curing (Brady and Prufer 1999:138; Saunders 2004:130; Dow 1986:108–10; Pearson 2002:142). Lewis-Williams and Pearce (2005:259) suggest that crystals can be used to induce altered states of consciousness. Reichel-Dolmatoff (1988:22) explains how Colombian shamans facilitated trance states by concentrating on the reflections in multicolored crystals.

In the Eastern Woodlands, among the many peoples who associate quartz crystals with divination and curing are the Ojibway, Seneca, and Cherokee (Hamell 1983:13–14). In fact, Charles Hudson notes that "the means of divination which the Cherokees regarded as most authoritative entailed the use of certain crystals, presumably quartz" (1976:356).

Evidently, quartz was also considered special by the Hopewell. Among the items the Hopewell made from quartz were projectile points, plummets, and boatstones. Quantities of unworked quartz crystals suitable for divination and curing are also found. For example, in addition to a variety of exotic Hopewell points, quartz crystals were found in a cache near the parallel walls at Fort Ancient (Converse 2001). Unworked quartz crystals and several bushels of broken quartz points were similarly found by Squier and Davis (1848:213) in mound 3 at Mound City. Also found in the same mound were large fragments of garnet crystals (151). Moorehead (1922:130, 283, 284) noted that nearly a bushel of quartz was found in burial mounds at the Hopewell site. Figure 6.5b shows some of the quartz crystals Moorehead found.

While it is not possible to prove that the Hopewell used crystals for divination or curing, what does seem certain is that, as was the case for mica, the Hopewell attributed special powers to quartz. That conclusion is supported by an observation made by Mills with reference to bear teeth found at the Seip site. As will be recalled from chapter 5, Mills (1909:312) reported that many of the bear teeth he found had been cut into two and perforated with holes so that the two halves could be fastened together. Further, these teeth were hollowed out, and pigments, colored flint, or quartz crystals were often placed within the cavity.

The deliberate placement of quartz crystals or colored flint inside bear teeth suggests that special significance was attributed to these substances. In the case of quartz, perhaps the life force of the crystal was intended to augment the power of the bear tooth, resulting in a super-powerful protective or healing charm.

The notion that the Hopewell considered quartz (and also obsidian), to be special is further indicated by a discovery made by archaeologist Frank Cowan and his associates. Cowan discovered a buried cache consisting of chert, obsidian, and quartz. Known as the Koenig Cache, the deposit was located near the Stubbs earthwork, in southwestern Ohio. The cache contained 330 pounds (149.7 kg) of quartz and a lesser quantity of obsidian. Most of the quartz was vein quartz; however, some of it was quartz crystal. The many thousands of small quartz flakes and hundreds of obsidian flakes found in the deposit indicated that these materials were knapped. Importantly, Cowan recognized that for so many tiny flakes to be present, knapping must have been done using some sort of ground cloth or hide to catch the flake debris. The implications are revealing. As explained by Cowan:

> When flaking chert, "the chips could fall where they may," but such casual disposal was simply not appropriate for quartz and obsidian. For quartz and obsidian, the flakes, shatter, and production rejects had to be properly disposed of by gathering them up and returning them to the earth, removing them from the plane of "This World" and placing them into the "Underworld," either within a deep pit or beneath a mound. (2005:7–8)

Figure 6.5c shows one of several obsidian bifaces recovered from the Hopewell site. Whatever the use and meaning of these bifaces, it is obvious from their size and the rarity of obsidian for the Hopewell that these objects carried powerful symbolic messages. Because they were viewed as special objects, it is perhaps understandable why the flakes and shatter from knapping these objects might be considered special.

Summary

In this chapter, the roles Hopewell shamans engaged in were considered. First discussed was evidence for Hopewell shamans as curers. Individual curing sessions leave little trace in the material record. There are, however, tantalizing clues to Hopewell healing methods found in the occurrence of sucking and blowing tubes. Other healing methods may have included the use of crystals and "power" animal parts.

Additionally, though, there is something else that informs us with regard to Hopewell shamans as healers. In shamanic thought, "sickness is disruption, imbalance and the manifestation of malevolent forces in the flesh" (Davis 1998:148). In such cases, healing involves restoration of the individual's spiritual balance or equilibrium.

From the volume and variety of Hopewell deposits that appear to have been offerings, there seems to have been a strong emphasis on maintaining spiritual harmony and balance between this world and the Otherworld. Presumably, the Hopewell believed that if they maintained a reciprocal balance with the spirits or forces of the Otherworld, the result would be communal well-being, which essentially implies good health, good fortune, successful hunting and horticultural endeavors, as well as other things implicit in a good life. If this was the case, the Hopewell material record offers impressive evidence for Hopewell shamans doing what they did best, which was to maintain the spiritual well-being of the community.

Evidence supportive of the idea that Hopewell shamans were concerned with and acted as intermediaries to the Otherworld in connection with the renewal of plant and animal resources is strong. Among the evidence considered were artifact designs showing mating pairs, physical evidence of what appear to be world renewal rituals, and, again, large cache offerings.

The hypothesis that Hopewell shamans served as psychopomps was considered. In this, the evidence demonstrates that for the Hopewell, movement of the dead from this world to the spirit world was a process that proceeded over time, with proscribed steps at specific intervals, likely presided over by specialist shamans.

Lastly, the evidence for Hopewell shamans as diviners is convincing, especially if earthwork alignments are understood as providing the ability to anticipate future events. The use of specific objects such as astragali bones, marbles, crystals, and mica mirrors for divination is less certain, but certainly the data offer some intriguing possibilities.

CHAPTER SEVEN

Ways of the Hopewell Shaman

Shamanism is more than a list of beliefs about the universe; it is an experiential way of knowledge that includes a repertoire of techniques for causing changes in this world through interaction with the spirit world. In this chapter, some of the techniques Hopewell shamans used for this purpose are considered. Among these techniques are altered states of consciousness, animal transformation, and animal helpers.

Altered States of Consciousness

Ludwig's classic definition for altered states of consciousness (ASCs) was provided in chapter 1. Essentially, an ASC is any state of consciousness that is different from one's normal waking state. ASCs include lucid dreams, hypnagogic states, inebriation by alcohol, coma, and many other states. What generally distinguishes shamanic ASCs is that the shaman is able to use the ASC or trance for the purpose of contacting spirit entities or intentionally moving about within the spirit world, and the shaman is able to control that experience. ASCs are central to shamanism because they provide a way of seeing the spirit world and deliberately working with spirit entities. In shamanic trance, what is normally invisible becomes visible.

ASCs can be induced by a variety of methods, including meditation, prayer, concentration, guided visualization, and hypnosis. More physical methods include rhythmic dancing, auditory driving (drumming, chanting, clapping), pain stimulation, hyperventilation, prolonged isolation (sensory deprivation), fasting (hypoglycemia), thirst (dehydration), sleep deprivation, hypoxia, and use of psychoactive substances. Review of the literature reveals that Native Americans were aware of most of these methods.

Hayden summarizes an interesting argument as to why the more physical methods of inducing ASCs may have provided an evolutionary adaptive benefit:

> There is undoubtedly a rudimentary neurological basis for experiencing ecstatic states in many animals. This seems to consist of the tendency to enter altered states under conditions of starvation, stress, and intoxication. Such states may be adaptive. . . . The release of neurochemicals associated with ecstatic states under stress conditions may have also helped animals ignore pain and fatigue in critical struggles for survival. . . . I argue that it is no coincidence that the techniques most widely used for inducing altered and ecstatic states of consciousness in humans generally feature extremes of stress. (2003:32)

Perhaps for this reason, ASCs are able to be experienced by all people in all cultures. In fact, cross-cultural studies show that ASCs are universal. Bourguignon (1977:9) found ASCs involved in the religious practices of 90 percent of the 488 societies she looked at in a cross-cultural study. Bourguignon (11) further found ASCs to be institutionalized in 97 percent of the societies included for North America. More recently, in a study of 47 societies spanning a time period of almost four thousand years, Winkelman (1989) found that prior to Western influence, all the societies studied used ASCs for healing and religious purposes.

In line with the theory presented by Hayden, Winkelman (2004:208) suggests that many of the methods used to induce ASCs result in the release of endogenous opioids in the body. Perhaps the best known of the opioids are the endorphins. When released, endorphins produce pain relief and a sense of well-being. Also implicated in ASCs is activation of the mesolimbic dopamine system. There are several neural systems in the brain that utilize dopamine as their major neurotransmitter. Bozarth (1994) identifies the ventral tegmental dopamine system as the "pleasure system" or neural network that is activated by most psychoactive drugs, psychomotor activity, and even electrical stimulation (see, e.g., Olds and Milner 1954; Routtenberg and Lindy 1965).[1] Arguably, it is the release of endogenous opioids and consequent activation of the dopamine "pleasure system" that give rise to ecstatic states and sensations that ASC participants report, such as profound insight, a sense of rejuvenation, and feelings of the ineffable.

Pratt makes the point that shamanic ASCs can range from "a light diagnostic state, to a deep journey state, and to a full embodiment by spirit" (2007: xxxv). Much depends on the purpose of the ASC. In the case of spirit or soul flight ASCs, the shaman is able to direct his or her soul, spirit, or consciousness to other realms or dimensions. Once in the Otherworld, the shaman is able to directly interact with spirit beings, including deceased ancestors and animal masters, and from these entities gain information not available during ordinary consciousness. Such information may include diagnoses, healing practices and cures, songs, and rituals. While in the spirit world, the shaman is also able to locate objects and people, learn the outcome of future events, retrieve souls, and make changes to the fabric of reality, all of which affect the physical world.

Although Native American shamans often used fasts, isolation, sleep deprivation, and pain to induce ASCs, it is not likely that direct physical evidence for these techniques will be found in the Hopewell material record. What we do find, however, is evidence for the use of psychotropic substances and rhythmic dancing.

Psychotropic Substances

The term *psychotropic* refers to substances that, when taken into the body by any means, cause emotional, behavioral, or perceptual changes in the person. For a substance to have a psychotropic effect, it must cross the blood-brain barrier and alter neurotransmitter function. Several kinds of drugs are psychotropic, including depressants (barbiturates, benzodiazepene, alcohol), stimulants (amphetamine, cocaine, caffeine), opiates (opium, morphine, heroin), and hallucinogens (mescaline, LSD, psilocybin). Of course, for indigenous peoples who used such substances, they were not psychotropic drugs, but rather, sources of power. By eating, drinking, smoking, or otherwise introducing certain plant, cactus, or mushroom substances into their body, shamans assimilate the power of these living things, with the result being facilitated access to the spirit world. Among the psychotropic substances the Hopewell may have used are tobacco, black drink tea, and *Amanita* or *Psilocybe* mushrooms.

Smoking Pipes and Tobacco

Native American peoples smoked a variety of substances. Knight (1975:132–39) documented fifty different plant species that were smoked by Eastern Woodlands peoples. Yarnell (1964:180–82) identified twenty species smoked by Great Lakes–area Indians.

Of the plant substances smoked by Historic period Native Americans, tobacco is the most important. Anthropologist Joseph C. Winter explains: "First and foremost among the herbs and drugs used by shamans, medicine men, and other healers is tobacco. Almost every native group in North America . . . uses or used tobacco as a tool to divine and treat illness" (2000a:266). In fact, Winter makes the point that "[t]obacco is at the heart of Amerindian religion and at the core of Native American culture. . . . [Tobacco] binds the natural world with its supernatural counterpart, [and] eliminates the boundaries between them" (2000b:302). Whether offered to the spirit of an animal killed in the hunt, as a purifying fumigant for the deceased, or to the spirits of the Four Quarters, what tobacco does, in effect, is provide a communication link or pathway between this world and the Otherworld.

The tobacco used by Native Americans is not the same species that most modern Western cigarette smokers are familiar with. Commercial cigarettes contain *Nicotiana tabacum*, while the tobacco traditionally used by Native Americans is *Nicotiana rustica*. The difference is that *N. rustica* is far stronger than *N. tabacum*. Chemical analyses have shown, for example, that *N. rustica* grown by the Huichol Indians contains from 1.9 to 18.7 percent nicotine, while commercial tobacco contains only about 1.5 percent nicotine (Winter 2000b:307). Relatively small doses of nicotine provided by commercial cigarettes result in increased alertness and improved psychomotor performance (Mangan 1982; Hindmarch, Sherwood, and Kerr 1994). Based on ethnographic reports and personal accounts by modern-day investigators, however, it is clear that in higher dosages, *N. rustica* is capable of producing trances, catatonia, visions, and hallucinations (Rafferty 2006; Winter 2000b:307; von Gernet 1992b:176; Dobkin de Rios 1977; Joniger and Dobkin de Rios 1976). Von Gernet (1992b:177), for example, described his smoking experiences using *N. rustica*, including vertigo, sensations of flight, out-of-body sensations, and mild hallucinations. Several lines of evidence suggest that Hopewell people smoked tobacco.

First are the pipes. Smoking pipes date to at least 1000 B.C. in the Eastern Woodlands (Brown 1997:475; Rafferty 2004:2). Tube pipes are found in Late Archaic, Glacial Kame, and Adena contexts. Stylistically, there is nothing very remarkable about these pipes. During Hopewell times, however, things change. Whereas tube pipes predominate in earlier times, people of the Hopewell culture made platform pipes with curved bases, platform pipes with flat bases, smokestack pipes, and effigy pipes. Pipes and pipe fragments are found at dozens of Hopewell sites. The most well known are the caches from Mound City and Tremper. Whole pipes and fragments representing approximately 200 pipes were found at Mound City, while another 140 or so were found at the Tremper site.

What is important to recognize about smoking pipes is that, as explained by Sean Rafferty and Rob Mann, "smoking pipes are essentially drug delivery devices and that smoking instills varying degrees of altered states of consciousness. . . . Their function is no way utilitarian" (2004:xiii).

As to what the Hopewell were smoking in these pipes, unfortunately there are no published analyses of pipe residues that provide that information. Such analyses have been done, however, for pipes associated with earlier cultures. For example, mass spectrometry analysis of residue found in a pipe dating from 125 B.C. to 300 B.C. from the Boucher site in Vermont found significant levels of nicotine (Rafferty 2006). Artifacts from the site included pipes made from Ohio pipestone.

Closer to Ohio Hopewell, analysis of residue from a tube pipe found with a burial in the Cresap mound revealed nicotine (Rafferty 2002). The Cresap mound was built by people of the Adena culture between 500 B.C. and 200 B.C. (Dragoo 1963). The mound is located in West Virginia near the Ohio River, about sixty-five miles northeast of Marietta, Ohio, the site of a large Hopewell geometric complex.

The strongest evidence that the Hopewell used tobacco, however, comes from the discovery of tobacco seeds in Hopewell contexts. Notably, carbonized tobacco seeds were recovered from pit features at the Strait site, located in Fairfield County, Ohio (Dancey and Burks 2006). Radiocarbon dates for the pit features range from A.D. 220 to A.D. 260 (Burks 2001).

From the above, it seems certain that the Hopewell used tobacco. Ethnographic accounts (e.g., Morgan 1851; Freesoul 1987) tell us that tobacco was used throughout the Americas as a means of communicating and connecting with the spirit world. From this it is reasonable to presume that the Hopewell used tobacco in much the same way—that is, to facilitate ASCs in order to communicate with spirit beings and to soul travel to the Otherworld.

Magic Mushrooms
Although tobacco is a potent substance, there are other natural substances that are even more powerful. Jimsonweed and peyote, as well as certain *Amanita* and *Psilocybe* mushrooms, are examples. What these plants, cacti, and fungi have in common is that they produce hallucinogenic effects. While under the influence of a hallucinogen, the individual may experience vivid sensations of flight, as well as transformations into other life forms (Furst 1976b; Reichel-Dolmatoff 1975). Moreover, these experiences have a strong visual component. Through their effects, hallucinogenic substances allow one to experience flight to the upperworld and descent to the lowerworld, and engage in conversations with animals, spirit beings, and deceased persons.

The use of hallucinogenic substances has a long history north of Mexico. The use of jimsonweed and peyote dates back to at least A.D. 1 (Brown 1997:475), and use of red mescal bean may be earlier (Furst 1977:20). The use of hallucinogens in the Old World may be even earlier yet (Wasson and Wasson 1957). According to ethnographic research conducted by the Wassons and others, the hallucinogenic substance used by Siberian shamans was the mushroom *Amanita muscaria*. Of considerable interest is that A. *muscaria* is found not only in Siberia, but also across much of North America, including the Eastern Woodlands and Ohio.

In the Eastern Woodlands, A. *muscaria* was known to the Ojibway Indians. They called the mushrooms "death-dreamers" (Keewaydinoquay 1978:34). The power of the A. *muscaria* mushroom is revealed in a story told by Keewaydinoquay, an Ojibway medicine-woman. The story tells of how an evil sorcerer used the mushroom to seduce young women of the tribe:

> He would get them to come to him for some charm or other, and then have them drink this decoction he made from the *Oshtimisk*. Whatever was in it, it made them leave everything and everyone else and want to be with him. They said they saw colored lights and heard beautiful music and had at last found true happiness.
>
> They washed that salamander's slimy clothes, and mended his lodge, and cleaned up his filth, and didn't half know what they were doing . . . . [T]hey lived in a half-world where nothing was real. (36)

According to Keewaydinoquay (1978:34–35), *Oshtimisk* is the Ojibway name for the red top A. *muscaria* mushroom. Effects of A. *muscaria* intoxication can include illusions, hallucinations, wavelike shifts between sleepiness and wakefulness, and spontaneous episodes of signing and dancing (Jochelson, quoted in Wasson 1968:266).

In Ohio, A. *muscaria* is fairly common. During the course of forty-two mushroom-hunting forays made by members of the Ohio Mushroom Society over a period of thirty years, A. *muscaria* specimens were collected on twenty-three of the excursions (Hyatt 2005).[2] Figure 7.1a. shows two *Amanita* species mushrooms collected in October 2006 in northern Ohio.

The possibility that the Hopewell knew about the effects of *Amanita* mushrooms is suggested by a unique object found in mound 7 at Mound City (Mills 1922:547). Shown in figure 7.1b, the object is known as the "mushroom effigy wand." Carved out of wood and covered with thin copper, the object is about 13 1/2 inches (34.3 cm) in length. The effigy wand had been "placed on a large sheet of mica" and covered with cremated remains (547).

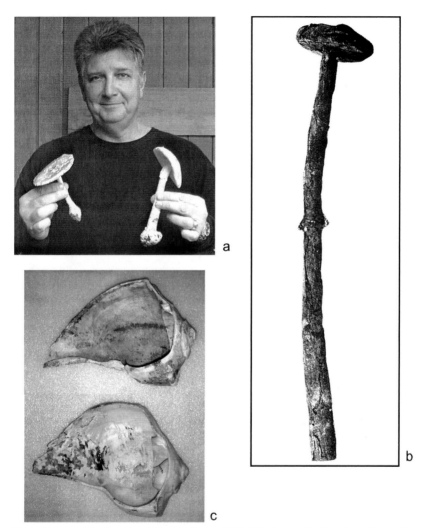

Figure 7.1.   a. Mushrooms collected during Ohio Mushroom Society foray in north-east Ohio, October, 2006. *Amanita muscaria* (Fly Agaric) (yellow var.) on left. *Amanita ocreata* (Death Angel) on right. Photo by Evie Romain. b. Mushroom effigy wand found in Mound City, mound 7. From Mills 1922:fig. 71, used with permission from the Ohio Historical Society; image scan by Arthur W. McGraw. c. Shell drinking cups (*Busycon contrarium*) from the Hopewell site. Photo by William Romain. Figures not to scale.

As can be seen by comparison with figure 7.1a and for reasons discussed in detail elsewhere (Romain 2000:214–16)—including the shape of the cap, the presence of an annulus on the effigy's stem, and the reddish-yellow color of the copper used to cover the wood—it is likely that the effigy wand represents an *Amanita* species mushroom. In particular, it may represent an *A. muscaria* mushroom. Mills (1922:547) and Moorehead (1922:174) both identified the effigy as an *Amanita*.

Alternatively, Rätsch (1998:678) identifies the effigy as a *Psilocybe* mushroom.[3] Psilocybin-producing mushrooms are found in the eastern, southeastern, and midwestern United States (Stamets 1996); and *Psilocybe caerulipes* and *Gymnopilus spectabilis* have been reported from Ohio.

If the effigy shows an *Amanita*, then it is important to know that most *Amanitas* are either poisonous or hallucinogenic—or both. Depending on the species, sometimes the difference is merely a matter of dosage. So too, *Psilocybe* mushrooms are well known for their hallucinogenic effects.

In either case, it seems doubtful the Hopewell would go through the trouble of making the mushroom effigy to commemorate its food value, which is negligible. The fact that the effigy is covered in precious copper, the time and care required to fashion it, and the unique characteristics of mushrooms in general, all indicate that the effigy wand was an object of special importance. Also of significance is that the effigy wand was deliberately positioned in a central location in a burial mound, on top of which were placed cremated human remains. From its liminal location in a burial mound and its association with the dead, it seems likely that the mushroom was important for its mind-altering capabilities. Irrespective of whether the mushroom effigy represents a helper used to facilitate hallucinogenic journeys or to cause death, it is reasonable to think that for the Hopewell, the mushroom provided access to the Otherworld—one way or another.

Black Drink
Another psychotropic substance possibly used by the Hopewell was black drink. Commonly known as yaupon or cassina, black drink—according to Rätsch (1998:285)—was made from both the *Ilex cassine* and *Ilex vomitoria* plants. Both plants belong to the holly family; both grow in the southeastern United States. To make the black drink, southeastern Native Americans brewed the leaves. Taken in large quantities—possibly with other substances, including salt water (Merrill 1979)—black drink was sometimes used by southeastern Indians as an emetic.[4] When consumed in this manner, the purpose was to purify the individual in preparation for vision quests, warfare, and ritual activities.

The psychoactive substance in *I. cassine* and *I. vomitoria* is caffeine (Rätsch 1998:286, 295). Caffeine is a central nervous system stimulant. Its effects are to reduce physical fatigue, heighten mental alertness, enable more focused thought, and speed reaction time (Hindmarch, Sherwood, and Kerr 1994).

Early European settlers who learned of black drink from the Indians consumed it in the same way that coffee is consumed today (Sturtevant 1979:150).

Among southeastern Indian groups, black drink was consumed, along with tobacco, prior to and during important council meetings (Hudson 1976:228). It was also offered to visitors. In this use, the shared smoking of tobacco and drinking of caffeinated beverages seems nearly universal as a way of promoting peace and friendship.[5] Black drink was also consumed during burial ceremonies (Merrill 1979:54). And according to Merrill (63, 70), it was used for divination by the Choctaw and Hasinai Indians. According to Rätsch (1998:285), fermenting agents were sometimes added to black drink, resulting in inebriating effects.

Although direct physical evidence is lacking, Milanich (1979) speculates that black drink was used by the Hopewell. His argument is based in the observation that Historic period southeastern Indians traditionally drank black drink from conch shell vessels (Adair, in Witthoft 1949:54; Swanton 1946:Pl. 98). Further, residues that may be from evaporated black drink have been found in shell cups at prehistoric Mississippian sites in the Southeast (Milanich 1979:83).

Notably, large marine shells fashioned into what appear to be drinking cups are found at Hopewell sites. Seeman (1979a:347) reports that "conch" shells have been found at eighty-four sites within the Hopewell Interaction Sphere.[6] As Milanich (1979:90) points out, the shell vessels are not found in habitation refuse, but usually with Hopewell burials, where they are often placed near the head of the body. Milanich (112–13) proposes that the leaves used to make black drink were likely obtained by the Hopewell at the same time they obtained the large marine shells, through trade with peoples in the South.

I agree with Milanich. In fact, I think it is very likely that the large marine shells found in Hopewell contexts were part of a ceremonial complex that included the drinking of black drink along with tobacco smoking. Perhaps the combined effects of caffeine and nicotine were sought during communal ceremonies, where the intended result was a relatively mild and controllable altered state of consciousness with attendant feelings of shared friendship and well-being. In this proposed use, like smoking pipes, marine shell cups were ritually important mind-altering devices. Like smoking pipes, too, from their burial contexts in accompaniment with individual burials, it appears that shell vessels were the personal property of individuals.

Figure 7.1c shows two shell vessels found with burials at the Hopewell site. Similar shells found at the Turner site were identified by Willoughby and Hooton (1922:21, 24, 25) as "busycon" shells. Mills (1922:496, fig.33,

1907:183, 1909:315, fig. 35) identifies shells found at the Mound City, Harness, and Seip sites as *Fulgar perversum*. *F. perversum* is an old name for the lightning whelk, or *Busycon contrarium*.

Based on these identifications, it appears that most—but not all—Hopewell shell vessels were made from the lightning whelk.[7] What makes lightning whelk shells of special interest is that they are "left-handed." Most large conch shells have a right-hand rotation. This means that when the shell is viewed from the front with the spire facing upward, the opening appears on the right. The lightning whelk, however, spirals to the left. As it happens, 90 percent of all people are right-handed (McManus 1999:199). I propose that left-handed lightning whelks were selected because they are easiest for right-handed people to drink from, with the narrowest part of the shell serving as a handle. Ethnographic support for this interpretation is found in a print from the year 1591 that shows the central figure of a southeastern Indian ceremonial gathering holding the narrow end of a drinking-cup shell with his right hand, with the lip of the shell toward his body (Merrill 1979:fig.4). If my interpretation is correct, then the left-handedness of the Hopewell shells brings us one step closer to establishing that the Hopewell used these shells as drinking cups, perhaps for the black drink.

Singing, Dancing, and Music

Rhythmic singing and dancing are well-known ways of bringing about altered states of consciousness (Winkelman 2004; Achterberg 1987:117). What singing and dancing have in common is that they—and related behaviors such as chanting and marching in drill—incorporate body movements and/or vocalization in time to a rhythmic beat. The effect of prolonged rhythmic stimulation or driving through dance, music, or singing is a change in the focus of awareness (Achterberg 1987:117), as well as a positive emotional experience. Moreover, as Tuan points out, music can "negate a person's awareness of directional time" and dance can abrogate "historical time and oriented space" (1977:128). Not surprising therefore, are the findings of Greeley (1975), who reports that among people who have had a "religious experience," music was the most important elicitor of the experience in 49 percent of the cases, followed by prayer in 48 percent of the cases. As to the neural processes involved, d'Aquili and Newberg propose the following:

[N]ormally either the arousal or the quiescent system predominates, and the excitation of one system normally inhibits the other. In the special case of prolonged rhythmic stimuli, it appears that the simultaneous strong discharge of both parts of the autonomic nervous system creates a state that consists not only of a pleasurable sensation but, also, under proper conditions, a sense of union with conspecifics and a blurring of cognitive boundaries. (1999:90)

The blurring of cognitive boundaries d'Aquili and Newberg refer to is precisely the kind of ASC that is useful in shamanic practices. In this kind of altered state, the boundaries between this world and the Otherworld are less distinct and more easily crossed. Perhaps for this reason, song and dance are closely intertwined with shamanic practices.[8] Indeed, singing, dancing, and music are integral to most shamanic performances.

Whether the participant is singing or dancing, the requirement that movement or vocalization be in time with a beat implies some way of establishing a rhythm. Among shamanic cultures, rattles, drums, tinklers, and other percussion instruments are typically used to produce rhythmic sounds. With reference to Hopewell, therefore, we might look for evidence of musical instruments as indicators of singing- and dancing-induced ASCs.

Rattles

Rattles are a form of musical instrument often used in shamanic activities. Like drums, rattles rely on rhythmic driving to induce shamanic trance. During curing rituals, rattles can be used to invoke helpful spirits, or, alternatively, drive away malevolent spirits (e.g., Vitebsky 2001 [1995]:49). In the Southeast, rattles were frequently used by shamans and served as symbols of shaman status (Emerson 2003:8).

Several examples of rattles are found in Ohio Hopewell contexts. As mentioned in an earlier chapter 4, eighteen small copper rattles were found at Mound City, with burial 12 in mound 7. Figure 7.2a shows two of these rattles. Mills (1922:494, 550) reported that the rattles were sewn to a leather belt that had been preserved, in part, from contact with the copper. The rattles are each about 2 inches (5.1 cm) in length and 1 1/2 inches (3.8 cm) in width. Each rattle is shaped like a small turtle and contains small beads or quartz pebbles.

Since the burial with which these rattles were found was cremated, it is difficult to know how the rattle belt was used. It could have been attached to the individual's clothing, or worn around the waist, knees, or ankles. Used in this way, the rattles would produce sound as the individual moved, presumably in dance. Alternatively, the belt could have been attached to a staff so that sounds would be produced as the staff was shaken.

Another example of a Hopewell rattle was discussed in chapter 4. In this case, however, the rattle, which was recovered from mound 3 at the Turner site, is comprised of two human parietal bone disks. What the Mound City

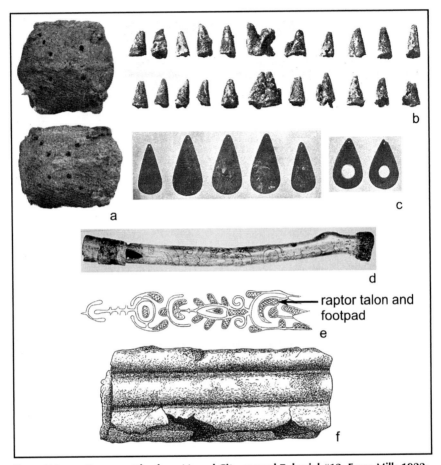

Figure 7.2.   a. Copper rattles from Mound City, mound 7, burial #12. From Mills 1922: fig. 74; used with permission from the Ohio Historical Society. Image scan by Arthur W. McGraw. b. Copper tinklers from the Turner site, mound 4. From Willoughby and Hooton 1922:Pl. 18(d), courtesy of the Peabody Museum, Harvard University. c. Copper bangles from the Turner site, mound 3, central altar. From Willoughby and Hooton 1922:Pl. 11, courtesy of the Peabody Museum, Harvard University. d. Bone whistle from the Bourneville mound. From Baby 1961:fig 1; used with permission from the Ohio Historical Society. e. Engraved design on bone whistle. From Baby 1961:fig 2; used with permission from the Ohio Historical Society. f. Panpipe from the Turner site. From Willoughby and Hooton 1922:fig. 21, courtesy of the Peabody Museum, Harvard University. Figures not to scale.

and Turner rattles have in common—and what suggests their association with shamanic activities—is that both are made of special substances: human bone in one case and precious copper in the other.

Tinklers and Bangles
Tinkling cones are small triangular pieces of metal bent into the shape of a cone. Typically, they are attached to clothing or accessories so that a tinkling sound is made as the person or item moves. Tinklers were often attached to the costumes of Siberian shamans. The noise was believed to frighten away evil spirits (Heissig 2000:23). Tinklers were also used by Native American peoples (e.g., Rockwell 1956:43–44).

What appear to be Hopewell tinklers were found at the Turner site. Dozens of "hollow cone-shaped objects . . . made by rolling together thin sheets of copper" were recovered from the central altar of mound 3 (Willoughby and Hooton 1922:49). Another two-dozen copper cones were found in mound 4, on altar 1, also at the Turner site (Pl. 18). Figure 7.2b shows the copper tinklers recovered from mound 4.

Willoughby and Hooton (1922:49) mention that similar objects made from hollowed-out deer antler tips were also found in mound 4. The tonal quality of these objects striking each other would have been different from their metal counterparts, but still quite capable of creating a rattling sound when shaken. Voegelin (1942:465) notes that deer hooves were used as tinklers by the Shawnee. In that usage, they were attached to the bottom edges, sleeves, and shoulder areas of men's shirts and garters.

Another sound-producing object that may have been used by the Hopewell are bangles. Bangles are attached to clothing, necklaces, or bracelets so they jingle when moved. Shown in figure 7.2c are several copper pieces found on the central altar of mound 3 at the Turner site. These objects could have functioned as earrings or some other kind of decorative device, Or they may have been bangles. Each has a small hole in one end. If these holes were used to attach the pieces to a necklace or bracelet, the result would be a jingling sound.

Similar objects are described as accompanying burial 12 in mound 7 at Mound City. Mills (1922:317) describes these objects as 6 inches (15.2 cm) to 8 inches (20.3 cm) long, in the shape of a laurel oak leaf. DeBoer (2004:99) interprets the burial 12 objects as bangles. DeBoer's interpretation is consistent with the observation that the small copper turtle rattles discussed earlier were found with this same burial. As DeBoer suggests, "Imagined on a costume, these bangles recall the classical garb of a Siberian shaman bedecked with metal disks . . . all jingling and jangling when the shaman danced to assume flight" (90).

Whistles
Whistles were used by Native Americans for a variety of purposes. War whistles were used to signal attack or retreat. Often, however, whistles

were used in ritual performances—for example, during the Plains Indians' Sun Dance.

Figure 7.2d shows a bone whistle found in the Bourneville mound (McBeth 1960). The Bourneville mound was a Hopewell burial mound situated near Paint Creek in Ross County, Ohio. Eight extended burials were found on the floor of the mound. The bone whistle was found with one these burials, along with four copper earspools, a copper plate, pearl beads, and two bear teeth.

According to archaeologist Raymond Baby (1961b), the whistle was fashioned from a piece of human radius bone. A thin copper band extends around the whistle near the lower head. From copper staining on the piece, it appears that a similar band extended around the bone near its opposite end. The use of copper to augment the piece suggests that the whistle was an object of some importance. As can be seen in figure 7.2d, a triangular opening has been cut into the bone, and the piece has extensive engraving.

Cross-culturally, whistles are sometimes used to imitate bird cries. It may be that the Bourneville whistle was used for similar purposes. I offer this suggestion based in the avian symbolism found in the engraved design. Figure 7.2e shows a rollout of the design. Visible in the design are the now-familiar Hopewell symbols of a raptor talon and footpad. Also found in the design, however, are two wishbone-shaped design elements. If these design elements represent actual wishbones, then, it is of interest to know that only birds have wishbones. Technically known as furcula, wishbones are fused collarbones that strengthen the chest for flight.

Also worth considering is that, given the single triangular opening cut into the bone, it seems the device was intended to produce only one note (unlike a flute, which might have several openings). Notably, most hawk species give what is essentially a high-pitched, one-note descending scream. Perhaps the Bourneville whistle was used to imitate the cries of a hawk. In this, the whistle could have been used in special rituals. Additionally, the whistle could have been used to either call in hawks or, alternatively, "freeze" game birds. Both tasks would be appropriate to a shaman—able to control life forces at a distance—and both tasks would be consistent with the avian symbols on the piece.

Panpipes
Panpipes are wind instruments made of conjoined tubes of reed, cane, or bone. Hopewell panpipes usually have three or four tubes and are covered with copper, silver, or meteoric iron. Figure 7.2f shows a panpipe recovered from the central altar of mound 3 at the Turner site (Willoughby and Hooton 1922:50).

According to Seeman (1979:327) panpipes are unique to Hopewell; they are not found in the Eastern Woodlands before or after Hopewell. Panpipes were apparently important to the Hopewell, however, given that more than seventy have been found at sites throughout the Hopewell Interaction Sphere (328). Of these seventy panpipes, eighteen were recovered from sites in the area of the Scioto Regional Tradition, the rest are from Copena, Santa Rosa–Swift Creek, Crab Orchard, and other areas. Since Seeman's report, additional panpipes have been found.

Discussion

From the physical evidence of rattles, tinklers, bangles, whistles, and panpipes, I think it is clear that Hopewell people made music, sang songs, and danced to the rhythm of musical instruments. Cross-culturally, music, songs, and dance accompany group-oriented rituals, especially those involving a transition from one state to another, such as initiation, marriage, healing, and mortuary services.[9] As Steven Mithen points out, throughout history, music-making has been "first and foremost a shared activity" (2006:205). For the shaman and audience, singing and dancing bring about changes in consciousness. As Ellen Basso explains,

> In such situations, a person feels, first, one with the group . . . and finally, there is a sense of "space without distinction of places" and "time in which past and future coexist within the present," that is, of the movement of tones which is music itself. (1985:254)

Additionally, though, singing, dancing, and music provide a means of communication not only with other humans but also with nonhuman listeners. Through singing and dancing, the shaman invokes and banishes spirits. In this sense, shamanic singing and dancing can be considered a special language—one that is understood by the spirits (Nettl 1956).

In summary, the shaman's songs, music, and dance have the power to link humans to the spirit world. From the evidence at hand, it appears that the Hopewell understood this, and, further, that they were quite proficient in the manufacture and use of these consciousness-altering devices.

Animal Transformations

In chapter 3, evidence was presented suggesting that the Hopewell had bear, deer, wolf, panther, and bird shamans. In chapter 5, it was suggested that one of the characteristics of the Hopewell universe was the predilection of things to transform or change appearance. Of interest to the present discussion is why Hopewell shamans—or any shaman, for that matter—might wish to transform into an animal.

The simplest answer is that shamans transform into animals in order to make use of the source animal's knowledge, attributes, and capabilities. Animals have special abilities that allow them to see, hear, and smell things beyond the reach of human senses. Consequently, they know things that humans do not. Animals also possess species-specific attributes—such as strength, cunning, and stealth—that can be useful for the shaman. And animals have the ability to go where humans cannot—underwater, underground, and across the sky. By identifying with or incorporating the spirit or power of an animal into his or her consciousness, the shaman is able to assimilate the capabilities and perspective of the source animal, thereby becoming something greater than human. By operation of conceptual blending and perspective shifting, the shaman becomes a were-animal.

Interestingly, there are people in Western society who experience were-animal transformations as real. According to Moselhy (1999), during these experiences, brain scans show changes in the region of the brain responsible for body image. More commonly, however, especially in shamanic cultures, psychoactive drugs are used to facilitate human to animal transformations. The question is: Why would Hopewell shamans want to change into or assimilate the perspective of bears, deer, birds, wolves, and panthers, specifically?

Were-Bears

Bears are represented in Hopewell contexts in copper, mica, and bone; in stone effigy pipes; and, most famously, in the Wray figurine. More than one thousand bear canine teeth have been recovered from Hopewell sites (Seeman 1979:372). Also found are multiple instances of bear mandibles and maxillae that have been polished, ground, and drilled for suspension. From these data it is obvious that the bear was of importance to the Hopewell.

Native Americans associate the bear with many things. Perhaps most revealing is that, based in his review of the ethnographic literature, researcher David Rockwell found that "[m]ost of the tribes in North America associated bears with curing" (1991:75). Rockwell (76–77) explains that for Native Americans, herbs and roots played an important role in the treatment of the sick and injured. For Native Americans, plants have the power to alleviate a wide variety of symptoms; thus plants hold the secrets to curing. Bears appear to know these secrets—that is, bears seem to know what plants are good to eat, where to find plant foods, and are often seen digging for edible roots. Many myths tell of Indians having learned the secrets of which plants are good for curing by watching bears.

Another common association for the bear is that of annual renewal, based in the animal's habit of hibernating through the winter. Buried deep in its den during the winter, the bear appears dormant. Each year at springtime, however, the bear is seemingly reborn as it emerges from its lowerworld den.

Bears have no natural enemies. They are intelligent, with good memories and keen senses. Moreover, they are at home in trees, caves, and water, as well as on land. For many North American and Eurasian peoples, the bear was considered the Master of Animals (Hollimon 2001:127; Hallowell 1926:62). In this role, bears are often associated with the lowerworld. In parts of Siberia, the bear was considered a mediator between the living and the dead (Hollimon 2001:127).

Among Native Americans, the size, strength, and hunting ability of the bear accounts for its being adopted by many as a protector and/or totem of warriors (Rockwell 1991:56). At the same time, however, the bear could also be associated with evil sorcery. Among the Ojibway, for example, there were sorcerers—known as Bearwalkers—who, in bear form, killed their enemies, robbed the graves of children at night, and feasted on the dead (Dewdney 1975:116–22).

For the Hopewell, given their emphasis on the collection of bear teeth, it may be that in certain contexts, the strength and power of the bear were important. Based on the occurrence of sucking or blowing tubes made from bear bones, discussed in chapter 6, the bear spirit may have played a role in Hopewell curing practices. It may also be that for the Hopewell, different species of bears—that is, brown and black bears—represented different capabilities and powers that could be utilized.

A clue as to why some Hopewell shamans might wish to transform into a bear is found in the Wray figurine. Presumably, as a function of his or her shaman status, the Wray figurine were-bear was able to move between this world and the Otherworld. Further, the Wray figurine were-bear is shown holding an upside-down human head. From this, as well as the ethnographic observation that bear shamans were sometimes considered mediators between the living and the dead, it may be that the Wray bear shaman was in some way engaged in the movement of the deceased to the Otherworld. In this case, transformation from human to bear may have facilitated the psychopomp role of the shaman.

Were-Deer

As a source of food, deer were of critical importance to many Native American peoples. In Eurasia, reindeer were important. Seldom, however, were deer valued only for their meat. The deer was almost universally associated with shamanism and was thought to have special abilities. Deer are known for their speed and agility, as well as their spectacular jumping abilities, and people in Siberia frequently ride reindeer. Thus, in northern Eurasia and also in North America, the deer is often considered the shaman's spirit mount that carries him or her to the Otherworld (Furst 1976b:170). In this context, the deer can be associated with either the upperworld or the lowerworld (La Barre 1970:176; Shirokogoroff 1935:295).

Deer are prolific breeders, with successful herds becoming quite large. Thus the deer is also associated with fecundity. According to Furst:

> Sometimes the supernatural deer is male—Deer as patron of hunting, for example,—sometimes female, as supernatural mistress of the species or even of all animals. . . . Deer ceremonials to obtain supernatural power and other benefits . . . from the spirit of a particular deer or from the species as a whole—are so widespread in North America as to be near universal, not only among hunters but among agricultural Indians as well. (1976b:166)

Association of the deer with fecundity is sometimes symbolically represented by reference to the male deer's annual growth of antlers (La Barre 1970:414). The deer sheds its antlers in autumn and re-grows them in spring. Thus the annual cycle of renewal is dramatically expressed in the deer's physical appearance. As Furst writes, "[I]t is the [deer] horn that since time immemorial has embodied the concept of supernatural power and eternal renewal" (170).

Given the explicit representation of antler growth stages found in Hopewell contexts (figures 3.1d and 4.26d), we can speculate that for the Hopewell, the deer was associated with regeneration, renewal, and fertility. If that was the case, then perhaps in their deer guises, Hopewell shamans were concerned with plant and animal fecundity.

Were-Raptors

The association of shamans with birds is common among indigenous peoples around the world (Eliade 1964:403). Perhaps the simplest explanation for this is that shamans use bird spirits to carry them in soul travels to the upperworld. As explained by Shirokogoroff (1935:296) with reference to Siberian shamans, the bird costume is used when shamans need a "light flying body" for travel to the sky world. From this it follows that avian representations are often used to symbolize shamanic soul flight. In these representations, human and avian elements are combined.

Among the Hopewell there is extensive evidence for human-to-bird transformations. As discussed earlier, bird headdresses and actual raptor heads, as well as interrelated bird talon and human hand design elements, are suggestive of transformation. So too, several Adena tablets show creatures that are part human and part bird (also see Webb and Baby 1957:83–95; Otto 1975a; Romain 1991b; Carr and Case 2005b).

Lewis-Williams and Pearce (2005) suggest that sensations of flight are often experienced during altered states of consciousness. These sensations include the feeling of moving or flying through a tunnel or vortex to another world. Thus there is an association between altered states of consciousness, flight, and bird symbolism. From this it is reasonable to conclude that Hopewell bird shamans, who either incorporate bird symbolism in their costumes or are depicted as part bird and part human, were involved in shamanic soul flight.

Were-Wolves and Were-Panthers

In chapter 3, evidence was presented suggestive of were-wolf and were-panther transformations. It is difficult to know what attributes Hopewell shamans might wish to gain when assimilating their spirits or transforming into these animals. Historically, though, in the Eastern Woodlands, both wolves and panthers had hunter and warrior associations, with the added association of close social bonding in the case of the wolf and sorcery in the case of the panther.

What is impressive about the were-wolf evidence is the personal commitment Adena shamans made in furtherance of their transformations. As will be recalled from chapter 3, several wolf shamans apparently had their front teeth removed so that a wolf maxilla could be inserted into the space where their teeth had been.

Of course, it could be argued that the Adena wolf-persons were not shamans, but rather wolf clan warriors or some other such role. In either case, however, what we have in these occurrences are dramatic examples of conceptual blending in which wolf and human attributes are combined to form anomalous and liminal creatures. For the individuals who underwent these operations, whatever their social role, human-to-animal transformation was not a casual matter. In these examples, we have dramatic evidence for the belief that human and animal body parts were interchangeable. Moreover, it is clear that these persons lived with the effects of their transformations throughout the course of their daily lives. These were not part-time or casual shamans.

Guardian Spirits and Spirit Helpers

Beliefs about guardian spirits vary among peoples. In general, however, guardian spirits provide protection as well as conferring special powers or abilities to the individual. Guardian spirits are most often obtained through vision quests and dreams, but may also be purchased, inherited, or adopted (Benedict 1923:19). Guardian spirits are almost always animals; however, they can also assume human form during a vision or dream. Often, the guardian spirit represents the collective spirit of an entire animal species, thereby giving the guardian spirit extraordinary capabilities. Thus, calling upon one's guardian spirit, who happens to be a wolf, empowers one with the special abilities of the collective Wolf spirit.

Spirit helpers are a bit different from guardian spirits. While most shamans have one guardian spirit, a powerful shaman can have dozens—or even hundreds—of spirit helpers. Spirit helpers are generally limited in their role and are dismissed once they have performed some specific task. Spirit helpers protect, provide knowledge, and otherwise assist the shaman. Spirit helpers can be ancestors, dead enemy warriors, or spirits of plants, mushrooms, particular mountains, bodies of water, or even the Four Directions. Usually, however, they are animals. Animals are typically enlisted as spirit helpers because they possess abilities and powers not available to humans. Thus, when shamans require more than their own power to cure, hunt, foresee the future, or perform some other task, they can supplement their personal power with the power gained from a spirit helper. An example is provided by Joan Vastokas with reference to the Goldi shamans of Siberia:

> The shaman's journey to the Underworld is most perilous; only the shaman may go there and return. He must travel over high mountains, through dense forests, across wide rivers, lakes and treacherous swamps, and is only able to do so with the aid of his spirit helpers. He flies through the air on the back of a mythical bird, Koori; tigers help him through the woods, while lizards, snakes, and toads aid his passage across lakes and swamps. (1977:98)

Given their cross-cultural ubiquity and reported occurrence among Historic period Native American peoples, it is likely that the Hopewell utilized both guardian spirits and spirit helpers.

Wolf Guardian Spirit

At least one case suggests that the wolf served as a guardian spirit for a Hopewell individual. The case in point is found outside of Ohio. It occurs in connection with burial 1 in mound 5 at the Lawrence Gay Mounds site, in Pike County, Illinois. Burial 1 was an adult male. The skull of this individual had been painted with red ocher. Among the objects found with the burial were two platform pipes, three antler points, and three knapping tools made of antler. The most interesting item, however, was what appears to have been a medicine bag. Archaeologist Gregory Perino describes the bag and its contents as follows:

> A pouch or bag once lay to the left of the skull. All that remained of the bag was a black powder . . . in which were the following artifacts: 17 obsidian flakes struck from a large blade; two sections of a cut, undrilled wolf mandible ornament; a turkey claw; 19 unfired, yellow clay beads 7/16 inch [1.1 cm] in diameter covered with pulverized mica; a small conch shell; and toe bones of a wolf. (2006:514–20)

Virtually every item in this bag is unusual in its own right. Historically, turkey claws were sometimes attached to dance sticks. The conch shell was perhaps used to drink special concoctions. The black obsidian flakes had their origin in a far distant source and provide a color and texture contrast to the rounded clay beads covered with silvery mica. The wolf mandible and toe bones, however, are of special interest. Seemingly emphasized by their collection are the two most representative parts of the wolf: its powerful canine jaws and paws. I would propose that together, the wolf jaw and paw embodied the spirit of the Wolf. If this interpretation is correct, then in this medicine bag we have suggestive evidence for the Wolf as a guardian spirit.

Avian Spirit Helpers

As discussed earlier, in the North Benton mound, two extended burials were found on the wings of the raptor effigy located at the base of the mound. A human female extended across the north wing, while a human male extended across the south wing. In this case, it is tempting to speculate that perhaps the raptor was intended to carry the souls of the deceased to the Otherworld. If that was the case, then the North Benton mound provides an example of a spirit helper.

A second case concerns a triple burial found in mound 3 of the Gibson Mound Group in Illinois (Parmalee and Perino 1971). In this instance, the skeleton of a roseate spoonbill (*Ajaia ajaja*) was found laid out alongside a human child. Equidistant from the child on the other side was an elderly male person. What is intriguing is that the bird had been decapitated; its head was not found in the grave. Given this, it may be that the bird was sacrificed so that it could carry or guide the deceased to the Otherworld. This interpretation finds support in the comments of Converse (1908:96), who notes that among certain Native American peoples, it was the custom to kill a bird over the grave of the deceased in the belief that the bird's spirit would transport the deceased to the Otherworld.

Effigy Pipes

Effigy pipes are one of the defining attributes of Hopewell. Figures 7.3a and 7.3b show two examples of Hopewell effigy pipes, recovered, in this case, from the Tremper site. What make Hopewell effigy pipes special are the exquisitely carved likenesses of animals carved on the pipes' bowls.[10] Flying creatures represented in the sculpted designs include hawks, falcons, owls, ducks, herons, cranes, and others. Four-legged earth walkers include squirrels, raccoons, rabbits, wolves, bears, panthers, opossums, and others. Swimming creatures include otters, beavers, and turtles. Jumpers include frogs and toads. Crawlers include a very few snakes.

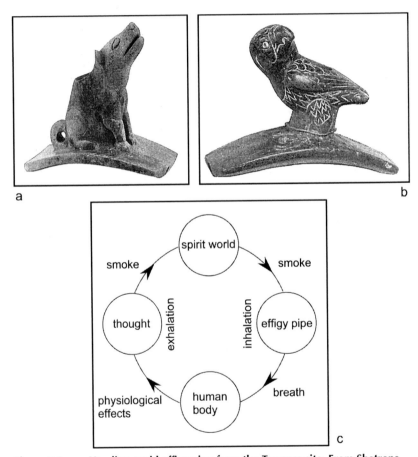

a   b

c

Figure 7.3.   a. Howling canid effigy pipe from the Tremper site. From Shetrone 1930:69. b. Bird effigy smoking pipe from Tremper site. From Shetrone 1930:fig. 96. c. Hypothetical representation of the process underlying effigy pipe smoking. Drawing by William Romain.

The idea that Hopewell effigy pipes might represent spirit helpers, spirit guardians, or personal tutelaries has been proposed by others (e.g., Penny 1989:194; Cowan 1996:134; Brown 2006:481–82; also see von Gernet and Timmins 1987). Support for this idea is found in the observation that the creatures on most Hopewell effigy pipes face the smoker. As pointed out by Brown, the result was that when smoking an effigy pipe, the smoker would have been "eye-to-eye—with the effigy animal" (2006:481). Along similar lines, I note that many of the animals shown on the effigy pipes are depicted in a seated position—perhaps analogically equivalent to two persons in a relaxed setting sitting across from one another when communicating.

Based on ethnographic data from Iroquoian and Algonkian tribes, it is archaeologist Ted Brasser's (1980:96) opinion that self-directed effigy pipes served as "mental devices" to concentrate the smoker's thoughts on the represented effigy. Both Brown and Brasser's ideas make sense. To fully understand how Hopewell effigy pipes relate to spirit helpers, however, we need to explore one more concept: the phenomenon of breath.

In most Native American traditions, breath is associated with the soul and life (Hultzkrantz 1953:180–87; Saunders 2004:135). Breath is the animating aspect of living things. Breath is the essence of life. Life stops when breathing stops. According to Smith (1992:59), many Native American peoples have a single word that means breath, life, and wind. Among the Cheyenne, for example, the word *taxtavoom* means breath, air, and wind, and it is that essence that animates physical life (Schlesier 1987:6). Among the Creek Indians, the Master of Breath was the supreme power in the cosmos (Swanton 1928).

In most Native American belief systems, objects such as smoking pipes are believed to have their own spirit, or life essence. Applying these observations to the typical Hopewell effigy pipe, we note that a hollow cavity courses through the effigy creature's body as created by the bowl and stem. The result is that when the smoker inhales, he or she is causing the breath/smoke to flow from the outside world, down into and through the effigy animal's body, and into the smoker himself. By causing the flow of breath through the animal effigy, the smoker metaphorically gives "life" to the effigy and at the same time incorporates the breath or life essence of the effigy animal into his own body. The life forces are commingled. This hypothetical process is represented in figure 7.3c.

In figure 7.3c, pipe smoke embodies the spirit essence of the Otherworld. As the smoke is drawn down through the pipe effigy, the animal spirit is selected for—let us say, in this case, the hawk. As the smoker inhales, the Hawk spirit smoke is combined with the human breath. The Hawk spirit smoke and human breath merge in the body and mind of the smoker, so that

Hawk spirit and human are combined. By operation of the pipe smoker's focus on the effigy, as well as the physiological effects of the substance being smoked, the merging of hawk and human intensifies with each successive breath. What is being assimilated by the smoker is not the personality of a particular hawk, but rather the "spirit" or representative characteristics of the hawk species. In the exhalation phase, the thoughts or prayers of the smoker-human-hawk are carried to the spirit world. If the substance being smoked has hallucinogenic properties—such as *Nicotiana rustica*, then presumably the smoker-shaman would be able to intentionally direct his or her soul flight to the spirit world.

In the hypothetical process just described, we have a conceptual blend of human and effigy animal. The emergent result is that the smoker has become something more than human, something more than animal.

With reference, then, to Hopewell pipes, depending on which animal effigy was selected, the smoker-shaman would have been able to assimilate all manner of useful attributes (Brown 2006:482). The ability to fly, obtained from the hawk and other bird effigies, would be useful for traveling to the upperworld. The abilities of the squirrel might be useful for gaining a better vantage. Swimming abilities possessed by otters, beavers, and frogs might be useful for journeying to the lowerworld. Powers of the owl and raccoon might be useful for stealth movements, night vision, and so on.

If Hopewell effigy pipes were used in this way, that might account for the variety of species represented. Depending on the requirements of the task to be undertaken, a Hopewell shaman could have drawn from a repertoire of spirit helpers, as represented by the different pipes. This might also account for the observation that there seems to have been a selection preference for mostly social animals. What we find represented in the Hopewell effigy pipes are birds, bears, otters, beavers, and others. Few snakes are included in the menagerie, and no insects whatsoever. After all, who wants to mind-meld with a bug—even if there is an equivalency among life forces?

Summary

From the data presented in this chapter, I do not think there is any doubt that the Hopewell used altered states of consciousness, animal transformations, and spirit helpers to interact with the Otherworld. Music, dance, and psychotropic substances were part of Hopewell life. So too, were-bears, were-panthers, and were-wolves moved among the people. In the Hopewell world, things were not always as they seemed. As demonstrated by Hopewell designs, first appearances could be deceiving.

Physical evidence for the use of musical instruments—and, by implication, dance—is clear. Undoubtedly, tobacco was smoked. Most likely it was mixed with other plant substances. If, as suggested, conch shells were use for drinking black drink, then, based on the number of shells found, it would appear that concoction was a favorite drink.

Physical evidence shows that in at least one instance, mushrooms were important enough to make a special effigy wand and situate it in a central location in a burial mound. As suggested, it is likely that Hopewell shamans used mushrooms for their mind-altering effects.

Multiple lines of evidence indicate that shamanic trances and interaction with the Otherworld were of considerable importance. Manifestations of altered states are widespread throughout Hopewell and are reflected in design motifs involving flight and human-to-animal transformations, in physical evidence for psychoactive substance use, and in rhythmic dancing to percussion instruments. What is impressive is the repertoire of techniques the Hopewell used to interact with the spirit world. This repertoire can be described as a continuum. Depending on the desired result, Hopewell shamans could bring about mild states of altered consciousness through the drinking of black drink and rhythmic dancing. Or they could significantly increase the depth of trance through tobacco smoking. When a strong visual component was required, the eating of hallucinogenic mushrooms provided a way to intensify interaction with spirit beings and soul travel to the Otherworld. In their ability to manipulate of states of consciousness, Hopewell shamans appear to have been masters.

CHAPTER EIGHT

Afterword

The phenomenon that was Hopewell represents a "lost world"—a world that has, in large measure, been erased by time and faded from memory. Thus Hopewell is mostly unknown territory. What I have offered in the preceding pages is not a map, but rather a sketch of that territory—an outline, if you will—limited to a few structural components. Others will view the same territory and draw a different picture. No matter how careful the explorer, however, what sketches reveal are unknown areas and gaps in our knowledge. Not discussed in the present study, for example, were matters of religious training and initiation. Nor were the roles of prayer, vision questing, and dreaming discussed. There simply are no data I am aware of that provide insight into these areas. Only the dimmest of outlines is visible with regard to Hopewell mythology. No insights into any moral code associated with Hopewell shamanism were gleaned from the archaeological record. Nor are we ever likely to know much about the spiritual experiences of individual people of the Hopewell culture. Like mapmakers of old, the best we can do is fill in these empty spaces with informed conjecture.

In truth, however, that is the nature of archaeology. Archaeology is not a science, like mathematics, where every problem has an answer and answers are precise. We must admit that in some cases, we may never know the answers. There is no cosmic mandate that by cleverness or diligence scientists can come to know everything. As evolutionary psychologists Leda Cosmides and John Tooby point out, "[T]here is no warrant for thinking that [natural] selection would have favored cognitive mechanisms that are well-engineered for solving classes of problems beyond those encountered by Pleistocene hunter-gatherers" (1994:87).

Since archaeologists were not present during the events that shaped the past, the best we can do is to ask whether the evidence at hand tends to support or weaken the idea under consideration. Using that criterion as a compass, future explorers will continue to make new and exciting discoveries that better delineate the territory outlined herein.

There is a positive side to offering a sketch, however. Sketches are similar to models, and models can be used to assess multiple data sets. So in the case of the shamanic worldview model, it might prove interesting to apply it to other places and other times. I wonder, for example, what aspects of the shamanic worldview model would be most strongly supported by archaeological data from ancient Egypt, Mesopotamia, or predynastic China? In what manner would we find core elements of the archetypal shamanic worldview represented?

Identifying prehistoric expressions of the shamanic worldview, however, is only part of the story. Increasingly it is becoming clear that if we wish to understand—if we truly want to know just what sort of creature we are—then, as anthropologists and archaeologists, we need to look deeper into ourselves and integrate theories and data from the cognitive sciences into our hypotheses and interpretations. Undoubtedly, initial efforts will provide ample opportunity for embarrassment and mistakes. Ultimately, however, archaeology and anthropology will benefit in extraordinary ways from such collaborations.

To return to the Hopewell, I think it is virtually certain that shamanic beliefs permeated Hopewell life. For the Hopewell, this meant there was little or no separation between religious worldview and everyday life, and that, in daily life, Hopewell people were ever mindful of the spirit world around them. We can imagine that to drink from a stream meant to partake of the life force of the river. To hunt and eat required ritual preparation and favor of the animal spirits. To cut from the forest involved requests, permissions, and thanks to the spirit entities. To mold the earth into vessels or monumental earthworks was to facilitate the transformation of life force from one form to another.

In these thought-guided actions and the material evidence left behind, the Hopewells' vision of the universe is reflected in a set of recurring themes. These themes are the common heritage of humankind and comprise the archetypal shamanic worldview.

Arguably, shamanism in its various forms reflects humankind's oldest expression of religious belief. Certain of its core elements are visible by at least

50,000 B.C.—or roughly forty-eight thousand years earlier than Christianity, Buddhism, or any of the world's other major religions. We might ask why that is.

The answer, I think, has several interrelated parts. First, shamanism corresponds to the world as humans perceive it. There really does seem to be a dual aspect to the cosmos as evidenced by Self and Everything Else. So too, as far as our senses tell us, the world really is vertically layered into earth, sky, and water. And there are four horizontal directions, as our bodies confirm: left, right, front, back. The world is indeed cyclic in its alternation of night and day, winter and summer, life and death. And there truly is a hidden aspect to things, as evidenced by the myriad of unseen forces that act upon us. At the same time, everything seems to have its own spirit or inner essence that defines what it is like to be that thing. So too, the world is a place of metamorphosis and transformation. All around us, things change as they move through their respective life cycles. Lastly, the world really is a predatory place where the rule is eat or be eaten.

Shamanism also endures because it seems to work. Earlier I mentioned the behavior of pigeons as they danced in ritualized patterns in the hope of food pellets from heaven. Our own thought processes are not much different. We think our shamanic rituals work because sometimes there happens to be a correspondence between our ritual movements and events in the real world.

Who can deny, too, that shamanism just feels good. By operation of rituals that incorporate rhythmic movement, auditory driving, psychotropic drugs, and other mind-altering techniques, we are able to voluntarily change our brain chemistry with the result that we feel a sense of oneness with the universe and people around us. Through activation or stimulation of various brain cells, we feel "at home in the universe." Through changes in our brain chemistry brought about by shamanic rituals, we find resolutions to the paradoxes and problems of existence.

Equally important, shamanism provides a myth telling us we are special, that the universe is stable and orderly, that it has meaning, and that we play an important role in that meaning. Who does not feel special in the sense of being at the center of time and space? Indeed, by operation of our mind-brain's agency detection tools, we are compelled to believe that anything showing signs of order or movement has a teleological purpose and hence, meaning. And, as the research of psychologist Deborah Kelemen (1999) demonstrates and as aptly summarized by Tremlin, "We seem to want to see things as being the way they are for specific reasons rather than as the result of random chance" (2006:102). In this, we believe we are not alone in the universe, that gods and spirits are our companions, and that we play a participatory role in the purpose of the universe.

Lastly, shamanism provides a story telling us that we live in a universe that accommodates our continued existence. If the shamanic world is one of spirits and souls, then death has no hold over us. Thus shamanism provides a positive and hopeful alternative to death and extinction.

Unfortunately, the archetypal shamanic worldview in its various iterations probably does not correspond to the structure and workings of the universe as it might appear from a God's-eye view. Rather, the shamanic worldview describes the universe as seen through the mind-brains of humans. This is to be expected, given that natural selection has equipped us with the mental tools we need to survive in the particular kind of world in which we find ourselves. In every sense, therefore, shamanism is contingent on our embodiment in the world. As emphasized throughout the preceding pages, shamanism is a worldview that is constrained by the operation of our mind-brains, the physical limitations of our bodies, and the nature of the world around us. At the same time, it is a worldview that is primed by adaptive behaviors initiated long ago by our evolutionary predecessors. The creatures and worlds of the shamanic worldview—ghosts and spirits, thunderbirds and serpents—are things of our imagination, created through the attribution of intentional agency, conceptual blending, and other mind-brain operations.

Moreover, shamanism is humancentric. Born out of human activities, its focus is on the needs and desires of humans. I would venture to guess that more cumulative prayer time has been spent petitioning the gods for salvation from hell than has ever been devoted to asking that the suffering of nonhuman creatures be relieved.

Ultimately, the reason the shamanic worldview endures—even today, in the guise of modern religions—is because as humans, we share with our earliest ancestors the same basic mind-brain-body relationships to the real world that generated the shamanic worldview in the first place.

We are the creators of the gods and goddesses, spirits and monsters that dance through the shamanic worldview. As the result of how our mind-brains are structured and function, our gods, spirits, and monsters bear distinct resemblances to ourselves in their physical attributes and social relationships. In an interesting twist to things, we are self-organized matter that has evolved the capacity to invent the imaginary worlds and imaginary beings that we presume to interact with.

We are each nodes of matter and energy that have become self-aware. Human awareness, however, is a double-edged sword that brings with it the intuition that there are unseen forces and entities that cause all manner of bad things, including suffering, disease, and death. The result, as Eleanor Ott explains, is that

> all people share basic human needs for the nourishment and well-being of the body, mind, and spirit. So long as these aspects of life remain ephemeral and uncertain, there will always be a place for the person who can provide relief from the illnesses, pains, and insecurities that humans suffer. (2001 [1995]:285)

And so it is that, as long as by operation of our mind-brains humans imagine monsters and devils in the shadows, there will always be shamans and Shaman-priests to step forward and engage. It's in our nature; it's in our biogenetic makeup. It's who we are.

Notes

Chapter 1: Introduction

1. Ludwig provides the classic definition for the phrase *altered states of consciousness*:

> any mental state(s), induced by various physiological, psychological, or pharmacological maneuvers or agents, which can be recognized subjectively by the individual himself (or by an objective observer of the individual) as representing a sufficient deviation, in subjective experience or psychological functioning from certain general norms for that individual during alert, waking consciousness. (1969:11)

2. Complicating the matter is that traditionally, many Native Americans who are not shamans engage in many of the same practices as shamans (e.g., acquisition of a guardian spirit, vision questing, altered states to contact spirits).

Chapter 2: Theoretical Background and Methods

1. The phrase *biogenetically generated shamanic worldview* is similar in meaning to the phrase *neurologically generated worldview* used by Lewis-Williams and Pearce (2005:122)—except that *biogenetically generated* is intended to be more explicit with regard to the cognitive evolutionary basis of the worldview.

2. Although I have relied on a number of authorities in developing this model, many of its key attributes are directly attributable to Mircea Eliade. Eliade is widely recognized as an expert in the history of religions. A number of specialists, however, have been critical of Eliade (e.g., Bahn 2001:55–56; Balzer 1997:47–48; Kehoe 2000; Lawson and McCauley 1990:13; also see Rennie 1996:179–212). Criticisms range

from assertions that his ideas are inadequately grounded in empirical data to charges that his model of shamanism is too static and lacks historical context.

I am not an apologist for Eliade. Indeed, I recognize that there are problems with aspects of his work. I agree with Bloch (1992:3), for example, that the "character of his archetypes . . . [are] vague and mystical." Unfortunately, Eliade did not have the benefit of recent findings in cognitive neuroscience—which, I propose, anchor several of his archetypes in mind-brain structures and operations common to all humans.

In any case, Eliade's explication of several key attributes of the shamanic world-view remains a valuable contribution. Among these attributes are the *axis mundi*, layered cosmos, cyclic time and eternal return, initiatory dismemberment, and soul flight to the upper and lower worlds. Several of these attributes—especially as found in indigenous Siberian cultures, were identified earlier by others. It was Eliade, however, who presented the case that these attributes are universal to shamanism.

3. Several terms are conceptually related to animism, including panpsychism, hylozoism, pantheism, panentheism, and panexperientialism. David Skrbina (2005:19–22) provides a useful explanation for each. In animistic belief, things such as lakes, trees, mountains, and other material objects are believed to possess a spirit. Typically, spirits have humanlike personalities and qualities, including intelligence, emotion, memory, and intention.

4. Assertions are sometimes made that there are nonshamanic indigenous cultures (e.g., Francfort 2001:37). The assertion is also sometimes made that certain religions—such as Buddhism, for example—are not shamanic.

I do not find these arguments compelling. All religions exhibit core attributes of the archetypal shamanic worldview including but not limited to a layered cosmos, belief in nonhuman counterintuitive agents or forces that can effect changes in the visible world (including spirits, gods, or karma), and use of altered states of consciousness to contact counterintuitive agents and realities (including psychotropic substances, prayer, meditation, fasting, and so on).

Chapter 3: Hopewell Shamans

1. Archaeologist Bradley Lepper (2005) finds that the illusion of bear-to-human transformation can also be caused by pitching the Wray figurine up and down. Thus the transformation illusion can be effected in multiple ways.

2. Of course, the avian symbols could be clan symbols, identifying the burials as belonging to a raptor clan. Even if that were the case, however, the size and shape relationships between the mica hand and claw suggest an equivalency between life forms and fluidity of outward shape suggestive of the capabilities exhibited by bird shamans who might also be clan leaders.

3. Carr and Case (2005a:figure 1.3 caption) state that the paw print is that of a cat. I do not agree. My opinion is that a canine paw print is shown. Felines have retractable claws. As a result, their claws' impressions do not show up in their paw prints or tracks. Canines, on the other hand, do not have retractable claws. Their

tracks show claw impressions. Since the copper headdress paw print shows claws, my assessment is that it represents a canine paw print.

4. Animal disguises, including wolf and deer, were sometimes used by Native Americans for hunting purposes (e.g., Pickett 1962 [1851]:69). Based on this, it may be that the idea of human to animal transformation had its origins, in part, in hunting strategies involving animal disguises that evolved deep in our past.

The idea of human to animal transformation may also have developed from our early experiences wearing animal furs or skins as protection against the sun, cold, wind, insects, and brush. From wearing a favorite wolf, bear, or other fur, the mental leap would not have been very great in thinking that by wearing a fur, one might take on not only the source animal's appearance, but also its other attributes.

5. In this and similar instances, red ocher may have been used to vivify or imbue the consecrated object or bones with the essence of life as incorporated in blood and symbolized by the color red.

Chapter 4: Hopewell Cosmology: Part I

1. Thought of in another way, the human organism differentiates between self and nonself. The reason this differentiation is necessary in the first place is explained by d'Aquili and Newberg:

> It is likely a fundamental need of animals to recognize self from nonself at least in some form since this lies at the heart of behaviors such as finding food, mating, and avoiding danger. . . . [I]f everything is perceived as self, then the organism would never eat, try to mate, or avoid danger because it obviously would have no reason to do this. If the organism ate, it would be eating itself. In such a case, all dangers would be perceived only as an extension of self and would not need to be avoided. . . . [T]he organism would have similar difficulties if it had the opposite perception such that nothing is self. In this case there is no self to feed, no self to take care of, and no self to live. Thus this ability to resonate with oneself to develop an awareness of self as distinct from nonself is highly adaptive and absolutely necessary for survival. (1999:63)

2. The Gaitskill stone tablet is about 4 inches (10.2 cm) in length and 3 inches (7.6 cm) in width (Webb and Baby 1957:82). The design carved into the tablet is done in bas-relief. If the Gaitskill stone tablet image is rotated and placed next to the Rutledge copper piece, an interesting set of correspondences result. The shape of the head is the same for both the Gaitskill tablet creature and the Rutledge salamander. The eyes of the creatures are shaped the same, and the position of the eyes on both heads is nearly identical. Both creatures have four toes on each of their feet. And in both cases, the feet and toes extend in such a way as to frame the head. On the Rutledge salamander, external plumelike gills are located behind the front legs; similar features are located just behind the front legs on the Gaitskill tablet creature. In sum, these correspondences suggest that the creature represented in the Gaitskill tablet is also a salamander.

What makes the correspondences between these two pieces more remarkable is that the Gaitskill stone tablet was found in an Adena mound in Mount Sterling, Kentucky, while the Rutledge copper salamander piece is from a presumed Hopewell mound in central Ohio. (But see Morton and Carskadden [1983] for a discussion of how artifacts and burials associated with the Rutledge mound show Adena attributes.) Given that the salamander motif is represented in the same way in both contexts, it is likely that the creature held similar meanings for the two geographically separated groups.

3. When looking at the Turner turtle and other pieces, we need to keep in mind that there is no requirement that Hopewell designs conform to our sense of reality or expectations about what an animal "should" look like. Indigenous designs reflect the world as the design creator wishes to show it, subject to the stylistic conventions of his or her society, not ours.

Hopewell designs often combine body parts in ways that defy natural order. What is intriguing about the Hopewell fragmented design technique is that it provides an unexpected way of seeing a subject. We are shown the subject—whether turtle, deer, wolf, or other creature, not from the limited perspective afforded by normal vision; rather, we see simultaneous and multiple fragmented views of the subject. We are, in effect, presented with a view of the subject as it might appear in another reality. It may be that this perspective is based in a real psychological effect.

What I mean is this: In the Turner turtle and several other designs discussed later, the subject's body parts are disjointed and fragmented. This way of viewing things is remarkably reminiscent of the "fragmentation" noted by Lewis-Williams and Dowson (1988), Whitley (2005:112), and others as one of the characteristics of trance imagery. That is, during certain altered states, things sometimes appear to break up into their constituent parts. Hallucinogenic drugs, in particular, trigger this effect. Given this, it may be that certain Hopewell designs (e.g., Turner turtle, Hopewell deer, Cincinnati wolf) were inspired by the appearance of things during hallucinogenic states.

Another remarkable thing about Hopewell designs is that, from large-scale earthworks to small-scale engravings, Hopewell designs reflect a sophisticated ability to manipulate shapes in mental space. In addition to multiple meanings, Hopewell designers apparently felt at ease in their use of rotated images, simultaneous views, and conflated images in addition to fragmented views. Considered in this context, the fragmented perspective offered by the Turner turtle is simply another design expression drawn from a wide range of available techniques.

4. Alternatively, Greber and Ruhl (2000:221) and Trevelyan (2004:263) argue that the outline of the copper piece resembles a deer ear. There are problems with the deer ear interpretation, however. First, if a deer ear was intended, then we might expect to find a second copper ear, since ears occur in pairs. No second ear was ever found. Further, the deer ear interpretation fails to account for the copper forked "tongue" elements found in the same mound.

Also, as can be seen in representations of deer ears elsewhere in this chapter, deer ears are not symmetrically shaped. Serpent heads, on the other hand, are quite symmetrical in top view—as is the copper piece.

5. As to why the head and tongue pieces might be separately fashioned and then placed together to form a composite image, it may be that the intention was to provide flexibility to the design. By making the design in two separate pieces, the resulting figure would be able to bend along with whatever supporting material it was attached to. A one-piece rendering would be more likely to break or be ripped from the underlying material when flexed. It may also be that the head and tongue pieces were made separately so that when the underlying material moved, the copper serpent's tongue would also move, thereby imitating the flickering of a snake's tongue in life.

Occasionally it is argued that because several "tongue" elements—but only one serpent head—were found, the forked copper designs must not be tongues (Ruhl, in Greber and Ruhl 2000:121). While we cannot know exactly why the Hopewell designer made additional tongue elements, one possibility is that the multiple tongue elements were intended to represent multiple directions, as might correspond, for example, to the four-armed cross in the center of the serpent's head. Also important to note is that the posited tongue elements correspond in shape and proportion to real serpent tongues—an observation not otherwise accounted for by Ruhl.

6. Greber and Ruhl's (2000:221) interpretation again differs from mine in that they see a bear's face in the internal design. I see a panther. Several features support the panther interpretation. In the copper piece, the eyes of the posited panther are quite large. Compared to the overall size of their heads, bears have proportionately smaller eyes. The proportionate size of the copper eye elements therefore seems to be a better match to the panther than bear.

It is also the case that bears do not have distinguishing markings on their face. Panthers, on the other hand, have prominent face markings. These markings are black, contrasting with their tawny fur. The black face markings on panthers occur on both sides of the muzzle and extend from the upper area of the muzzle down toward the mouth. In the copper piece, there are two more-or-less teardrop-shaped design elements on each side of the muzzle. These design elements correspond to the facial markings on panthers in life (cf. figures 4.12d and 4.12e).

7. In both the panther and owl designs, eye elements seem emphasized. As to why this might be the case, it may be relevant that both the owl and panther are well adapted to nighttime hunting. Both have excellent night vision—far better than humans. Part of the reason for this enhanced night vision is that owls and panthers have a reflective layer behind the retinas of their eyes called the *tapetum lucidum*. The *tapetum lucidum* reflects light back through the retina, causing it to strike additional sensory cells in the retina. As light is reflected off the *tapetum lucidum*, the panther's and owl's eyes appear to glow. Seeing these glowing eyes at night would undoubtedly have been an impressive sight and may account for their emphasis in the copper piece.

8. Brose, Brown, and Penny (1985:203) give the dimensions of the bird effigy shown in figure 4.10a as 21.9 cm (8.62 inches) in length and 9 cm (3.54 inches) in height. According to Field Museum collections assistant Daniela Bono (personal communication, July 11, 2006), the copper fish shown in figure 4.10b (Field Museum accession #56174) is 21 cm (8.26 inches) in length by 10.2 cm (4 inches) in width. In figure 4.10c, I have made the images to the proportionate sizes provided by Brose, Brown, Penny and Bono.

9. It is interesting to note how this image supports J. L. Barrett's observation that when humans imagine a "new" animal from another world, "the 'new' animal carries basic features of the concept 'animal.' New animals look suspiciously like old ones, having properties such as bilateral symmetry, eyes, limbs, etc., that are assumptions of the organizing concept" (1997:136).

10. Among the Cheyenne, the lowerworld was thought to begin where the roots of trees and grass end (Schlesier 1987:6). Hopewell burial mound construction practices may incorporate a similar belief. In the case of mound 7, for example, as well as other mounds and earthen structures where the original topsoil layer has been removed, the intent may have been to provide direct physical contact with "deep earth," or the lowerworld (also see Charles, Van Nest, and Buikstra [2004], who propose the same thing for Illinois Hopewell). Subsequent to the last burials within Hopewell wooden structures used to hold the dead, those structures were burned and buried beneath layers of earth, sand, and gravel. Upon final capping of the resulting burial mound, the contents of the mound would have been merged with the deep earth, or the lowerworld.

11. The azimuths of 59°.7, 122°.3, 237°.7, and 300°.3 are calculated for the area of Chillicothe using a horizon elevation of 1°.0, center of the sun, for the year A.D. 100. Because the declination of the sun changes so slowly over the course of thousands of years, for a naked-eye observer, the sun would have appeared to rise and set in virtually the same place on the horizon during the entire Hopewell episode.

12. I suspect that Hopewell copper plates comprised the core elements of sacred bundles. Historically, sacred bundles were typically made of organic material such as animal skin, feathers, or woven plant material. Wrapped or contained within the bundle were selected objects having spiritual significance. Historically known medicine bundles have been found to contain projectile points, shells, crystals, beads, fossil teeth, seeds, bird beaks, as well as special rocks and minerals. Some contained metal plates (e.g., Pickett 1962 [1851]:82; Howard 1968:68–69). Sacred bundles generally belong to a tribe, lineage, or clan, although the care and protection of the bundle is often entrusted to one individual as its Keeper. Sacred bundles are believed to possess intrinsic power that provides spiritual protection and well-being for the group.

In the case of Hopewell copper plates, from their raptor and solar associations I suspect they were power objects—perhaps intended to gather and manipulate, in their reflective brilliance, sunlight, or upperworld forces. Manipulated in just the right way, perhaps during public ceremonies, the plates would give the shaman the apparent ability to bring the upperworld power of the sun down to earth.

13. Please note: I am not proposing that the Mound City raptor plate, Hopewell site raptor talon plate, or any other copper pieces were used as astronomical sighting devices. They simply incorporate solstice azimuths in much the same way that we might incorporate the cardinal directions in a contemporary drawing or design.

14. My decision to use the replica bald eagle talon for these comparisons was constrained by the availability of replicas. Available options included the bald eagle, golden eagle, red-tailed hawk, and peregrine falcon. Comparison of the bald eagle and peregrine falcon talon reveal that once the size difference between the two is equalized, both talons have essentially identical shape and curvature.

Given that the raptors shown in the Mound City plates lack the peregrine falcon's distinctive eye markings, I think it is likely that eagles are represented in this particular plate. Of the available eagle talons, only the bald eagle (*Haliaeetus leucocephalus*) is native to Ohio. In fact, during early pioneer days in Ohio, the bald eagle was fairly common. Although dwindling in numbers, small populations are still found along the Scioto, Muskingum, and Ohio rivers. Bald eagle remains have been found in Illinois Hopewell contexts (Parmalee 2006:233).

15. The stone outline of the center stone circle and mounds that make up the North Fort Square have been restored. For reasons discussed elsewhere (Romain 2004b), however, it appears that what we see at ground level today accurately reflects their original location.

16. In the present study, the terms *periodic* and *cyclic* are used interchangeably, with the understanding that for time to be considered cyclic, "all that is necessary is that the phases of a process should be both distinguished from one another, and identified with the equivalent phases of the same process in previous and subsequent cycles" (Gell 1992:33).

17. As explained by Jones (1976), in a world where things move in rhythmic cycles, it is preferable for creatures that have nervous systems to entrain their internal body rhythms to the rhythms of the outside world. This allows the individual to track changes and movement in the world, anticipate its next cyclic movement, and act accordingly.

Chapter 5: Hopewell Cosmology: Part II

1. In a similar explanation, Baron-Cohen (1995:31–58) describes four interrelated modules or mechanisms: the Intentionality Detector, Eye Direction Detector, Shared Attention Mechanism, and Theory of Mind Mechanism. Together, these mechanisms compel us to interpret motion in terms of agent goals and desires.

2. Forward-facing human ears are also prominently represented in the Low tablet. The Low tablet (Otto 1975a, 1975b) features two mirror images of a human face, each with huge ears that seem to be taking on characteristics of bird wings. Surrounding the two human faces are four raptorial bird heads similar to the one shown in the Berlin tablet.

It is usually proposed that the Cincinnati tablet was made by people of the Adena culture. Of interest is that several Hopewell designs show the human ear in the same way. These designs include a copper piece from the Hopewell site (Willoughby 1916:Pl. 3) and five leather objects recovered from the Mount Vernon site in Posey County, Indiana (Tomak 1994:34–35; Tomak and Burkett 1996). As pointed out by Tomak and Burkett (360–61), the morphological features of the Mount Vernon leather pieces match the anatomical features of human ears, and the Mount Vernon designs match the design of the solitary copper ear found at the Hopewell site.

3. While effigy deer and elk antlers made from copper are found, they are likely indicators of shamanic and/or political power. The origin of antlers as power symbols is perhaps based in their use by bucks for fighting. Hopewell representations of entire deer made out of copper or mica are unknown.

4. Although in this section I make the argument for teeth and claws as sources of power and protection, I should point out that many Hopewell burials are found without these power symbols. Rather, many Hopewell burials are found with hundreds, or even thousands of freshwater pearls and/or shell beads. In yet other cases, Hopewell burials are accompanied by both animal teeth and claws and pearls and shell beads. Pearls and shell beads were typically made into necklaces and used to adorn clothing. Both males and females wore pearls and shell beads.

Presumably, different kinds of accouterments, including necklaces, had different symbolic meanings. For example, whereas bear claw necklaces might have projected strength, power, and spiritual protection, drawing upon Hamell (1983, 1987, 1992), pearl and shell bead necklaces might have referenced purity, well-being, and life.

Chapter 6: Roles of the Hopewell Shaman

1. After Evans-Pritchard (1937), a distinction is made between witch and sorcerer. Witches are generally believed to have the ability to cause harm directly through their innate powers. Sorcerers, on the other hand, use specific spells, incantations, or rituals to invoke Otherworld entities to cause harm. For purposes of the present discussion, the distinction—if indeed it has any actual basis in ethnographic reality—is not important. What is common to both is that the practitioner is believed to have the ability to cause harm by superhuman means.

2. As to the punctuated design around the rim of the pipe, it may be that design element represents water. If so, then the fact that the birds' heads are upside down when the pipe is held right side up is consistent with the observation that the roseate spoonbill and northern shoveler duck both feed by immersing their beak, and sometimes head and neck, into the water. The deeper the bird's beak is immersed, the more the head seems to rotate from right side up to upside down.

3. Gell explains this seeming contradiction in the following way:

We have copious ethnographic testimony to the effect that various cultures do not consider that the temporal relationship of the present to the mythic/ancestral past is one that is affected by the passage of time. . . . I suggest that it would be more precise to say . . . that there are relationships between events or epochs which are temporal to the extent that epoch A precedes epoch B in time, but that the relationship between the events of epochs A and B is unaffected by the durational interval A/B. There is priority, there is order, but there is no measure. (1992:22)

4. In connection with their collections of precious substances, it is often proposed that the Hopewell obtained these materials from far-distant sources, sometimes as the function of a shamanic quest (e.g., DeBoer 2004; Charles, Van Nest, and Buikstra 2004; Carr 2005b; also see Helms [1998:10] for a more general discussion of the principle). Clearly, marine shell came from the Atlantic and Gulf coasts, obsidian from the Far West, and mica from the Appalachian Mountains.

The source for Hopewell copper, however, presents an interesting case. Traditionally it has been presumed that Hopewell copper was obtained from the Lake Superior region. Indeed, trace element analysis of Hopewell copper, at least from the Turner site, shows that it is "indistinguishable from sources in the Great Lakes region" (Tankersley 2007:282). Moreover, extensive evidence for prehistoric copper mining is found in the Lake Superior region on Isle Royale and the Keweenaw Peninsula.

Tankersley, however, points out that, in the immediate vicinity of the Turner site, there are glacial deposits of copper, gold, and silver that likely account for the Turner artifacts. Tankersley explains:

Nuggets of copper, gold, and silver from local Pleistocene outwash deposits exceed the size and weight of all the heavy mineral deposits from Turner. Therefore, it is probable that they were procured in the immediate vicinity of Turner, if not on site. . . . In other words, heavy minerals such as copper, gold, and silver from the Keweenaw Peninsula were naturally transported by Pleistocene glaciers and outwash to the Turner site complex and the immediate vicinity. (2007:282–83)

5. Although most large Hopewell caches or deposits probably represent gift offerings to lowerworld (and, perhaps, upperworld) chiefs and grandfathers, this is not to say that every object accompanying all burials were offerings. Some items—such as drinking cups, necklaces, bone awls, flake knives, and copper bracelets—found with specific burials may represent personally owned items placed with the deceased for sentimental or other nongifting reasons. Where deposits such as the Sunkle, Powell, and Koenig caches were made without accompanying human burials, they were perhaps intended as direct offerings to the Otherworld chiefs. Where large deposits accompany individual burials, it may be that the deceased was expected to act as a gift bearer to the Otherworld chiefs on behalf of the community. Some large caches may also represent sacred items possessed by a particular clan or lineage. In either case, it seems unlikely that large deposits were accompaniments of "wealth," either personally owned by the deceased or intended for the material comfort of the deceased in the afterlife. As Hall points out, "Acquisitiveness was quite remote from any Indian ethic . . . North American Indians gained prestige not from possessing but

from giving to others, often to the point of impoverishing themselves" (1997:156). If the same was true in even in small measure for the Hopewell, then it is doubtful that Hopewell individuals would stockpile and later be buried with things they presumably hoarded in life.

Second, large deposits comprised of one kind of item, such as the Mound City and Tremper pipe caches or the large deposits of earspools at the Hopewell site, were likely contributed by multiple persons. It is doubtful that one individual possessed hundreds of pipes or earspools. The more likely alternative is that individual donations of precious items were made by community members and then offered as a single collective gift to the Otherworld chiefs. Presumably, the display and destruction of valuable objects—by burying them—would have added to the social prestige of those who were willing and able to conspicuously dispose of valuable items and precious materials. Thus, there was likely an important social component to the gifting of material things to the Otherworld chiefs.

6. As to why humans would believe in an afterlife, I find cognitive psychologist Jesse Bering's explanation persuasive: "because it is impossible to ever know what it is like to be dead; our phenomenological systems are literally forced to construe theoretical models of a subjective existence beyond death" (2005:8). Empirical research that led to this conclusion includes a fascinating experiment conducted by Bering and Bjorklund (2004; also see Bering 2002; Bering, McLeod, and Shackelford 2005; Bloom 2004:207; Barrett 2004:57). Bering and Bjorklund told four- to six-year-old children a story wherein an alligator pursued, caught, and ate a mouse. The children were then asked questions about the deceased mouse's biological and psychological functioning. Consistently, the children recognized the biological consequences of death and reported that the mouse would no longer need to go to the bathroom, that its ears wouldn't work, and that its brain no longer worked. More than half the children, however, said that even though it was dead, the mouse would continue to experience hunger, have thoughts about the alligator, and want to go home. For all practical purposes, most of the children appeared to believe in what we would call a soul that survives physical death of the body.

7. It is difficult to know why the Hopewell cremated some people, while giving others extended or other kinds of burials. In many cultures the cause of death determines final disposition; in other instances, disposition of the body is related to age and status. In some cases, the choice of how a body is disposed of is made by the individual before death, or by family members or religious specialists after death. Often, the decision is in some way related to cosmological beliefs. Thus, inhumation might anticipate resurrection sometime in the future (e.g., Naji 2005:176). Mummification can be with the idea of continuing the presence of the deceased in the world of the living (e.g., Rakita and Buikstra 2005:105). Cremation may be intended to remove the corpse from this world in its entirety (104). Sky burial may be intended to dispose of the body in such as way that it contributes to the well-being of other living things by being eaten by birds and other creatures (e.g., Malville 2005).

8. Hertz finds this is a common theme among indigenous peoples:

[D]eath is not completed in one instantaneous act; it implies a lasting procedure, which, at least in a great many instances, is considered terminated only when the dissolution of the body has ended. . . . [D]eath is not a mere destruction but a transition: as it progresses so does the rebirth; while the old body falls to ruins, a new body takes shape, with which the soul—provided the necessary rites have been performed—will enter another existence, often superior to the previous one. (1960 [1907]:48)

9. Hopewell de-fleshing may reflect a belief that flesh binds the soul to the world of the living; hence its disintegration is necessary before the deceased can cross to the Otherworld (see Bloch and Parry [1982] for a general discussion of the concept). In this scenario, de-fleshing can be accomplished by leaving the body exposed on a scaffold as a sky burial or by interment in the ground. De-fleshing can be accomplished by vultures, or by human "bone pickers," as traditionally practiced by the Choctaw (Swanton 1931:173). In either case, de-fleshing is often followed by secondary burial, which marks the final separation of the dead from the living and movement of the deceased to the Otherworld.

Interestingly, dissolution of the body—especially rapid dissolution—can serve a useful psychological purpose for the living. With reference to the Kayabi of Brazil, Oakdale (2005:107) points to disarticulation and cremation of the body as a way of helping mourners "let go of their dead." In other words, such mortuary treatments are intended to "help people forget about their dead," thereby helping the bereaved to better cope with their loss.

10. Forensic studies indicate that prior to cremation, Hopewell deceased were dismembered (Baby 1954:2–4; also see Binford 1963; Baker 1974:10). The procedure seems to have included removal of the head and of the legs at the level of the upper third of the femora.

Of interest is that the dismemberment pattern identified by Baby for real Hopewell bodies is represented in Hopewell designs. Figure 6.3a shows a copper effigy recovered from Mound City. Figure 6.3b shows two effigies cut out of mica that were recovered from the Hopewell site. In all cases, the effigies are headless. In one of the three cases, lower parts of the legs have been removed. In all three cases, the forearms have been removed. In other words, the effigies replicate what was apparently done in real life. (Due to the angle of the camera, the effigy's neck is not visible in figure 6.3a. For a published photograph of this piece that shows the neck, however, see Trevelyan 2004:fig. 8.)

What these effigy pieces seem to indicate is that, for the Hopewell, dismemberment was not simply a field expedient intended to facilitate burning of the body. Rather, dismemberment was ritualized; the procedure followed a specific series of events involving the alteration of selected body parts in a very particular manner. In all three effigy pieces, for example, the designs show that heads were removed at the base of the skull, leaving most of the neck intact and attached to the body. Torsos were not chopped in half, legs were not cut off at the pelvis, and so on. The evidence suggests that there was a proscribed, ritualized way of carrying out the dismemberment process.

Ritual actions carry with them embedded symbolic meanings. The implication is that, at least for these persons, ritualized dismemberment was part of the transformation process from life into death. In this, there is a parallel with a Seneca Indian legend that tells of a requirement for ritual de-fleshing and dismemberment before an individual can enter the Otherworld (Hewitt 1918:614). Perhaps the Hopewell believed that ritual dismemberment was required before the individual could enter the Otherworld.

Worth pointing out, too, is the possibility that Hopewell dismemberment may have additionally served to prevent the deceased from coming back, or reentering the land of the living. Cross-culturally, the fear of ghosts is common. Removal of the deceased person's head and limbs certainly would make it more difficult for the dead person to cause harm to the living.

11. Psychologist Richard Coss and his colleagues think our attraction to shiny, glossy surfaces results from our evolutionary development involving the long-distance detection of water. According to Coss, early hominids, especially in the drier conditions that characterized east Africa during early hominid development, needed to be able to locate water on a daily basis in order to survive. As Coss and Moore explain, "for the last 5 million years, failure to find drinking water has probably acted as a major source of selection on the ways our hominid progenitors perceived optical information signifying the presence of water. That is, individuals not sensitive to the optical information for water would not survive" (1990: 369).

In support of their theory, Coss, Ruff, and Simms (2003) conducted research showing that the response by infants and toddlers to shiny, reflective surfaces is to place their heads on these surfaces and make sucking motions with their mouths, as if drinking water. Coss and Moore (1990) also cite substantial research that children and adults prefer landscape pictures that include water. Lastly, Coss and Moore show that adults associate glossy and glittering surfaces with the properties of wet rather than dry, and that glossy and glittering panels elicit more positive emotional ratings than matte and sandy panels.

If Coss and his colleagues are correct, this theory could help explain the occurrence of mica beds sometimes found in Hopewell burial mounds. Although it is pure conjecture, given the glossy, reflective surfaces provided by these mica beds, it may be that they were intended as symbolic representations of water. (I appreciate the comments of George Horton, who made this suggestion to me many years ago.) This interpretation is consistent with Hamell's association of mica with the lowerworld, noted earlier. It is also consistent with the observation that Hopewell burials are often found in direct association with other water-related substances—specifically, water-borne soils such as muck and puddled clay (Hall 1979:260).

Carr and Case (2005a:44) likewise propose that mica was used as a water symbol. Carr and Case's argument does not develop from evolutionary psychology, nor do they utilize Hamell's findings. Rather, their argument proceeds from the observation that mica, shells, galena, and other substances are associated with water by virtue of their silvery, white, transparent, or reflective properties. Expanding on this thesis,

Carr and Case point out that Hopewell burials are sometimes surrounded not only by mica but also other water-associated substances, including shell beads, conch shells, and pearls. Citing Hall's (1976) work showing that in the Eastern Woodlands water barriers were believed to inhibit the movement of ghosts, Carr and Case (2005a) propose a similar purpose for the water-associated substances often surrounding Hopewell burials.

I believe Hall, Carr, and Case have identified an important aspect of Hopewell belief. Fear of the dead is common. In indigenous cultures, the dead are often believed capable of causing illness and harm to the living (e.g., Heissig 2000:14). By surrounding the dead with symbolic water barriers, including mica, it may be that the Hopewell hoped to contain the soul of the deceased within its grave.

At the heart of this argument is the observation that both mica and water reflect the image of the person looking. In many shamanic cultures, reflected images are believed to be manifestations of one's soul. Consider Kalweit's comments: "The soul is described as wind, vapor, a shadow, an image, a sketch, a mirror image in water, a phantom, an outline, a reflection" (1988:27). Continuing this line of reasoning, if a soul were to try to cross a water barrier, it follows that the water (or mica) barrier would capture the errant soul in its reflectivity (Hall 1976:361).

Chapter 7: Ways of the Hopewell Shaman

1. For a contrary opinion, see Benzon, who asserts that "the nervous system doesn't have neural centers specifically for pleasure, nor does it have anything that can be called a pleasure system" (2001:83–86).

2. Other *Amanita* species were also collected during these forays, including *Amanita vaginata* on twenty-four forays and *Amanita rubescens* on twenty-one forays (Hyatt 2005).

3. It is notoriously difficult to correctly identify mushroom species even when found in their living habitat. This difficulty is significantly increased when attempting to make an identification from a carved effigy nearly two thousand years old.

The reason there is some question as to whether the effigy is an *Amanita* is that the stem of the Hopewell effigy wand is proportionately longer than that found on *Amanitas*. Based strictly on this characteristic, the effigy resembles a *Psilocybe* mushroom, of which several species have an annulus.

On the other hand, the proportions of the Hopewell effigy wand correspond to actual *Amanitas* if allowance is made for grasping the effigy. Held in the hand as a wand, the lower 5 inches (12.7 cm) or so of the effigy piece would not be visible. To an observer, the resulting appearance would resemble the size and shape of most *Amanitas*.

4. Although *Ilex vomitoria* is often claimed to have been used as an emetic by Native Americans, that effect does not seem to result when brewed as a tea and taken in moderate quantities. As Fairbanks explains, "Apparently, Europeans were not expected to disgorge black drink, and none of them describe it as a violent emetic"

(1979:137). Further, according to Fairbanks, "Certainly *Ilex vomitoria* tea does not in itself seem to produce this effect, because no European travelers mention that they themselves were inconvenienced by drinking it. It was always the Indians who vomited" (141).

5. Feinhandler notes that "[b]oundaries between people and groups are both maintained and mediated with the use of tobacco, alcohol, coffee, and tea" (1994:82).

6. "Conch" is the common name given to a number of marine gastropod mollusks that belong to several genera, including *Strombus* and *Cassis*. Conchs are often confused with whelks, which are also marine gastropods. Whelks generally have more slender shells.

7. Hale (1976:134) reports that out of 251 identifiable shell vessels from twenty-nine midwestern sites from Hopewell, Mississippian, and Historic periods, 92 percent were made from *Busycon contrarium*. Hale (89–98) identifies the shell vessels from Turner, Seip, and Hopewell sites as *Busycon contrarium*.

8. Freeman (2000, 1995:121–32) suggests that rituals involving transitions from one state to another require changes in the relationships between people. For example, as the body of the deceased is transitioned to its final resting place, the living need to disengage their attachments to the deceased. The "collective neural tissue" needs to be changed. Conversely, when a baby is born, the collective neural tissue needs to establish connections to this new person. According to Freeman, ritual and music help in this regard by stimulating release of the neuropeptide oxytocin. Freeman explains that

> [oxytocin] . . . appears to act by dissolving preexisting learning by loosening the synaptic connections in which prior knowledge is held. This opens an opportunity for learning new knowledge. The meltdown does not instill knowledge. It clears the path for the acquisition of new understanding through behavioral actions that are shared with others. (2000:418)

If Freeman's hypothesis is correct, the implication is that music and ritual activity are biologically adaptive. In this we are reminded of Hayden's (2003:29–34, 1987) thesis that ecstatic religious rituals result in emotional bonds between people—the result being mutual aid alliances. These bonds are especially strong since they result from very strong emotions driven by the release of "brain opioids" (2003:33).

An alternative hypothesis originally proposed by Charles Darwin and recently revived by Geoffrey Miller (2000) suggests that music making is primarily a young male activity and evolved as a means to attract sexual partners.

9. McNeill suggests that communal dancing at times of festive occasions is nearly universal among indigenous groups (e.g., wedding dances, war dances, harvest dances, initiation dances), with the effect that participants "feel good about themselves and those around them" (1995:37). Further, McNeill proposes that the "shared emotion of this vaguely euphoric tone . . . binds the community more firmly together and makes cooperative efforts of every kind easier to carry through" (37).

McNeill (30) argues that dancing provided early humans with a survival advantage by increasing group cohesiveness and social bonding—an important consideration when dependent upon group hunting.

Explained another way by cognitive scientist William Benzon: "Music is a medium through which individual brains are coupled together in shared activity" (2001:23). Further, "[m]usicking allows individuals to couple their nervous systems together while language gives them an access to one another's minds that is impossible for other animals" (184).

Psychologist Robin Dunbar (2004:133–35) proposes that communal singing and dancing result in the release of endorphins, which, in turn, result in positive emotional experiences.

10. Brown (2006:482) makes the point that the vast majority of animal species represented in the effigy pipes are not animals that were of real economic importance to the Hopewell. As explained by Brown, "Rather, they emphasize animals that could plausibly have been encountered in the supernatural realm and the tutelaries that a shaman might have brought to this realm as protection" (484).

References

Abel, Timothy, David M. Stothers, and Jason M. Koralewski. 2001. The Williams Mortuary Complex: A Transitional Archaic Regional Interaction Center in Northwestern Ohio. In *Archaic Transitions in Ohio & Kentucky Prehistory*, edited by K. M. Prufer, S. E. Pedde, and R. S. Meindl, 290–327. Kent, OH: Kent State University Press.

Achterberg, Jeanne. 1987. The Shaman: Master Healer in the Imaginary Realm. In *Shamanism: An Expanded View of Reality*, edited by S. Nicholson, 103–24. Wheaton, IL: Theosophical Publishing House.

Allen, Douglas. 2002. *Myth and Religion in Mircea Eliade*. New York: Routledge.

Andresen, Jensine, ed. 2001. *Religion in Mind: Cognitive Perspectives on Religious Belief, Ritual, and Experience*. Cambridge: Cambridge University Press.

Applegate, Darlene. 2005. Woodland Taxonomy in the Middle Ohio Valley: A Historical Overview. In *Woodland Period Systematics in the Middle Ohio Valley*, edited by D. Applegate and R. C. Mainfort Jr., 1–18. Tuscaloosa: University of Alabama Press.

Ashbrook, James B., and Carol Rausch Albright. 1997. *The Humanizing Brain: Where Religion and Neuroscience Meet*. Cleveland, OH: Pilgrim Press.

Ashmore, Wendy, and Pamela L. Geller. 2005. Social Dimensions of Mortuary Space. In *Interacting with the Dead: Perspectives on Mortuary Archaeology for the New Millennium*, edited by G. F. M. Rakita, J. E. Buikstra, L. A. Beck, and S. R. Williams, 81–92. Gainesville: University Press of Florida.

Atran, Scott. 2002. *In Gods We Trust: The Evolutionary Landscape of Religion*. Oxford: Oxford University Press.

Aveni, Anthony F. 2002. *Empires of Time: Calendars, Clocks, and Cultures* (revised edition). Boulder: University Press of Colorado.

———. 2005. *The First Americans: The Story of Where They Came From and Who They Became*. New York: Scholastic.

Babcock, Harold L. 1919. *Turtles of New England*. Boston: Memoirs of the Boston Society of Natural History, vol. 8, no. 3.

Baby, Raymond S. 1954. Hopewell Cremation Practices. *Papers in Archaeology, No. 1*. Columbus: Ohio Archaeological Society.

———. 1961a. A Unique Hopewellian Breastplate. *Ohio Archaeologist* 11(1):13–15.

———. 1961b. A Hopewell Human Bone Whistle. *American Antiquity* 27(1):108–10.

Bacon, Willard S. 1993. Factors in Siting a Middle Woodland Enclosure in Middle Tennessee. *Midcontinental Journal of Archaeology* 18(2):245–81.

Bahn, Paul. 2001. Save the Last Trance for Me: An Assessment of the Misuse of Shamanism in Rock Art Studies. In *The Concept of Shamanism: Uses and Abuses*, edited by H. P. Francfort and R. N. Hamayon, 51–93. Budapest, Hungary: Akademiai Kiado.

Bailey, Garrick A., ed. 1995. *The Osage and the Invisible World from the Works of Francis La Flesche*. Norman: University of Oklahoma Press.

Baker, Lea. 1974. Report on Analysis of Mound City Cremation. In *Excavation of Section L, Mound 15, Mound City Group National Monument*, edited by B. C. Drennen, 7–10. Columbus: Ohio Historical Society.

Balzer, Marjorie Mandelstam, ed. 1997. *Shamanic Worlds: Rituals and Lore of Siberia and Central Asia*. London: North Castle Books.

Barkow, J., L. Cosmides, and J. Tooby. 1992. *The Adapted Mind: Evolutionary Psychology and the Generation of Culture*. New York: Oxford University Press.

Baron-Cohen, Simon. 1995. *Mindblindness: An Essay on Autism and Theory of Mind*. Cambridge, MA: MIT Press.

Barrett, H. Clark. 1999. Human Cognitive Adaptations to Predators and Prey. PhD dissertation, University of California, Santa Barbara.

Barrett, Justin L. 1997. Anthropomorphism, Intentional Agents, and Conceptualizing God. PhD dissertation, Cornell University, Ithaca, NY.

———. 2004. *Why Would Anyone Believe in God?* Lanham, MD: AltaMira Press.

Basso, Ellen B. 1985. *A Musical View of the Universe: Kalapalo Myth and Ritual Performances*. Philadelphia: University of Pennsylvania Press.

Bean, Lowell John. 1977. Power and Its Application in Native California. In *The Anthropology of Power: Ethnographic Studies from Asia, Oceania, and the New World*, edited by R. D. Fogelson and R. N. Adams, 117–29. New York: Academic Press.

Becker, Ernest. 1975. *Escape from Evil*. New York: Free Press.

Beers, F. W. 1866. *Atlas of Licking County*. New York: Beers, Soule, and Co.

Behler, John L., and F. Wayne King. 1979. *National Audubon Society Field Guide to North American Reptiles and Amphibians*. New York: Alfred A. Knopf.

Benedict, Ruth Fulton. 1923. *The Concept of the Guardian Spirit in North America*. Memoirs of the American Anthropological Association, Number 29.

Benson, Elizabeth P., ed. 1972. *The Cult of the Feline*. Washington, DC: Dumbarton Oaks.

Benzon, William L. 2001. *Beethoven's Anvil: Music in Mind and Culture*. New York: Basic Books.

Bering, Jesse M. 2002. Intuitive Conceptions of Dead Agents' Minds: The Natural Foundations of Afterlife Beliefs as Phenomenological Boundary. *Journal of Cognition and Culture* 2(4):263–308.

————. 2005. Death as an Empirical Backdoor to the Representation of Mental Causality. Paper presented at the CNRS Web-based Conference for the Société de l'Information, Causal Cognition in Human and Non-human Animals. The Institute for Cognitive Sciences, Lyon, France. (Invited online symposium: www.interdisciplines.org).

Bering, Jesse M., and David F. Bjorklund. 2004. The Natural Emergence of Reasoning about the Afterlife as a Developmental Regularity. *Developmental Psychology* 40:217–33.

Bering, J. M., K. A. McLeod, and T. K. Shackelford. 2005. Reasoning about Dead Agents Reveals Possible Adaptive Trends. *Human Nature* 16:360–81.

Bernardo, José M., and Adrian F. M. Smith. 1994. *Bayesian Theory*. New York: John Wiley & Sons.

Berres, Thomas E., David M. Stothers, and David Mather. 2004. Bear Imagery and Ritual in Northeast North America: An Update and Assessment of A. Irving Hallowell's Work. *Midcontinental Journal of Archaeology* 29(1):5–42.

Binford, Lewis R. 1963. An Analysis of Cremations from Three Michigan Sites. *Wisconsin Archaeologist* 44:98–110.

————. 1972. Archaeological Systematics and the Study of Culture Process. In *Contemporary Archaeology: A Guide to Theory and Contributions*, edited by M. P. Leone, 125–32. Carbondale: Southern Illinois University Press.

Birmingham, Robert A., and Leslie E. Eisenberg. 2000. *Indian Mounds of Wisconsin*. Madison: University of Wisconsin Press.

Blanke, Olaf, Stephanie Ortigue, Theodor Landis, and Margitta Seeck. 2002. Stimulating Illusory Own-body Perceptions: The Part of the Brain That Can Induce Out-of-body Experiences Has Been Located. *Nature* 419:269–70.

Bloch, Maurice. 1992. *Prey into Hunter*. Cambridge: Cambridge University Press.

Bloch, Maurice, and Jonathan Parry. 1982. Introduction: Death and the Regeneration of Life. In *Death and the Regeneration of Life*, edited by M. Block and J. Parry, 1–37. Cambridge: Cambridge University Press.

Bloom, Paul. 2004. *Descartes' Baby: How the Science of Child Development Explains What Makes Us Human*. New York: Basic Books.

Bourguignon, Erika. 1977. Altered States of Consciousness, Myths, and Rituals. In *Drugs, Rituals and Altered States of Consciousness*, edited by B. M. Du Toit, 7–23. Rotterdam: A. A. Balkema.

Bowie, F. 2000. *The Anthropology of Religion*. Oxford: Blackwell.

Boyer, Pascal. 1994. *The Naturalness of Religious Ideas: A Cognitive Theory of Religion*. Berkeley and Los Angeles: University of California Press.

————. 2001. *Religion Explained: The Evolutionary Origins of Religious Thought*. New York: Basic Books.

————. 2008. Religion: Bound to Believe? *Nature* 455:1038–39.

Boyer, Pascal, and Pierre Liénard. 2006. Why Ritualized Behavior? Precaution Systems and Action Parsing in Developmental, Pathological, and Cultural Rituals. *Behavioral and Brain Sciences* 29:595–613.

Boyer, Pascal, and Charles Ramble. 2001. Cognitive Templates for Religious Concepts: Cross-Cultural Evidence for Recall of Counter-Intuitive Representations. *Cognitive Science* 25:535–64.

Bozarth, Michael A. 1994. Pleasure Pathways in the Brain. In *Pleasure, the Politics and the Reality*, edited by D. M. Warburton, 5–14. New York: John Wiley & Sons.

Brady, James E., and Keith M. Prufer. 1999. Caves and Crystalmancy: Evidence for the Use of Crystals in Ancient Maya Religion. *Journal of Anthropological Research* 55(1):129–44.

Brasser, Ted J. 1980. Self-Directed Pipe Effigies. *Man in the Northeast* 19:95–104.

Brose, David S., James A. Brown, and David W. Penney. 1985. *Ancient Art of the American Woodland Indians*. New York: Harry N. Abrams, Inc., in association with the Detroit Institute of Arts.

Brown, Donald E. 1991. *Human Universals*. New York: McGraw-Hill.

Brown, James A. 1997. The Archaeology of Ancient Religion in the Eastern Woodlands. *Annual Review of Anthropology* 26:465–85.

———. 2006. The Shamanic Element in Hopewellian Period Ritual. In *Recreating Hopewell*, edited by D. K. Charles and J. E. Buikstra, 475–88. Gainesville: University Press of Florida.

Brown, Joseph Epes. 1975 [1953]. *Hanblecheyapi*: Crying for a Vision. In *Teachings from the American Earth*, edited by D. Tedlock and B. Tedlock, 20–41. New York: W. W. Norton.

Buck, Caitlin E., William G. Cavanagh, and Clifford D. Litton. 1996. *Bayesian Approach to Interpreting Archaeological Data*. New York: John Wiley & Sons.

Buikstra, Jane E., and Douglas K. Charles. 1999. Centering the Ancestors: Cemeteries, Mounds, and Sacred Landscapes of the Ancient North American Midcontinent. In *Archaeologies of Landscape: Contemporary Perspectives*, edited by W. Ashmore and A. B. Knapp, 201–28. Oxford: Blackwell.

Buikstra, Jane E., Douglas K. Charles, and Gordon F. M. Rakita. 1998. *Staging Ritual: Hopewell Ceremonialism at the Mound House Site, Greene County, Illinois, Kampsville Studies in Archeology and History, No. 1*. Kampsville, IL: Center for American Archeology.

Burkert, Walter. 1983. *Homo Necans: The Anthropology of the Ancient Greek Sacrificial Ritual and Myth*. Translated by by P. Bing. Berkeley and Los Angeles: University of California Press.

Burks, Jarrod. 2001. Strait Site Radiocarbon Dates Revealed. *Ohio Archaeological Council Newsletter* 13(1):7.

Byers, A. Martin. 1987. The Earthwork Enclosures of the Central Ohio Valley: A Temporal and Structural Analysis of Woodland Society and Culture. PhD dissertation, State University of New York at Albany.

———. 1996. Social Structure and the Pragmatic Meaning of Material Culture: Ohio Hopewell as an Ecclesiastic-Communal Cult. In *A View from the Core: A Synthesis of*

Ohio Hopewell Archaeology, edited by P. J. Pacheco, 174–92. Columbus: Ohio Archaeological Council.

———. 2004. *The Ohio Hopewell Episode: Paradigm Lost and Paradigm Gained*. Akron, OH: University of Akron Press.

———. 2005. The Mortuary "Laying-In" Crypts of the Hopewell Site: Beyond the Funerary Paradigm. In *Interacting with the Dead: Perspectives on Mortuary Archaeology for the New Millennium*, edited by G. F. M. Rakita, J. E. Buikstra, L. A. Beck, and S. R. Williams, 124–41. Gainesville: University Press of Florida.

Byrne, Richard W. 1995. The Ape Legacy: The Evolution of Machiavellian Intelligence and Anticipatory Interactive Planning. In *Social Intelligence and Interaction: Expressions and Implications of the Social Bias in Human Intelligence*, edited by E. Goody, 37–52. Cambridge: Cambridge University Press.

Campbell, Jonathan A., and William W. Lamar. 2004. *The Venomous Reptiles of the Western Hemisphere*. Vol. 1. Ithaca, NY: Cornell University Press.

Carr, Christopher. 2005a. The Tripartite Ceremonial Alliance among Scioto Hopewellian Communities and the Question of Social Ranking. In *Gathering Hopewell: Society, Ritual, and Ritual Interaction*, edited by C. Carr and D. T. Case, 258–338. New York: Kluwer Academic/Plenum Publishers.

———. 2005b. Rethinking Interregional Hopewellian "Interaction." In *Gathering Hopewell: Society, Ritual, and Ritual Interaction*, edited by C. Carr and D. T. Case, 575–623. New York: Kluwer Academic/Plenum Publishers.

Carr, Christopher, and D. Troy Case. 2005a. The Gathering of Hopewell. In *Gathering Hopewell: Society, Ritual, and Ritual Interaction*, edited by C. Carr and D. T. Case, 19–50. New York: Kluwer Academic/Plenum Publishers.

———. 2005b. The Nature of Leadership in Ohio Hopewellian Societies: Role Segregation and the Transformation from Shamanism. In *Gathering Hopewell: Society, Ritual, and Ritual Interaction*, edited by C. Carr and D. T. Case, 177–237. New York: Kluwer Academic/Plenum Publishers.

Charles, Douglas K., Julieann Van Nest, and Jane E. Buikstra. 2004. From the Earth: Minerals and Meaning in the Hopewellian World. In *Soils, Stones and Symbols*, edited by N. Boivin and M. A. Owoc, 43–70. London: UCL Press.

Clay, R. Berle. 1992. Chiefs, Big Men, or What? Economy, Settlement Patterns, and Their Bearing on Adena Political Models. In *Cultural Variability in Context: Woodland Settlements of the Mid-Ohio Valley*. MCJA Special Paper No. 7, edited by M. F. Seeman, 77–80. Kent, OH: Kent State University Press.

Clottes, Jean, and David Lewis-Williams. 1998. *The Shamans of Prehistory: Trance and Magic in the Painted Caves*. New York: Harry N. Abrams.

Conant, Roger, and Joseph T. Collins. 1998. *A Field Guide to Reptiles and Amphibians: Eastern and Central North America*. Boston: Houghton Mifflin.

Conner, Randy P. 1993. *Blossom of Bone: Reclaiming the Connections between Homoeroticism and the Sacred*. San Francisco: HarperCollins.

Connolly, Robert P., and Bradley T. Lepper, eds. 2004. *The Fort Ancient Earthworks: Prehistoric Lifeways of the Hopewell Culture in Southwestern Ohio*. Columbus: Ohio Historical Society.

Converse, Harriet M. 1908. *Myths and Legends of the New York Iroquois*. Edited and annotated by Arthur C. Parker. New York State Museum Bulletin No. 125.

Converse, Robert N. 1994. Engraved Bone Objects from the Harness Site. *Ohio Archaeologist* 44(3):32.

———. 2001. The Powell Cache. *Ohio Archaeologist* 51(4):23.

———. 2003. *The Archaeology of Ohio*. Columbus: Archaeological Society of Ohio.

Cordy-Collins, Alana. 1983. The Dual Divinity Concept in Chavin Art. In *Chavin Art*, edited by P. G. Roe and A. Cordy-Collins, 42–72. Miscellaneous Series No. 48. Greeley: University of Northern Colorado, Museum of Anthropology.

Cosmides, Leda, and John Tooby. 1994. Origins of Domain Specificity: The Evolution of Functional Organization. In *Mapping the Mind: Domain Specificity in Cognition and Culture*, edited by L. Hirschfeld and S. Gelman, 85–116. Cambridge: Cambridge University Press.

Cosmides, L., J. Tooby, and J. Barkow. 1992. Introduction: Evolutionary Psychology and Conceptual Integration. In *The Adapted Mind: Evolutionary Psychology and the Generation of Culture*, edited by J. Barkow, L. Cosmides and J. Tooby, 3–15. New York: Oxford University Press.

Coss, Richard G. 2003. The Role of Evolved Perceptual Biases in Art and Design. In *Evolutionary Aesthetics*, edited by E. Voland and K. Grammer, 197–213. Berlin: Springer.

Coss, Richard G., and Michael Moore. 1990. All That Glistens: Water Connotations in Surface Finishes. *Ecological Psychology* 2:367–80.

Coss, Richard G., Saralyn Ruff, and Tara Simms. 2003. All That Glitters II: The Effects of Reflective Surface Finishes on the Mouthing Activity of Infants and Toddlers. *Ecological Psychology* 15:197–213.

Cowan, C. Wesley. 1996. Social Implications of Ohio Hopewell Art. In *A View From the Core: A Synthesis of Ohio Hopewell Archaeology*, edited by P. J. Pacheco, 128–48. Columbus: Ohio Archaeological Council.

Cowan, Frank L. 2005. Black and White and Buried All Over. Paper presented at the Midwest Archaeological Conference, Dayton, OH.

Culin, Stewart. 1975 [1907]. *Games of the North American Indians*. New York: Dover Publications. Originally published in the Twenty-fourth Annual Report of the Bureau of American Ethnology.

Dancey, William S., and Jarrod Burks. 2006. Middle Woodland Period Settlement as Seen from the Overly and Strait Sites in Central Ohio. Paper presented at the Archaeological Society of Ohio Conference, Hopewell: Origins, Artistry and Culture, Columbus.

d'Aquili, Eugene G. 1993. The Myth-Ritual Complex: A Biogenetic Structural Analysis. In *Brain, Culture, and the Human Spirit: Essays From an Emergent Evolutionary Perspective*, edited by J. B. Ashbrook, 45–75. Lanham, MD: University Press of America.

d'Aquili, Eugene G., Charles D. Laughlin Jr., and J. McManus. 1979. *The Spectrum of Ritual*. New York: Columbia University Press.

d'Aquili, Eugene G., and Andrew Newberg. 1999. *The Mystical Mind: Probing the Biology of Religious Experience*. Minneapolis: Fortress Press.

———. 2002. The Neuropsychology of Aesthetic, Spiritual & Mystical States. In *Neuro Theology: Brain, Science, Spirituality, Religious Experience*, edited by R. Joseph, 233–42. San Jose: University Press, California.

Davis, Wade. 1998. *Shadows in the Sun*. Washington, DC: Island Press.

DeBoer, Warren R. 1997. Ceremonial Centres from the Cayapas (Esmeraldas, Ecuador) to Chillicothe (Ohio, USA). *Cambridge Archaeological Journal* 7(2):225–53.

———. 2004. Little Bighorn on the Scioto: The Rocky Mountain Connection to Ohio Hopewell. *American Antiquity* 69(1):85–107.

Dennett, Daniel C. 2006. *Breaking the Spell: Religion as a Natural Phenomenon*. New York: Penguin.

Dewdney, Selwyn H. 1975. *The Sacred Scrolls of the Southern Ojibway*. Toronto: University of Toronto Press (for the Glenbow-Alberta Institute).

Dobkin de Rios, Marlene. 1977. Plant Hallucinogens, Out-of-Body Experiences and New World Monumental Earthworks. In *Drugs, Rituals and Altered States of Consciousness*, edited by B. M. Du Toit, 237–49. Rotterdam: A. A. Balkema.

Douglas, Mary. 1966. *Purity and Danger: An Analysis of Concepts of Pollution and Taboo*. New York: Frederick A. Praeger.

Dow, James. 1986. *The Shaman's Touch: Otomi Indian Symbolic Healing*. Salt Lake City: University of Utah Press.

Dragoo, Don W. 1963. *Mounds for the Dead: An Analysis of the Adena Culture*. Annals of the Carnegie Museum, No. 37. Pittsburgh, PA: Carnegie Museum.

Dragoo, Donald W., and Charles Wray. 1964. Hopewellian Figurine Rediscovered. *American Antiquity* 30:195–99.

Driver, Harold E. 1969. *Indians of North America* (revised second edition). Chicago: University of Chicago Press.

Dunbar, Robin. 2004. *The Human Story: A New History of Mankind's Evolution*. London: Faber and Faber.

Eliade, Mircea. 1954. *The Myth of the Eternal Return*. Translated by W. R. Trask. Bollingen Series 46. New York: Pantheon Books.

———. 1959. Methodological Remarks on the Study of Religious Symbolism. In *The History of Religions: Essays in Methodology*, edited by M. Eliade and J. M. Kitagawa, 86–107. Chicago: University of Chicago Press.

———. 1962. *The Two and The One*. New York: Harper & Row.

———. 1964. *Shamanism: Archaic Techniques of Ecstasy*. New York: Pantheon Books.

———. 1987. Shamanism: An Overview. In *Encyclopedia of Religion*, edited by M. Eliade. New York: Macmillan.

Emerson, Thomas E. 1995. Settlement, Symbolism, and Hegemony in the Cahokian Countryside. PhD dissertation, University of Wisconsin–Madison.

———. 1997. Cahokian Elite Ideology and the Mississippian Cosmos. In *Cahokia: Domination and Ideology in the Mississippian World*, edited by T. R. Pauketat and T. E. Emerson, 190–228. Lincoln: University of Nebraska Press.

———. 2003. Materializing Cahokia Shamans. *Southeastern Archaeology* 22(2):1–20.

Evans-Pritchard, E. E. 1937. *Witchcraft, Oracles, and Magic among the Azande.* Oxford: Clarendon.

Fairbanks, Charles H. 1979. The Function of Black Drink among the Creeks. In *Black Drink: A Native American Tea*, edited by C. Hudson, 120–49. Athens: University of Georgia Press.

Fauconnier, Gilles, and Mark Turner. 2002. *The Way We Think: Conceptual Blending and the Mind's Hidden Complexities.* New York: Basic Books.

Feinhandler, S. J. 1994. Take P-leisure Whilst Ye May. In *Pleasure, the Politics and the Reality*, edited by D. M. Warburton, 77–83. New York: John Wiley & Sons.

Fenton, William N. 1962. "This Island, The World on the Turtle's Back." *Journal of American Folklore* 75:283–300.

Feit, Harvey A. 1994. Dreaming of Animals: The Waswanipi Cree Shaking Tent Ceremony in Relation to Environment, Hunting, and Missionization. In *Circumpolar Religion and Ecology: An Anthropology of the North*, edited by T. Irimoto and T. Yamada, 289–316. Tokyo: University of Tokyo Press.

Fletcher, Alice C., and Francis La Fleshe. 1911. The Omaha Tribe. In *Twenty-seventh Annual Report of the Bureau of American Ethnology.* Washington, DC: Government Printing Office.

Fodor, Jerry A. 1983. *The Modularity of Mind.* Cambridge, MA: MIT Press.

Fogelson, Raymond D., and Amelia R. Bell. 1983. Cherokee Booger Mask Tradition. In *The Power of Symbols: Masks and Masquerade in the Americas*, edited by N. R. Crumrine and M. Halpin, 48–69. Vancouver: University of British Columbia.

Fowke, Gerard. 1902. *Archaeological History of Ohio.* Columbus: Ohio State Archaeological and Historical Society.

Francfort, Henri-Paul. 2001. Prehistoric Section: An Introduction. In *The Concept of Shamanism: Uses and Abuses*, edited by H. P. Francfort and R. N. Hamayon, 31–49. Budapest: Akademiai Kiado.

Freeman, Walter J. 1995. *Societies of Brains: A Study in the Neuroscience of Love and Hate.* Hillsdale, NJ: Lawrence Erlbaum Associates.

———. 2000. A Neurobiological Role of Music in Social Bonding. In *The Origins of Music*, edited by N. L. Wallin, B. Merker, and S. Brown, 411–24. Cambridge, MA: MIT Press.

Freesoul, John Redtail. 1987. The Native American Prayer Pipe: Ceremonial Object and Tool of Self-Realization. In *Shamanism: An Expanded View of Reality*, edited by S. Nicholson, 204–10. Wheaton, IL: Theosophical Publishing House.

Freidel, David, Linda Schele, and Joy Parker. 1993. *Maya Cosmos: Three Thousand Years on the Shaman's Path.* New York: HarperCollins.

Furst, Peter T. 1968. The Olmec Were-Jaguar Motif in the Light of Ethnographic Reality. In *Dumbarton Oaks Conference on the Olmec, October 28th and 29th, 1967*, edited by E. P. Benson, 143–78. Washington, DC: Dumbarton Oaks.

———. 1976a. Shamanistic Survivals in Mesoamerican Religion. *Actas del XLI Congreso Internacional de Americanistas* 3:149–57.

———. 1976b. *Hallucinogens and Culture.* Novato, CA: Chandler & Sharp.

———. 1977. The Roots and Continuities of Shamanism. In *Stones, Bones and Skin: Ritual and Shamanic Art*, edited by A. Brodzky, R. Danesewich, and N. Johnson, 1–28. Toronto: Society for Art Publications. Original edition, 1973/1974 ArtsCanada.

———. 1994a. Introduction: An Overview of Shamanism. In *Ancient Traditions: Shamanism in Central Asia and the Americas*, edited by G. Seaman and J. S. Day, 1–28. Niwot: University Press of Colorado.

———. 1994b. "The Mara'akame Does and Undoes": Persistence and Change in Huichol Shamanism. In *Ancient Traditions: Shamanism in Central Asia and the Americas*, edited by G. Seaman and J. S. Day, 113–77. Niwot: University Press of Colorado.

Gabriel, Kathryn. 1996. *Gambler Way: Indian Gaming in Mythology, History and Archaeology in North America*. Boulder, CO: Johnson Books.

Gazzaniga, Michael S. 1988. Brain Modularity: Towards a Philosophy of Conscious Experience. In *Consciousness in Contemporary Science*, edited by A. J. Marcel and E. Bisiach. Oxford: Clarendon.

Geertz, Clifford. 1973. Religion as a Cultural System. In *The Interpretation of Cultures*, edited by C. Geertz, 87–125. New York: BasicBooks.

Gell, Alfred. 1992. *The Anthropology of Time*. Oxford: Berg.

Giovannoli, Joseph. 1999. *The Biology of Belief: How Our Biology Biases Our Beliefs and Perceptions*. New York: Rosetta Press.

Gintis, Herbert, Eric A. Smith, and Samuel Bowles. 2001. Costly Signaling and Cooperation. *Journal of Theoretical Biology* 213(1):103–19.

Goldberg, Elkhonon. 2001. *The Executive Brain: Frontal Lobes and the Civilized Mind*. Oxford: Oxford University Press.

Gombrich, E. H. 1979. *The Sense of Order: A Study in the Psychology of Decorative Art*. London: Phaidon.

Goody, Esther. 1995. Social Intelligence and Prayer as Dialogue. In *Social Intelligence and Interaction: Expressions and Implications of the Social Bias in Human Intelligence*, edited by E. Goody, 206–20. Cambridge: Cambridge University Press.

Greber, N'omi B. 1979. A Comparative Study of the Site Morphology and Burial Patterns at Edwin Harness Mound and Seip Mounds 1 and 2. In *Hopewell Archaeology: The Chillicothe Conference*, edited by D. S. Brose and N. B. Greber, 27–38. Kent, OH: Kent State University Press.

———. 1996. A Commentary on the Contexts and Contrasts of Large to Small Ohio Hopewell Deposits. In *A View from the Core: A Synthesis of Ohio Hopewell Archaeology*, edited by P. J. Pacheco, 150–72. Columbus: Ohio Archaeological Council.

———. 2005. Adena and Hopewell in the Middle Ohio Valley: To Be or Not to Be? In *Woodland Period Systematics in the Middle Ohio Valley*, edited by D. Applegate and R. C. Mainfort, 19–39. Tuscaloosa: University of Alabama Press.

Greber, N'omi B., and Katherine C. Ruhl. 1989. *The Hopewell Site: A Contemporary Analysis Based on the Work of Charles C. Willoughby*. Boulder, CO: Westview.

———. 2000. *The Hopewell Site: A Contemporary Analysis Based on the Work of Charles C. Willoughby* (revised edition). Ft. Washington, PA: Eastern National.

Greeley, A. 1975. *The Sociology of the Paranormal*. London: Sage.

Guthrie, Stewart. 1993. *Faces in the Clouds: A New Theory of Religion*. Oxford: Oxford University Press.

———. 2002. Animal Animism: Evolutionary Roots of Religious Cognition. In *Current Approaches in the Cognitive Science of Religion*, edited by I. Pyysiainen and V. Anttonen, 38–67. New York: Continuum.

Hale, H. Stephen. 1976. Marine Shells in Midwestern Archaeological Sites and the Determination of their Most Probable Source. Master's thesis, Florida Atlantic University, Boca Raton.

Hall, Robert L. 1976. Ghosts, Water Barriers, Corn, and Sacred Enclosures in the Eastern Woodlands. *American Antiquity* 41(3):360–64.

———. 1979. In Search of the Ideology of the Adena-Hopewell Climax. In *Hopewell Archaeology: The Chillicothe Conference*, edited by D. S. Brose and N. B. Greber, 258–65. Kent, OH: Kent State University Press.

———. 1993. Red Banks, Oneota, and the Winnebago: Views from a Distant Rock. Special issue: "Exploring the Oneota-Winnebago Direct Historical Connection," edited by David F. Overstreet. *Wisconsin Archaeologist* 74(1–4):10–79.

———. 1997. *An Archaeology of the Soul: North American Indian Belief and Ritual*. Chicago: University of Illinois Press.

———. 2006. The Enigmatic Copper Cutout from Bedford Mound 8. In *Recreating Hopewell*, edited by D. K. Charles and J. E. Buikstra, 464–74. Gainesville: University Press of Florida.

Hallowell, A. Irving. 1926. Bear Ceremonialism in the Western Hemisphere. *American Anthropologist* 28(1):1–175.

———. 1964 [1960]. Ojibwa Ontology, Behavior, and World View. In *Primitive Views of the World*, edited by S. Diamond, 49–82. New York: Columbia University Press.

Halsey, John. 1992 [1983]. *Miskwabik—Red Metal. The Roles Played by Michigan's Copper in Prehistoric North America*. Eagle Harbor, MI: Keweenaw County Historical Society.

Hamayon, Roberte N. 1994. Shamanism in Siberia: From Partnership in Supernatural to Counter-power in Society. In *Shamanism, History, and the State*, edited by N. Thomas and C. Humphrey, 76–89. Ann Arbor: University of Michigan Press.

———. 2001. Shamanism: Symbolic System, Human Capability and Western Ideology. In *The Concept of Shamanism: Uses and Abuses*, edited by H. P. Francfort and R. N. Hamayon, 1–27. Budapest, Hungary: Akademiai Kiado.

Hamell, George R. 1983. Trading in Metaphors: The Magic of Beads. Another Perspective upon Indian-European Contact in Northeastern North America. In *Proceedings of the 1982 Glass Trade Bead Conference*, edited by C. F. Hayes III, N. Bolger, K. Karklin, and C. F. Wray, 5–28. Rochester, NY: Rochester Museum and Science Center Research Records.

———. 1987. Strawberries, Floating Islands, and Rabbit Captains: Mythical Realities and European Contact in the Northeast During the Sixteenth and Seventeenth Centuries. *Journal of Canadian Studies* 21:72–94.

———. 1992. The Iroquois and the World's Rim: Speculations on Color, Culture, and Contact. The American Indian Quarterly: *Journal of American Indian Studies* 16:451–69.

———. 1998. Long-Tail: The Panther in Huron-Wyandot and Seneca Myth, Ritual, and Material Culture. In *Icons of Power: Feline Symbolism in the Americas*, edited by N. J. Saunders, 258–87. London: Routledge.

Harkness, Barbara. 1982. Implications for Ohio Hopewell Polity Suggested by Lithic and Iconographic Analysis. PhD dissertation, Ohio State University, University Microfilms, Ann Arbor, Michigan.

Harner, Michael J. 1988. What Is a Shaman? In *Shaman's Path: Healing, Personal Growth, & Empowerment*, edited by G. Doore, 7–15. Boston: Shambala.

———. 1990 [1980]. *The Way of the Shaman* (tenth anniversary edition). San Francisco: Harper.

Hayden, Brian. 1987. Alliances and Ritual Ecstasy: Human Responses to Resource Stress. *Journal for the Scientific Study of Religion* 26: 81–91.

———. 2003. *Shamans, Sorcerers, and Saints: A Prehistory of Religion*. Washington, DC: Smithsonian Books.

Heider, Fritz, and Marianne Simmel. 1944. An Experimental Study of Apparent Behavior. *American Journal of Psychology* 57(1):243–59.

Heissig, Walther. 2000. *The Religions of Mongolia*. Translated by G. Samuel. New York: Kegan Paul.

Helms, Mary A. 1998. *Access to Origins: Affines, Ancestors, and Aristocrats*. Austin: University of Texas Press.

Hertz, Robert. 1960 [1907]. *Death & The Right Hand*. Translated by R. A. C. Needham. Glencoe, IL: Free Press.

Hewitt, John Napolean Brinton. 1894. The Iroquoian Concept of the Soul. *Journal of American Folklore* 7:107–16.

———. 1918. Seneca Fiction, Legends, and Myths. In *Thirty-second Annual Report of the Bureau of American Ethnology*. Washington, DC: Government Printing Office.

Hill, James N. 1994. Prehistoric Cognition and the Science of Archaeology. In *The Ancient Mind: Elements of Cognitive Archaeology*, edited by C. Renfrew and E. Zubrow, 83–92. Cambridge: Cambridge University Press.

Hindmarch, Ian, Neil Sherwood, and John S. Kerr. 1994. The Psychoactive Effects of Nicotine, Caffeine and Alcohol. In *Pleasure, the Politics and the Reality*, edited by D. M. Warburton, 50–57. New York: John Wiley & Sons.

Hively, Ray, and Robert Horn. 1982. Geometry and Astronomy in Prehistoric Ohio. *Archaeoastronomy*. Supplement to Vol. 13, *Journal for the History of Astronomy* 4:S1–S20.

———. 1984. Hopewellian Geometry and Astronomy at High Bank. *Archaeoastronomy* Supplement to Vol. 15, *Journal for the History of Astronomy* 7:S85–S100.

Hodder, Ian. 1992. *Theory and Practice in Archaeology*. London: Routledge.

Hollimon, Sandra E. 2001. The Gendered Peopling of North America: Addressing the Antiquity of Systems of Multiple Genders. In *The Archaeology of Shamanism*, edited by N. S. Price, 123–34. London: Routledge.

Holmes, William H. 1883. Art in the Shell of the Ancient Americans. In *Second Annual Report of the Bureau of American Ethnology*. Washington, DC: Government Printing Office.

Holyoak, Keith J., and Paul Thagard. 1995. *Mental Leaps: Analogy in Creative Thought.* Cambridge, MA: MIT Press.

Holzapfel, Elaine. 1994. The Harness Hopewell Cache. *Ohio Archaeologist* 44(1):10–11.

Howard, James H. 1965. *The Plains Ojibwa or Bungi.* Anthropological Paper No. 1, South Dakota Museum. Vermillion: University of South Dakota.

———. 1968. *The Southeastern Ceremonial Complex and Its Interpretation.* Columbia: Missouri Archaeological Society, University of Missouri.

Hubert, Henri, and Marcel Mauss. 1964 [1898]. *Sacrifice: Its Nature and Function.* Translated by W. D. Halls. Chicago: University of Chicago Press.

Hudson, Charles. 1976. *The Southeastern Indians.* Knoxville: University of Tennessee Press.

Hultzkrantz, Åke. 1953. *Conceptions of the Soul among North American Indians.* Monograph Series, No. 1. Stockholm: Museum of Sweden.

———. 1979. *The Religions of the American Indians.* Translated by M. Setterwall. Berkeley and Los Angeles: University of California Press.

Hutton, Ronald. 2001. *Shamans: Siberian Spirituality and the Western Imagination.* London: Hambledon and London.

Hyatt, Shirley. 2005. Top Ohio Mushrooms. In Ohio Mushroom Society, The Mushroom Log. www.ohiomushroom.org/oldoms/julaug05.html (August 27, 2006).

Ingold, Tim. 1987. *The Appropriation of Nature: Essays on Human Ecology and Social Relations.* Iowa City: University of Iowa Press.

Jaffe, Eric. 2006. Mental Leap: What Apes Can Teach Us about the Human Mind. *Science News* 170(10):154–56.

Jones, M. R. 1976. Time, Our Lost Dimension: Toward a New Theory of Perception, Attention, and Memory. *Psychological Review* 83:323–54.

Joniger, O., and M. Dobkin de Rios. 1976. Nicotiana an Hallucinogen? *Economic Botany* 30:149–51.

Kalweit, Holger. 1988. *Dreamtime & Inner Space: The World of the Shaman.* Boston: Shambala.

Kearney, Michael. 1984. *World View.* Novato, CA: Chandler & Sharp.

Keewaydinoquay. 1978. *Puhpohwee for the People: A Narrative Account of Some Uses of Fungi among the Ahnishinaubeg.* Ethnomycological Studies No. 5. Cambridge, MA: Botanical Museum of Harvard.

Kehoe, Alice B. 2000. *Shamans and Religion: An Anthropological Exploration in Critical Thinking.* Long Grove, IL: Waveland Press.

Kelemen, Deborah. 1999. Beliefs about Purpose: On the Origins of Teleological Thought. In *The Descent of Mind: Psychological Perspectives on Hominid Evolution,* edited by M. C. Corballis and S. E. G. Lea, 278–94. Oxford: Oxford University Press.

Kinietz, W. Vernon. 1965. *The Indians of the Western Great Lakes, 1615–1760.* Ann Arbor: University of Michigan Press.

Kirkpatrick, Lee A. 2005. *Attachment, Evolution, and the Psychology of Religion.* New York: Guilford Press.

———. 2008. Religion Is Not an Adaptation: Some Fundamental Issues and Arguments. In *The Evolution of Religion: Studies, Theories, & Critiques,* edited by J. Bulbulia, R.

Sosis, E. Harris, R. Genet, C. Genet, and K. Wyman, 61–66. Santa Margarita, CA: Collins Foundation Press.

Klein, Cecelia F., Eulogio Guzman, Elisa C. Mandell, Maya Stanfield-Mazzi, and Josephine Volpe. 2001. Shamanitis: A Pre-Columbian Art Historical Disease. In *The Concept of Shamanism: Uses and Abuses*, edited by H.-P. Francfort and R. N. Hamayon, 207–41. Budapest, Hungary: Akademiai Kiado.

Knight, Vernon J., Jr. 1975. Some Observations Concerning Plant Materials and Aboriginal Smoking in Eastern North America. *Journal of Alabama Archaeology* 21:120–44.

Koerper, Henry C., and Nancy A. Whitney-Desautels. 1999. Astragalus Bones: Artifacts or Ecofacts? *Pacific Coast Archaeological Society Quarterly* 35(2+3):69–80.

La Barre, Weston. 1970. *The Ghost Dance. Origins of Religion*. New York: Dell.

———. 1972. Hallucinogens and the Shamanic Origins of Religion. In *Flesh of the Gods: The Ritual Use of Hallucinogens*, edited by P. J. Furst, 261–78. New York: Praeger.

Lakoff, George, and Mark Johnson. 1999. *Philosophy in the Flesh: The Embodied Mind and Its Challenge to Western Thought*. New York: Basic Books.

———. 2003 [1980]. *Metaphors We Live By*. Chicago: University of Chicago Press.

Lakoff, George, and Zoltan Kovecses. 1987. *Women, Fire, and Dangerous Things*. Chicago: University of Chicago Press.

Lamberg-Karlovsky, Martha, ed. 2000. *The Breakout: The Origins of Civilization*. Cambridge, MA: Peabody Museum of Archaeology and Ethnology, Harvard University.

Lankford, George E., ed. 1987. *Native American Legends. Southeastern Legends: Tales from the Natchez, Caddo, Biloxi, Chicasaw, and Other Nations*. Little Rock, AR: August House.

———. 2007. The Great Serpent in Eastern North America. In *Ancient Objects and Sacred Realms: Interpretations of Mississippian Iconography*, edited by F. K. Reilly III and J. F. Garber, 107–35. Austin: University of Texas Press.

Laughlin, Charles D., Jr., and Eugene G. d'Aquili. 1974. *Biogenetic Structuralism*. New York: Columbia University Press.

Lawson, E. Thomas, and Robert N. McCauley. 1990. *Rethinking Religion: Connecting Cognition and Culture*. Cambridge: Cambridge University Press.

Leach, Edmund. 2001 [1982]. Genesis as Myth. In *Magic, Witchcraft, and Religion: An Anthropological Study of the Supernatural*, edited by A. C. Lehmann and J. E. Myers, 39–45. Mountain View, CA: Mayfield.

Le Doux, Joseph. 2003. The Emotional Brain, Fear, and the Amygdala. *Cellular and Molecular Neurobiology* 23(4–5):727–38.

Lepper, Bradley T. 1996. The Newark Earthworks and the Geometric Enclosures of the Scioto Valley: Connections and Conjectures. In *A View from the Core: A Synthesis of Ohio Hopewell Archaeology*, edited by P. J. Pacheco, 224–41. Columbus: Ohio Archaeological Council.

———. 1998. The Archaeology of the Newark Earthworks. In *Ancient Earthen Enclosures of the Eastern Woodlands*, edited by R. C. Mainfort Jr. and L. P. Sullivan, 114–34. Gainesville: University Press of Florida.

———. 2004. The Newark Earthworks: Monumental Geometry and Astronomy at a Hopewellian Pilgrimage Center. In *Hero, Hawk, and Open Hand: Ancient Indian Art of the Woodlands*, edited by R. F. Townsend and R. V. Sharp, 72–81. New Haven, CT: Art Institute of Chicago and Yale University Press.

———. 2005. Virtual Explorations of Ancient Newark, Ohio. CD-ROM. Center for the Reconstruction of Historical and Archaeological Sites (CERHAS), University of Cincinnati.

Leslie, Alan. 1995. A Theory of Agency. In *Causal Cognition: A Multidisciplinary Debate*, edited by D. Sperber, D. Premack and A. J. Premack, 121–41. Oxford: Clarendon.

Lévi-Strauss, Claude. 1963. *Structural Anthropology*. Translated by C. Jacobson and B. Schoepf. New York: BasicBooks.

———. 1966. *The Savage Mind*. Chicago: University of Chicago Press.

Lewis-Williams, David. 2002. *The Mind in the Cave: Consciousness and the Origins of Art*. London: Thames & Hudson.

Lewis-Williams, David, and David Pearce. 2005. *Inside the Neolithic Mind: Consciousness, Cosmos and the Realm of the Gods*. London: Thames & Hudson.

Lewis-Williams, J. D., and T. A. Dowson. 1988. The Signs of All Times; Entopic Phenomena and Upper Paleolithic Art. *Current Anthropology* 29:201–45.

Liénard, Pierre, and Pascal Boyer. 2006. Whence Collective Rituals? A Cultural Selection Model of Ritualized Behavior. *American Anthropologist* 108(4):814–27.

Lindbergh, Charles A. 1953. *The Spirit of St. Louis*. New York: Scribner.

Lommel, A. 1967. *Shamanism. The Beginnings of Art*. New York: McGraw-Hill.

Lovisek, Joan A. 2007. Human Trophy Taking on the Northwest Coast: An Ethnohistorical Perspective. In *The Taking and Displaying of Human Body Parts as Trophies by Amerindians*, edited by R. J. Chacon and D. H. Dye, 45–64. New York: Springer.

Ludwig, Arnold. 1969. Altered States of Consciousness. In *Altered States of Consciousness*, edited by C. T. Tart, 11–24. New York: Anchor Books.

Lyford, Carrie. 1989 [1945]. *Iroquois: Their Art and Crafts*. Blaine, WA: Hancock House.

Lyon, William S. 1998. *Encyclopedia of Native American Shamanism: Sacred Ceremonies of North America*. Santa Barbara, CA: ABC-CLIO.

MacDonald, George F., John L. Cove, Charles D. Laughlin, and John McManus. 1989. Mirrors, Portals, and Multiple Realities. *Zygon* 24(1):39–64.

Machery, Edouard, and H. Clark Barrett. 2006. Essay Review: Debunking Adapting Minds. *Philosophy of Science* 73(2):232–46. www.sscnet.ucla.edu/anthro/faculty/barrett (December 12, 2008).

Magrath, Willis H. 1945. The North Benton Mound: A Hopewell Site in Ohio. *American Antiquity* 11(1):40–46.

Mainfort, Robert C., Jr. 1986. *Pinson Mounds: A Middle Woodland Ceremonial Center*. Tennessee Department of Conservation, Division of Archeology, Research Series, No. 7.

Mallam, R. Clark. 1982. Ideology from the Earth: Effigy Mounds in the Midwest. *Archaeology* 35(4):60–64.

Malville, Nancy J. 2005. Mortuary Practices and Ritual Use of Human Bone in Tibet. In *Interacting with the Dead: Perspectives on Mortuary Archaeology for the New Millennium*, edited by G. F. M. Rakita, J. E. Buikstra, L. A. Beck, and S. R. Williams, 190–204. Gainesville: University Press of Florida.

Mangan, G. L. 1982. The Effects of Cigarette Smoking on Vigilance Performance. *Journal of General Psychology* 106:77–83.

Martin, Susan R. 1999. *Wonderful Power: The Story of Ancient Copper Working in the Lake Superior Basin*. Detroit: Wayne State University Press.

Mayor, Adrienne. 2005. *Fossil Legends of the First Americans*. Princeton, NJ: Princeton University Press.

McBeth, Donald. 1960. Bourneville Mound, Ross County, Ohio. *Ohio Archaeologist* 10(1):12–14.

McCauley, Robert N., and E. Thomas Lawson. 2002. *Bringing Ritual to Mind: Psychological Foundations of Cultural Forms*. Cambridge: Cambridge University Press.

McCord, Beth K., and Donald R. Cochran. 2008. The Adena Complex: Identity and Context in East-Central Indiana. In *Transitions: Archaic and Early Woodland Research in the Ohio Country*, edited by M. P. Otto and B. G. Redmond, 334–59. Athens: Ohio University Press.

McManus, I. C. 1999. Handedness, Cerebral Lateralization, and the Evolution of Language. In *The Descent of Mind: Psychological Perspectives on Hominid Evolution*, edited by M. C. Corballis and S. E. G. Lea, 194–217. Oxford: Oxford University Press.

McNeill, William H. 1995. *Keeping Together in Time: Dance and Drill in Human History*. Cambridge, MA: Harvard University Press.

Merriam, Clinton Hart. 1923. Erroneous Identifications of "Copper Effigies" from the Mound City Group. *American Anthropologist* 25:424–25.

Merrill, William L. 1979. The Beloved Tree: *Ilex vomitoria* among the Indians of the Southeast and Adjacent Regions. In *Black Drink: A Native American Tea*, edited by C. Hudson, 40–82. Athens: University of Georgia Press.

Milanich, Jerald T. 1979. Origins and Prehistoric Distributions of Black Drink and the Ceremonial Shell Drinking Cup. In *Black Drink: A Native American Tea*, edited by C. Hudson, 83–119. Athens: University of Georgia Press.

Miller, Geoffrey. 2000. Evolution of Human Music Through Sexual Selection. In *The Origins of Music*, edited by N. L. Wallin, B. Merker, and S. Brown, 329–60. Cambridge, MA: MIT Press.

Miller, Jay. 1988. *Shamanic Odyssey: The Lushootseed Salish Journey to the Land of the Dead*. Menlo Park, CA: Ballena Press.

———. 1999. *Lushootsee Culture and the Shamanic Odyssey*. Lincoln: University of Nebraska Press.

———. 2001. Instilling the Earth: Explaining Mounds. *American Indian Culture and Research Journal* 25(3):161–77.

Miller, Mary, and Karl T. Taube. 1993. *An Illustrated Dictionary of the Gods and Symbols of Ancient Mexico and the Maya*. New York: Thames & Hudson.

Mills, William C. 1902. Excavations of the Adena Mound. *Ohio Archaeological and Historical Quarterly* 10:452–79.

———. 1907. The Exploration of the Edwin Harness Mound. *Ohio Archaeological and Historical Quarterly* 16:113–93.

———. 1909. Exploration of the Seip Mound. *Ohio Archaeological and Historical Quarterly* 18:269–321.

———. 1916. Exploration of the Tremper Mound. *Ohio Archaeological and Historical Quarterly* 25:262–398.

———. 1922. Exploration of the Mound City Group. *Ohio Archaeological and Historical Quarterly* 31:423–584.

Mithen, Steven. 1996. *The Prehistory of the Mind: The Cognitive Origins of Art, Religion and Science*. New York: Thames & Hudson.

———. 2006. *The Singing Neanderthals: The Origins of Music, Language, Mind, and Body*. Cambridge, MA: Harvard University Press.

Mooney, James. 1900. Myths of the Cherokee. In *Nineteenth Annual Report of the Bureau of American Ethnology, Pt. 1*. Washington, DC: Government Printing Office.

Moorehead, Warren K. 1922. The Hopewell Mound Group of Ohio. *Field Museum of Natural History Anthropological Series* 6(5):73–184.

———, ed. 1892. *Primitive Man in Ohio*. New York: G. P. Putnam's Sons.

Morgan, Lewis H. 1851. *League of the Ho-de-no-sau-nee or Iroquois*. New York: M. H. Newman.

Morgan, Richard G. 1946. *Fort Ancient*. Columbus: Ohio State Archaeological and Historical Society.

Morrisseau, Norval. 1998. *Travels to the House of Invention*. Toronto: Key Porter Books.

Morton, J., and M. Johnson. 1991. CONSPEC and CONLEARN: A Two-Process Theory of Infant Face Recognition. *Psychological Review* 98:164–81.

Morton, James, and Jeff Carskadden. 1983. The Rutledge Mound, Licking County, Ohio. *Ohio Archaeologist* 33(3):4–9.

Moselhy, H. F. 1999. Lycanthropy: New Evidence of Its Origin. *Psychopathology* 32(4):173–76.

Myerhoff, Barbara. 1976. Shamanic Equilibrium: Balance and Mediation in Known and Unknown Worlds. In *American Folk Medicine, A Symposium*, edited by W. D. Hand, 99–107. Berkeley and Los Angeles: University of California Press.

Naji, Stephan. 2005. Death and Remembrance in Medieval France. In *Interacting with the Dead: Perspectives on Mortuary Archaeology for the New Millennium*, edited by G. F. M. Rakita, J. E. Buikstra, L. A. Beck, and S. R. Williams, 173–89. Gainesville: University Press of Florida.

National Park Service. 2001. *Long Range Interpretive Plan for the Hopewell Culture National Historical Park*. Washington, DC: Government Printing Office.

Nelson, Sarah Milledge. 2008. *Shamanism and the Origin of States: Spirit, Power, and Gender in East Asia*. Walnut Creek, CA: Left Coast Press.

Nettl, Bruno. 1956. *Music in Primitive Culture*. Cambridge, MA: Harvard University Press.

Newberg, Andrew, Eugene G. d'Aquili, and Vince Rause. 2001. *Why God Won't Go Away: Brain Science and the Biology of Belief*. New York: Ballantine Books.

Oakdale, Suzanne. 2005. Forgetting the Dead, Remembering Enemies. In *Interacting with the Dead: Perspectives on Mortuary Archaeology for the New Millennium*, edited by

G. F. M. Rakita, J. E. Buikstra, L. A. Beck, and S. R. Williams, 107–23. Gainesville: University Press of Florida.

Okladnikova, E. A. 1989. The Shamanistic Aspect of the Crystal Magic. In *Shamanism: Past and Present. Part 2*, edited by M. Hoppal and O. von Sadovszky, 343–48. Budapest: Budapest Ethnographic Institute Hungarian Academy of Sciences/Fullerton International Society for Trans-Oceanic Research.

Olds, J., and P. Milner. 1954. Positive Reinforcement Produced by Electrical Stimulation of the Septal Area and Other Regions of Rat Brain. *Journal of Comparative and Physiological Psychology* 47:419–27.

Ortiz, Alfonso. 1969. *The Tewa World. Space, Time, Being, and Becoming in a Pueblo Society*. Chicago: University of Chicago Press.

Ott, Eleanor. 2001 [1995]. Shamans and Ethics in a Global World. In *Shamans Through Time: 500 Years on the Path to Knowledge*, edited by J. Narby and F. Huxley, 280–85. New York: Jeremy P. Tarcher/Penguin.

Otto, Martha Potter. 1975a. A New Engraved Adena Tablet. *Ohio Archaeologist* 25:31–36.

———. 1975b. A New Engraved Adena Tablet Identified. *Echoes* 14(11):1–2.

Otto, Martha Potter, and Brian G. Redmond. 2008. *Transitions: Archaic and Early Woodland Research in the Ohio Country*. Athens: Ohio University Press.

Parmalee, Paul W. 2006. Animal Remains from the Snyders Site. In *Illinois Hopewell and Late Woodland Mounds: The Excavations of Gregory Perino 1950–1975*, edited by K. B. Farnsworth and M. D. Wiant, 232–35. Studies in Archaeology No. 4. Urbana: Illinois Transportation Archaeological Research Program.

Parmalee, Paul W., and Gregory Perino. 1971. A Prehistoric Archaeological Record of the Roseate Spoonbill in Illinois. *Central States Archaeological Journal* 18:80–85.

Pascalis, O., S. de Schonen, J. Morton, C. Deruelle, et al. 1995. Mother's Face Recognition by Neonates: A Replication and an Extension. *Infant Behavior and Development* 18(1):79–85.

Pasztory, Esther. 1982. Shamanism and North American Indian Art. In *Native North American Art History*, edited by Z. P. Mathews and A. Jonaitis, 7–30. Palo Alto, CA: Peek.

Pearson, James L. 2002. *Shamanism and the Ancient Mind*. Walnut Creek, CA: AltaMira.

Penny, David W. 1985. Continuities of Imagery and Symbolism in the Art of the Woodlands. In *Ancient Art of the American Woodland Indians*, edited by D. S. Brose, J. A. Brown, and D. W. Penny, 147–98. New York: Harry N. Abrams.

———. 1989. Hopewell Art. PhD dissertation, Columbia University.

Perino, Gregory. 2006. The 1970 Lawrence Gay Mounds Excavations, Pike County, Illinois. In *Illinois Hopewell and Late Woodland Mounds: The Excavations of Gregory Perino 1950–1975*, edited by K. B. Farnsworth and M. D. Wiant, 505–36. Studies in Archaeology No. 4. Urbana: Illinois Transportation Archaeological Research Program.

Phillips, Philip, and James A. Brown. 1975. *Pre-Columbian Shell Engravings from the Craig Mound at Spiro, Oklahoma*. Cambridge, MA: Peabody Museum of Archaeology and Ethnology, Harvard University.

Pickard, William H. 1996. 1990 Excavations at Capitolium Mound (33WN13), Marietta, Washington County, Ohio: A Working Evaluation. In *A View from the Core: A Synthesis of Ohio Hopewell Archaeology*, edited by P. J. Pacheco, 274–85. Columbus: Ohio Archaeological Council.

Pickett, Albert. 1962 [1851]. *History of Alabama and Incidentally of Georgia and Mississippi from the Earliest Period*. Birmingham, AL: Birmingham Book and Magazine Co.

Pijoan, Teresa. 1992. *White Wolf Woman and Other Native American Transformation Myths*. Little Rock, AR: August House.

Pinker, Steven. 1997. *How the Mind Works*. New York: W. W. Norton.

Pratt, Christina. 2007. *An Encyclopedia of Shamanism*. New York: Rosen.

Premack, David, and Guy Woodruff. 1978. Does the Chimpanzee Have a Theory of Mind? *Behavioral and Brain Sciences* 1(4):515–26.

Priebe, Mac. 2000. *The Peregrine Falcon: Endangered No More*. Norwalk, CT: Mindful Publishing.

Prufer, Olaf H. 1996. Core and Periphery: The Final Chapter on Ohio Hopewell. In *A View from the Core: A Synthesis of Ohio Hopewell Archaeology*, edited by P. J. Pacheco, 406–25. Columbus: Ohio Archaeological Council.

Pyysiäinen, Ilkka. 2003. *How Religion Works: Towards a New Cognitive Science of Religion*. Boston: Brill.

Pyysiäinen, Ilkka, and Veikko Anttonen, eds. 2002. *Current Approaches in the Cognitive Science of Religion*. New York: Continuum.

Quimby, George I. 1960. *Indian Life in the Upper Great Lakes*. Chicago: University of Chicago.

Radin, Paul, and Albert Reagan. 1928. Ojibwa Myths and Tales. *Journal of American Folklore* 41:61–146.

Rafferty, Sean M. 2002. Identification of Nicotine by Gas Chromatography/Mass Spectroscopy Analysis of Smoking Pipe Residue. *Journal of Archaeological Science* 29(8):897–907.

———. 2004. "They Pass Their Lives in Smoke, and at Death Fall into the Fire": Smoking Pipes and Mortuary Ritual during the Early Woodland Period. In *Smoking and Culture: The Archaeology of Tobacco Pipes in Eastern North America*, edited by S. M. Rafferty and R. Mann, 1–41. Knoxville: University of Tennessee Press.

———. 2006. Evidence of Early Tobacco in Northeastern North America? *Journal of Archaeological Science* 33:453–58.

Rafferty, Sean M., and Rob Mann. 2004. Introduction: Smoking Pipes and Culture. In *Smoking and Culture: The Archaeology of Tobacco Pipes in Eastern North America*, edited by S. M. Rafferty and R. Mann, xi–xx. Knoxville: University of Tennessee Press.

Railey, Jimmy A. 1996. Woodland Cultivators. In *Kentucky Archaeology*, edited by R. B. Lewis. Lexington: University Press of Kentucky.

Rajnovich, Grace. 1994. *Reading Rock Art: Interpreting the Indian Rock Paintings of the Canadian Shield*. Toronto: Natural Heritage/Natural History.

Rakita, Gordon F. M., and Jane E. Buikstra. 2005. Corrupting Flesh: Reexamining Hertz's Perspective on Mummification and Cremation. In *Interacting with the Dead: Perspectives* on *Mortuary Archaeology for the New Millennium*, edited by G. F. M. Rakita, J. E. Buikstra, L. A. Beck, and S. R. Williams, 97–106. Gainesville: University Press of Florida.

Rappaport, Roy A. 1979. *Ecology, Meaning, and Religion*. Berkeley, CA: North Atlantic Books.

Rätsch, Christian. 1998. *The Encyclopedia of Psychoactive Plants: Ethnopharmacology and Its Applications*. Translated by J. R. Baker. Rochester, VT: Park Street Press.

Redfield, Robert. 1953. *The Primitive World and Its Transformations*. Ithaca, NY: Cornell University Press.

Reichel-Dolmatoff, Gerardo. 1975. *The Shaman and the Jaguar: A Study of Narcotic Drugs among the Indians of Colombia*. Philadelphia: Temple University Press.

———. 1988. *Goldwork and Shamanism: An Iconographic Study of the Gold Museum*. Medellin, Colombia: Compania Litographica Nacional S.A.

Reilly, F. Kent, III. 1996. Art, Ritual, and Rulership in the Olmec World. In *The Olmec World: Ritual and Rulership*, edited by J. Kerr and B. M. White, 27–45. Princeton, NJ: Art Museum, Princeton University.

Renfrew, Colin. 1985. *The Archaeology of Cult: The Sanctuary at Phylakopi*. London: Thames & Hudson and British School of Archaeology at Athens.

———. 1994. Towards a Cognitive Archaeology. In *The Ancient Mind: Elements of Cognitive Archaeology*, edited by C. Renfrew and E. B. W. Zubrow, 3–12. Cambridge: Cambridge University Press.

Renfrew, Colin, and Ezra Zubrow, eds. 1994. *The Ancient Mind: Elements of Cognitive Archaeology*. Cambridge: Cambridge University Press.

Rennie, Bryan S. 1996. *Reconstructing Eliade: Making Sense of Religion*. Albany: State University of New York.

Ridington, Robin, and Tonia Ridington. 1975 [1970]. The Inner Eye of Shamanism and Totemism. In *Teachings from the American Earth*, edited by D. Tedlock and B. Tedlock, 190–204. New York: W. W. Norton.

Riordan, Robert V. 1996. The Enclosed Hilltops of Southern Ohio. In *A View from the Core: A Synthesis of Ohio Hopewell Archaeology*, edited by P. J. Pacheco, 242–56. Columbus: Ohio Archaeological Council.

Ripinsky-Naxon, Michael. 1993. *The Nature of Shamanism: Substance and Function of a Religious Metaphor*. Albany: State University of New York Press.

Rockwell, David. 1991. *Giving Voice to Bear: North American Indian Rituals, Myths, and Images of the Bear*. Niwat, CO: Roberts Rinehart.

Rockwell, Wilson. 1956. *The Utes: A Forgotten People*. Denver: Sage.

Roe, Peter G. 1995. Style, Society, Myth, and Structure. In *Style, Society, and Person: Archaeological and Ethnological Perspectives*, edited by C. Carr and J. E. Neitzel, 27–76. New York: Plenum.

———. 1998. Paragon or Peril? The Jaguar in Amazonian Indian Society. In *Icons of Power: Feline Symbolism in the Americas*, edited by N. J. Saunders, 171–202. London: Routledge.

Romain, William F. 1991a. Symbolic Associations at the Serpent Mound. *Ohio Archaeologist* 41(3):29–38.

————. 1991b. Calendric Information Evident in the Adena Tablets. *Ohio Archaeologist* 41(4):41–48.

————. 1994. Hopewell Geometric Enclosures: Symbols of an Ancient Worldview. *Ohio Archaeologist* 44(2):37–43.

————. 1996. Hopewellian Geometry: Forms at the Interface of Time and Eternity. In *A View from the Core: A Synthesis of Ohio Hopewell Archaeology*, edited by P. J. Pacheco, 194–209. Columbus: Ohio Archaeological Council.

————. 2000. *Mysteries of the Hopewell: Astronomers, Geometers, and Magicians of the Eastern Woodlands.* Akron, OH: University of Akron Press.

————. 2004a. Hopewell Geometric Enclosures: Gatherings of the Fourfold. PhD dissertation, University of Leicester.

————. 2004b. Hidden Dimensions in Hopewell Art. Unpublished paper, privately circulated.

————. 2004c. Journey to the Center of the World: Astronomy, Geometry, and Cosmology of the Fort Ancient Enclosure. In *The Fort Ancient Earthwork: Prehistoric Lifeways of the Hopewell in Southwestern Ohio*, edited by R. P. Connolly and B. T. Lepper, 66–83. Columbus: Ohio Historical Society.

————. 2005a. Appendix 3.1: Summary Report on the Orientations and Alignments of the Ohio Hopewell Geometric Enclosures. In *Gathering Hopewell: Society, Ritual, and Ritual Interaction*, edited by C. Carr and T. Case. New York: Kluwer Academic.

————. 2005b. Hopewell Astronomy, Geometry, and Cosmology. Paper presented at the Archaeological Council of Ohio Annual Conference, Newark, OH.

Routtenberg, A., and J. Lindy. 1965. Effects of the Availability of Rewarding Septal and Hypothalamic Stimulation on Bar Pressing for Food under Conditions of Deprivation. *Journal of Comparative and Physiological Psychology* 60:158–61.

Ruggles, Clive. 1994. The Meeting of the Methodological Worlds? Towards the Integration of Different Discipline-Based Approaches to the Study of Cultural Astronomy. In *Time and Astronomy at the Meeting of Two Worlds*, edited by S. Iwaniszewski, A. Lebeuf, A. Wiercinski, and M. Ziolkowski, 497–515. Warsaw: Centro de Estudios Latinamericanos [CESLA] (Studies and Materials, 10).

Saunders, Nicholas J. 2004. The Cosmic Earth: Materiality and Mineralogy in the Americas. In *Soils, Stones and Symbols*, edited by N. Boivin and M. A. Owoc, 123–41. London: UCL Press.

————, ed. 1998. *Icons of Power: Feline Symbolism in the Americas.* London: Routledge.

Schlesier, Karl H. 1987. *The Wolves of Heaven: Cheyenne Shamanism, Ceremonies, and Prehistoric Origins.* Norman: University of Oklahoma Press.

Seeman, Mark F. 1979. The Hopewell Interaction Sphere: The Evidence for Interregional Trade and Structural Complexity. *Indiana Historical Society, Prehistory Research Series* 5(2).

————. 1988. Ohio Hopewell Trophy-Skull Artifacts as Evidence for Competition in Middle Woodland Societies circa 50 B.C.–A.D. 350. *American Antiquity* 53:565–77.

————. 1995. When Words Are Not Enough: Hopewell Interregionalism and the Use of Material Symbols at the GE Mound. In *Native American Interactions: Multiscalar Analyses and Interpretations in the Eastern Woodlands*, edited by M. S. Nassaney and K. E. Sassaman. Knoxville: University of Tennessee Press.

———. 2004. Hopewell Art in Hopewell Places. In *Hero, Hawk, and Open Hand: Ancient Indian Art of the Woodlands*, edited by R. F. Townsend and R. V. Sharp, 57–71. New Haven, CT: Art Institute of Chicago and Yale University Press.

———. 2007. Predatory War and Hopewell Trophies. In *The Taking and Displaying of Human Body Parts as Trophies by Amerindians*, edited by R. J. Chacon and D. H. Dye, 167–89. New York: Springer.

Seig, Lauren E. 2005. Valley View: Hopewell Taxonomy in the Middle Ohio Region. In *Woodland Period Systematics in the Middle Ohio Valley*, edited by D. Applegate and R. C. Mainfort, 178–96. Tuscaloosa: University of Alabama Press.

Shane, Orrin C., III. 1971. The Scioto Hopewell. In *Adena: The Seeking of an Identity*, edited by B. K. Swartz Jr. Muncie, IN: Ball State University.

Shanks, Michael, and Ian Hodder. 1995. Processual, Postprocessual and Interpretive Archaeologies. In *Interpreting Archaeology: Finding Meaning in the Past*, edited by I. Hodder, M. Shanks, A. Alexandri, V. Buchli, J. Carman, J. Last, and G. Lucas, 3–28. London: Routledge.

Shetrone, Henry C. 1925. Exploration of the Ginther Mound. *Ohio State Archaeological and Historical Quarterly* 34:154–68.

———. 1926. Explorations of the Hopewell Group of Prehistoric Earthworks. *Ohio Archaeological and Historical Quarterly* 35:5–227.

———. 1930. *The Mound-Builders*. New York: D. Appleton.

Shirokogoroff, S. M. 1935. *Psychomental Complex of the Tungus*. London: Kegan Paul, Trench, Trubner.

Skinner, B. F. 1948. "Superstition" in the Pigeon. *Journal of Experimental Psychology* 38:168–72.

Skinner, Shaune E. 1987. A Hopewell Trove: Excavations from Rutledge Mound. *Timeline* 4(2):51–54.

Skrbina, David. 2005. *Panpsychism in the West*. Cambridge, MA: MIT Press.

Slocum, Joshua. 1999 [1899]. *Sailing Alone around the World*. Dobbs Ferry, NY: Sheridan House.

Smith, Noel W. 1992. *An Analysis of Ice Age Art: Its Psychology and Belief System*. New York: Peter Lang.

Smith, Theresa S. 1995. *The Island of the Anishnaabeg: Thunderers and Water Monsters in the Traditional Ojibwe Life-World*. Moscow: University of Idaho Press.

Sosis, Richard. 2003. Why Aren't We All Hutterites? Costly Signaling Theory and Religious Behavior. *Human Nature* 14(2):91–127.

Speck, Frank G. 1977. *Naskapi: The Savage Hunters of the Labrador Peninsula*. Norman: University of Oklahoma Press.

Sperber, Dan. 1994. The Modularity of Thought and the Epidemiology of Representations. In *Mapping the Mind: Domain Specificity in Cognition and Culture*, edited by L. Hirschfeld and S. Gelman, 39–67. Cambridge: Cambridge University Press.

Squier, Ephraim G., and Edwin H. Davis. 1848. Ancient Monuments of the Mississippi Valley; Comprising the Results of Extensive Original Surveys and Explorations. *Smithsonian Contributions to Knowledge, Vol. 1*. Washington, DC: Smithsonian Institution.

Stamets, Paul. 1996. *Psilocybin Mushrooms of the World: An Identification Guide*. Berkeley, CA: Ten Speed Press.

Stevens, James R. 1971. *Sacred Legends of the Sandy Lake Cree*. Toronto: McClelland and Stewart.

Sturtevant, William C. 1979. Black Drink and Other Caffeine-Containing Beverages among Non-Indians. In *Black Drink: A Native American Tea*, edited by C. Hudson, 150–65. Athens: University of Georgia Press.

Sunderhaus, Ted S., and Jack K. Blosser. 2006. Water and Mud and the Recreation of the World. In *Recreating Hopewell*, edited by D. K. Charles and J. E. Buikstra, 134–45. Gainesville: University Press of Florida.

Swanton, John R. 1928. Social Organization and Social Usages of the Creek Confederacy. In *Forty-second Annual Report of the Bureau of American Ethnology*. Washington, DC: Smithsonian Institution.

———. 1931. Source Material for the Social and Ceremonial Life of the Choctaw Indians. *Bureau of American Ethnology Bulletin 103*. Washington, DC: Smithsonian Institution.

———. 1946. Indians of the Southeastern United States. *Bureau of American Ethnology, Bulletin 137*. Washington, DC: Smithsonian Institution.

Swentzell, Rina. 1997. An Understated Sacredness. In *Anasazi Architecture and American Design*, edited by B. H. Morrow and V. B. Price, 186–89. Albuquerque: University of New Mexico Press.

Tankersley, Kenneth B. 2007. Archaeological Geology of the Turner Site Complex, Hamilton County, Ohio. *North American Archaeologist* 28(4):271–94.

Tedlock, Barbara. 2005. *The Woman in the Shaman's Body: Reclaiming the Feminine in Religion and Medicine*. New York: Bantam Books.

Teilhard de Chardin, Pierre. 1959 [1955]. *The Phenomenon of Man*. Translated by B. Wall. New York: Harper & Row.

Thomas, Chad R., Christopher Carr, and Cynthia Keller. 2005. Animal-Totemic Clans of Ohio Hopewellian Peoples. In *Gathering Hopewell: Society, Ritual, and Ritual Interaction*, edited by C. Carr and D. T. Case, 339–85. New York: Kluwer Academic/Plenum.

Thomas, Cyrus. 1894. Report on the Mound Explorations of the Bureau of Ethnology for the Years 1890–1891. In *Twelfth Annual Report of the Bureau of American Ethnology*. Washington, DC: Smithsonian Institution.

Thomas, David Hurst. 1999. *Archaeology: Down to Earth* (second edition). Fort Worth, TX: Harcourt Brace.

Thomas, Nicholas, and Caroline Humphrey. 1994. Introduction. In *Shamanism, History, and the State*, edited by N. Thomas and C. Humphrey, 1–12. Ann Arbor: University of Michigan Press.

Thompson, Evan. 2007. *Mind in Life: Biology, Phenomenology, and the Sciences of Mind*. London: Belknap Press of Harvard University Press.

Tomak, Curtis H. 1994. The Mount Vernon Site: A Remarkable Hopewell Mound in Posey County, Indiana. *Archaeology of Eastern North America* 22:1–46.

Tomak, Curtis H., and Frank N. Burkett. 1996. Decorated Leather Objects from the Mount Vernon Site, a Hopewell Site in Posey County, Indiana. In *A View from the Core: A Synthesis of Ohio Hopewell Archaeology*, edited by P. J. Pacheco, 354–69. Columbus: Ohio Archaeological Council.

Tooby, John, and Leda Cosmides. 1992. The Psychological Foundations of Culture. In *The Adapted Mind: Evolutionary Psychology and the Generation of Culture*, edited by J. H. Barkow, L. Cosmides, and J. Tooby, 19–136. Oxford: Oxford University Press.

Tooker, Elisabeth. 1978. Iroquois since 1820. In *Handbook of North American Indians. Volume 15: Northeast*, edited by B. G. Trigger, 449–64. Washington, DC: Smithsonian Institution.

Tomak, Curtis H., and Frank N. Burkett. 1996. Decorated Leather Objects from the Mount Vernon Site, a Hopewell Site in Posey County, Indiana. In *A View from the Core: A Synthesis of Ohio Hopewell Archaeology*, edited by P. J. Pacheco, 354–69. Columbus: Ohio Archaeological Council.

Toynbee, Arnold. 1979. *An Historian's Approach to Religion* (second edition). Oxford: Oxford University Press.

Trautman, Milton B. 1981. *The Fishes of Ohio.* Columbus: The Ohio State University Press.

Tremlin, Todd. 2006. *Minds and Gods: The Cognitive Foundations of Religion.* Oxford: Oxford University Press.

Trevelyan, Amelia M. 2004. *Miskwabik, Metal of Ritual: Metallurgy in Precontact Eastern North America.* Lexington: University Press of Kentucky.

Tuan, Yi-Fu. 1974. *Topophilia: A Study of Environmental Perception, Attitudes and Values.* New York: Columbia University Press.

———. 1977. *Space and Place: The Perspective of Experience.* Minneapolis: University of Minnesota Press.

Turff, Gina M., and Christopher Carr. 2005. Hopewellian Panpipes from Eastern North America. In *Gathering Hopewell: Society, Ritual, and Ritual Interaction*, edited by C. Carr and D. T. Case, 648–95. New York: Kluwer Academic.

Turner, Victor. 1967. *The Forest of Symbols: Aspects of Ndembu Ritual.* Ithaca, NY: Cornell University Press.

———. 1969. *The Ritual Process: Structure and Anti-Structure.* Chicago: Aldine.

———. 1977 [1972]. Symbols in African Ritual. In *Symbolic Anthropology: A Reader in the Study of Symbols and Meanings*, edited by J. L. Dolgin, D. S. Kemnitzer, and D. M. Schneider, 183–94. New York: Columbia University Press.

van Baal, Jan. 2003 [1976]. Offering, Sacrifice and Gift. In *Understanding Religious Sacrifice: A Reader*, edited by J. Carter, 277–91. London: Continuum. Originally published in *Numen* 23(1976):161–78.

van Gennep, Arnold. 1960. *The Rites of Passage.* Translated by M. B. Vizedom and G. L. Caffee. Chicago: University of Chicago Press.

VanPool, Christine S. 2003. The Shaman-Priests of the Casas Grandes Region, Chihuahua, Mexico. *American Antiquity* 68(4):696–717.

Vastokas, Joan M. 1977. The Shamanic Tree of Life. In *Stones, Bones and Skin: Ritual and Shamanic Art*, edited by A. Brodzky, R. Danesewich, and N. Johnson. Toronto: Society for Art Publications. Original edition, 1973/1974 ArtsCanada.

Verwyst, Chrysostom. 2008 [1958]. *Missionary Labors of Fathers Marquette, Menard and Allovez in the Lake Superior Region (1886)*. Whitefish, MT: Kessinger Publishing.

Vitebsky, Piers. 1995. *Shamanism*. New York: Little, Brown.

———. 2001 [1995]. Shamanism and the Rigged Marketplace. In *Shamans Through Time: 500 Years on the Path to Knowledge*, edited by J. Narby and F. Huxley, 291–97. New York: Jeremy P. Tarcher/Penguin.

Voegelin, Ermine W. 1942. Shawnee Musical Instruments. *American Anthropologist* 44:463–75.

von Gernet, Alexander D. 1992a. New Directions in the Construction of Prehistoric Amerindian Belief Systems. In *Ancient Images, Ancient Thought: The Archaeology of Ideology*. Proceedings of the Twenty-third Annual Conference of the Archaeological Association of the University of Calgary, edited by A. S. Goldsmith, S. Garvie, D. Selin, and J. Smith, 133–40. Calgary: University of Calgary Archaeological Association.

———. 1992b. Hallucinogens and the Origins of the Iroquoian Pipe/Tobacco/Smoking Complex. In *Proceedings of the 1989 Smoking Pipe Conference*, edited by C. F. Hayes III, C. Cox Bodner, and M. Sempowski, 171–86. Rochester, NY: Rochester Museum and Science Center Research Records 22.

———. 1993. The Construction of Prehistoric Ideation: Exploring the Universality-Idiosyncrasy Continuum. *Cambridge Archaeological Journal* 3(1):67–81.

von Gernet, Alexander, and Peter Timmins. 1987. Pipes and Parakeets: Constructing Meaning in an Early Iroquoian Context. In *Archaeology as Long-Term History*, edited by I. Hodder, 31–42. Cambridge: Cambridge University Press.

Wallace, Anthony F. C. 1966. *Religion: An Anthropological View*. New York: Random House.

Wallace, Paul A.W., ed. 1958. *Thirty Thousand Miles with John Heckewelder*. Pittsburgh: University of Pittsburgh Press.

Wasson, R. Gordon. 1968. *Soma: Divine Mushroom of Immortality*. New York: Harcourt, Brace, Jovanovich.

Wasson, R. Gordon, and Valentina P. Wasson. 1957. *Mushrooms, Russia and History*. New York: Pantheon.

Webb, William S., and Raymond S. Baby. 1957. *The Adena People No. 2*. Columbus: Ohio Historical Society.

Webb, William S., and William D. Funkhouser. 1932. *Archaeological Survey of Kentucky. Reports in Archaeology and Anthropology*. Publications of the Department of Anthropology and Archaeology. Vol. 2. Lexington: University of Kentucky.

Webb, William S., and William G. Haag. 1947. The Fisher Site, Fayette County, Kentucky. *University of Kentucky, Reports in Anthropology* 7(2):47–104.

Webb, William S., and Charles E. Snow. 1945. *The Adena People*. Publications of the Department of Anthropology and Archaeology. Vol. 6. Lexington: University of Kentucky Press.

Wenegrat, Brant. 1990. *The Divine Archetype: The Sociobiology and Psychology of Religion.* Lexington, MA: Lexington Books.

Whitehouse, Harvey. 2004. *Modes of Religiosity: A Cognitive Theory of Religious Transmission.* Walnut Creek, CA: AltaMira.

———. 2007. The Evolution and History of Religion. In *Holistic Anthropology: Emergence and Convergence,* edited by D. Parkin and S. Ulijaszek, 212–33. New York: Berghahn Books.

Whitehouse, Harvey, and Luther H. Martin, eds. 2004. *Theorizing Religions Past: Archaeology, History, and Cognition.* Walnut Creek, CA: AltaMira.

Whitehouse, Harvey, and Robert N. McCauley, eds. 2005. *Mind and Religion: Psychological and Cognitive Foundations of Religiosity.* Walnut Creek, CA: AltaMira.

Whitley, David S. 2000. *The Art of the Shaman: The Rock Art of California.* Salt Lake City: University of Utah Press.

———. 2005. *Introduction to Rock Art Research.* Walnut Creek, CA: Left Coast Press.

Wilbert, Johannes. 1972. Tobacco and Shamanistic Ecstasy among the Warao Indians of Venezuela. In *Flesh of the Gods: The Ritual Use of Hallucinogens,* edited by P. T. Furst, 55–83. New York: Praeger.

Wiley, Martin L., and Bruce B. Collette. 1970. Breeding Tubercles and Contact Organs in Fishes: Their Occurrence, Structure, and Significance. *Bulletin of the American Museum of Natural History* 143:143–216.

Willoughby, Charles C. 1916. The Art of the Great Earthwork Builders of Ohio. In *Annual Report of the Smithsonian Institution.* Washington, DC: Smithsonian Institution.

Willoughby, Charles C., and Ernest A. Hooton. 1922. The Turner Group of Earthworks, Hamilton County, Ohio. *Papers of the Peabody Museum* 8(3).

Winkelman, Michael J. 1989. A Cross-Cultural Study of Shamanistic Healers. *Journal of Psychoactive Drugs* 21:17–24.

———. 1990. Shamans and Other "Magico-Religious" Healers: A Cross-Cultural Study of Their Origins, Nature, and Social Transformations. *Ethos* 18(3):308–52.

———. 1992. Shamans, Priests and Witches: A Cross-Cultural Study of Magico-Religious Practitioners. *Anthropological Papers,* No. 44. Tempe: Arizona State University.

———. 2000. *Shamanism: The Neural Ecology of Consciousness and Healing.* Westport, CT: Bergin & Garvey.

———. 2004. Shamanism as the Original Neurotheology. *Zygon* 39(1):193–217.

Winter, Joseph C. 2000a. From Earth Mother to Snake Woman: The Role of Tobacco in the Evolution of Native American Religious Organization. In *Tobacco Use by Native North Americans: Sacred Smoke and Silent Killer,* edited by J. C. Winter, 265–304. Norman: University of Oklahoma Press.

———. 2000b. Food of the Gods: Biochemistry, Addiction, and the Development of Native American Tobacco Use. In *Tobacco Use by Native North Americans: Sacred Smoke and Silent Killer,* edited by J. C. Winter, 305–28. Norman: University of Oklahoma Press.

Witthoft, John. 1949. Green Corn Ceremonialism in the Eastern Woodlands. *Occasional Contributions from the Museum of Anthropology* 13. University of Michigan, Ann Arbor.

Wylie, Alison. 1989. Archaeological Cables and Tacking: the Implications of Practice for Bernstein's "Options beyond Objectivism and Relativism." *Philosophy of Science* 19:1–18.

———. 2002. *Thinking from Things: Essays in the Philosophy of Archaeology*. Berkeley and Los Angeles: University of California Press.

Wymer, Dee Anne. 1996. The Ohio Hopewell Econiche: Human-Land Interaction in the Core Area. In *A View from the Core: A Synthesis of Ohio Hopewell Archaeology*, edited by P. J. Pacheco, 36–53. Columbus: Ohio Archaeological Council.

Yarnell, Richard A. 1964. Aboriginal Relationships between Culture and Plant Life in the Upper Great Lakes Region. *Anthropological Papers* 23. Museum of Anthropology, University of Michigan, Ann Arbor.

Index

Illustrations are in *italics*; some items appear in more than one illustration on the page.

About the Author

William F. Romain, Ph.D., is a research associate at The Ohio State University, Newark Earthworks Center. He is a Fellow of The Explorers Club and past recipient of the Ohio Archaeological Society's Robert Converse award for outstanding contributions to Ohio archaeology. He is the author of *Mysteries of the Hopewell: Astronomers, Geometers and Magicians of the Eastern Woodlands*.